SHEBA

Through the Desert

in Search of the

Legendary

Queen

Nicholas Clapp

Houghton Mifflin Company

Boston   New York   2001

For information about permission to reproduce selections from
this book, write to Permissions, Houghton Mifflin Company,
215 Park Avenue South, New York, New York 10003.

Visit our Web site: www.houghtonmifflinbooks.com.

LIBRARY OF CONGRESS CATALOGING-IN-PUBLICATION DATA

Clapp, Nicholas.
Sheba : through the desert in search of the
legendary queen / Nicholas Clapp.
p. cm.
Includes bibliographical references and
index.
ISBN 0-395-95283-2
1. Sheba, Queen of—Legends.   2. Clapp,
Nicholas— Journeys—Middle East.   3. Middle
East—Description and travel.   I. Title.
BS580.S48 C53   2001
939'.4—dc21   00-054123

Book design by Anne Chalmers
Type is Electra by Linotype-Hell
Line drawings and maps by Kristen Mellon

Printed in the United States of America

QUM 10 9 8 7 6 5 4 3 2 1

For Jennifer, Cristina, and Kay

Contents

Sheba

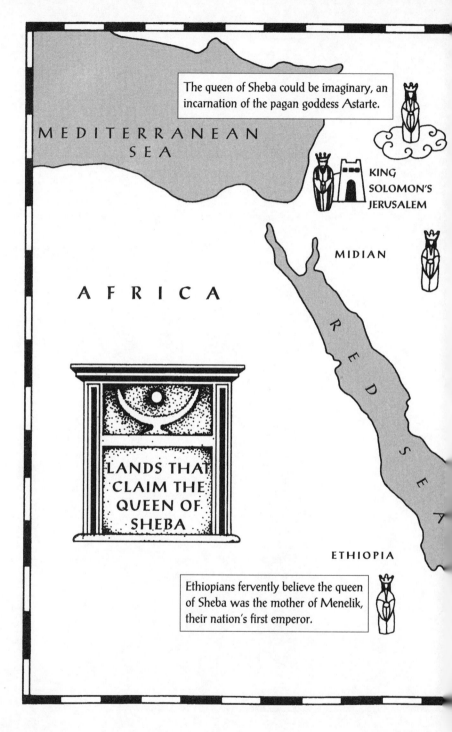

The queen of Sheba could be imaginary, an incarnation of the pagan goddess Astarte.

MEDITERRANEAN SEA

KING SOLOMON'S JERUSALEM

MIDIAN

AFRICA

RED SEA

LANDS THAT CLAIM THE QUEEN OF SHEBA

ETHIOPIA

Ethiopians fervently believe the queen of Sheba was the mother of Menelik, their nation's first emperor.

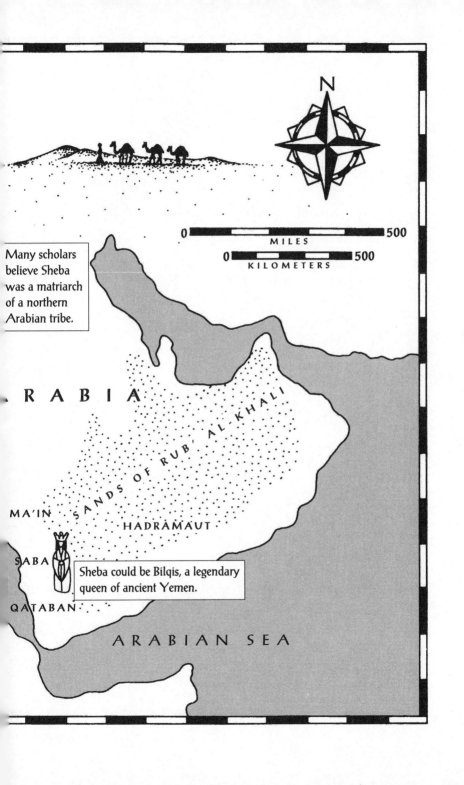

Many scholars believe Sheba was a matriarch of a northern Arabian tribe.

N

0 ⬛⬛⬛⬛⬛ 500
MILES

0 ⬛⬛⬛⬛⬛ 500
KILOMETERS

A R A B I A

SANDS OF RUB' AL-KHALI

MA'IN

HADRAMAUT

SABA

Sheba could be Bilqis, a legendary queen of ancient Yemen.

QATABAN

A R A B I A N   S E A

Prologue

ON A SLEET-STREAKED NOVEMBER afternoon I ducked into the New York Public Library, collapsed my umbrella—broken-spoked on the dash from the subway—sloshed up a grand marble staircase, and turned down a dark hallway leading to the Oriental Division. ("Oriental," in the nineteenth century's world-view, meant anything to the east of Greece, as in "We Three Kings of Orient Are . . .") In the hallway, the division's recent titles could be accessed on two computer terminals glowing green on a table to the right. To the left, shelves of black volumes recorded older entries, typed on antique machines and even handwritten. Both sources had pages of entries beginning: "Queen of . . ."

Queen of Bubbles, Queen of Frogs. Queens of Sorrows, Spies, the Swamp, Tears, Tomorrow, the Universe, Rage, and Ruin.

But on this damp day, one entry shone, the one I was looking for: the Queen of Sheba. Further crosschecking would pull up hundreds of entries bearing on her life—if she did ever live—and times.

I had no way of knowing it at the time, but the pursuit of the queen of Sheba would take me from Canterbury Cathedral to a Czech alchemist's tower. I would venture to the Orient of old and to Jerusalem, the city where Sheba appeared before King Solomon, a city so at the crux of Western religion that it was long held to be the center of the world.

Curiosity, that old cat-killer, would prod and beckon me on, through the cobbled streets of ancient caravansaries, through grassy green African highlands, across a stormy Strait of Tears, and into the trackless red sands of the Rub' al-Khali, the Empty Quarter of Arabia.

The desert, I've found, is a good place for the curious, for even on a short walk you can expect the unexpected, a glimpse of something you've never seen before, be it an oddly striped caterpillar, a rare ghost flower or, as I once found in California's Mojave, a barely tarnished fighter plane abandoned since World War II. This really doesn't make sense. One imagines the surprises of the world of nature and of man to be hidden in remote alpine canyons and mist-shrouded jungles. And certainly such places have their share of the unexpected. But it's in the desert—open, apparently lifeless, with few places to conceal anything—where secrets, perhaps the best secrets, are to be found. Or may still lie buried.

On again, off again, for a decade and more, I would seek Sheba in lands (like her?) exotic, sensuous, even sinister. Would the mists of her myth dissolve, and a real queen of a real country step forth? Or, upon investigation, might she prove to be Sheba, Queen of Illusion? I had no idea. But on a winter's day in New York, I scanned volume after worn volume and was warmed by the promise of adventure offered by Alexander Kinglake, a Victorian "traveling gent":

> There comes a time for not dancing quadrilles, not sitting in pews
> . . . and now my eyes would see the Splendor and Havoc of the
> East.

May, 2000

 In Which
the Queen of Sheba Appears
and Her Legend Unfolds

1

In the Monasteries of the East

JERUSALEM, *in the early spring of 1982, before the queen of Sheba cast her spell* . . .

Caught in the headlights of an idling pickup, the torn-eared goat looked to the bedouin, then to the butcher, then back again. I couldn't understand the Arabic, but the gestures that accompanied their haggling were unmistakable, particularly the butcher's rolled eyes and arms thrust heavenward, pantomime for "If this is your best goat, spare me the others."

It was a little before five in the morning at Friday's sheep market. I watched as trucks from the desert, packed with swaying sheep, goats, donkeys, even camels, struggled up the winding road to the eastern wall of Jerusalem's Old City and the foot of the Tower of Storks.

To the east the sun rose over the Mount of Olives and the Old City, a battered stone crown set upon a dusty Judean hill, glowed a biblical yellow-orange. Though it is encircled now by high-rises and urban sprawl, I found it easy to see in the mind's eye the Old City as it once was: walled and well defended but not very large, a remote and often troublesome corner of empires Roman, Arab, Crusader, Ottoman. A marginal city in the ancient world's network of trade, yet a city of prophets and poets, a city holy to Judaism, Christianity, and Islam.

As the chill of the night wore off, the pace of trading picked up, with goats bleating ever more balefully, as they have since the days of Christ and perhaps even the days of Solomon. And it was time to hasten back to my hotel to join my documentary film crew.

Passing through nearby St. Stephen's Gate, I threaded my way through the Old City's warren of twisting stone streets. Shops at this hour, normally the scene of mercantile tumult, were padlocked and shuttered tight. For several minutes I saw no one. Then a lone figure approached, moving in and out of the shadows cast by the arches of the Via Dolorosa. A tall black man, he wore a cylindrical black cap and a black cassock—a monk. But he was different from the other monks I'd seen in Jerusalem, who scuttle from cell to service, looking at you, if they give you even a glance, with furrowed frown. This man had an easy stride, and as we passed, he gave a genial nod and a smile, which I returned. Cheerful fellow, I thought. He didn't appear to be Roman Catholic or Greek Orthodox. When I paused and looked back, I saw only a patchy gray cat leaping onto a ledge to catch the warmth of the morning sun and heard footfalls receding down a side lane.

I had journeyed to Jerusalem in the company of cameraman Bert Van Munster to seek out ways of life that had survived in the Holy Land intact for hundreds, even thousands, of years. Our mostly Israeli crew—technicians, a couple of schleppers (if not in Israel, where?), and production manager Omri Meron—was filming sequences in and around Jerusalem, even exploring the Herodian tunnels that burrow beneath the city. We documented the city's markets, its ancient souks, with shoemakers, jewelers, and blacksmiths all on their particular streets, named long ago for their merchandise. Cotton merchants still held forth in the Suq-al-Qattin (*qattin* being the Arabic for "cotton"); and on the Malquisinat—"Street of Bad Cooking"—one could have as bad a meal as in Crusader days.

As time went by, quite a number of the Old City's vendors recognized us and spared us their imploring "Sir, mister . . . haff a look, haff a look." I began to feel as if in some way, fleetingly, I belonged here. And with this came the beginning of a renewed appreciation for the Bible as a vivid amalgam of history, myth, and morality play, a chronicle of a people's striving to behave themselves, with insights into human nature at its best and worst. At lunch breaks we talked about how life in Jerusalem was still and forever life in the shadow of the Bible. "But every day," said Omri, namesake of an Israelite king, "God around every corner—sometimes it can be a little too much." (Omri was not alone in this sentiment. As poet Yehuda Amichai pointed out, "The industry of Jerusalem is faith and prayer and, as in any industrialized city, the air can be difficult to breathe.")

One night at dinner, Omri reported that he had obtained permission for us to shoot within the fortified walls of holy Mar Saba.[1] In preparation for what we were doing, I had studied old etchings and lithographs of the Holy Land and had come across an imposing image of this Judean desert monastery drawn by the nineteenth-century Scottish artist David Roberts. The monastery was still intact, I learned, though rarely visited. Omri produced a letter that would gain us admission, signed by the Greek Orthodox "Ar-key-bishop" (as Israelis pronounce it) of all Jerusalem.

The next morning, our first view of Mar Saba mirrored the 1839 lithograph. Nothing had changed. The monastery walls, towers, living quarters, and many chapels stairstepped down a barren hillside overlooking the Dead Sea. It was an enormous compound, built to house a thousand or more monks. Pulling up in our van, we got out and walked to walled Mar Saba's wooden gate.

I knocked. No response. Omri knocked.

Then, from deep inside, an unseen someone shuffled toward us, stopped, and said nothing. Omri slipped the letter from the archbishop under the gate. An unseen hand picked it up and unfolded it. Then, after a very long pause, a gruff voice said, in English, "No. No television. Never. Go away."

"But the letter. It's from the arkeybishop!" Omri protested.

"Does not matter. Goodbye. No television never." The presumed monk slid the letter back under the gate and shuffled away.

"Looks as if our plans for the day, Nicholas, have taken an unexpected and disappointing turn," commented cameraman Bert.

Sullenly, we drove back to Jerusalem.

"Omri," I asked on the way. "That letter from the archbishop. Was there a donation involved?"

"Um, yes."

"How much?"

"A hundred and fifty."

"Dollars?"

"Dollars."

"Then at the very least," I said, "we must get it back. The letter didn't work."

"But we can't bother him about such a thing. He's the arkeybishop of Jerusalem! He's a holy man!"

"He's a holy man," chimed in Bert, "who owes us a hundred and fifty dollars. Are we *freiers?*"

As we made do, videotaping an alternate sequence for the rest of the day, Omri stewed. A *freier*—a sucker—is the last thing any Israeli wants to be called. At eleven o'clock that night, my hotel phone rang. It was Omri: "We have an appointment with the arkeybishop at eight tomorrow morning."

The archbishop's office overlooking Greek Patriarch Street was airy and well appointed. He greeted us warmly, removing his stovepipe hat and setting it on his tidy, polished desk. He had slicked-back hair and a nattily trimmed beard. A massive Byzantine gold crucifix nestled in the folds of his black robe. Diplomatically and with great respect, we told him that his letter of introduction to Mar Saba had been less than effective.

"Ah, those boys down there. Tch, tch. Not with the times," he mused in English, then rocked back in his chair and with his fingers made a little church. "But," he added, "everything could still work out."

"Yes?"

"I could write them a second letter, a letter that—how do you say it in America?—made them *an offer they couldn't refuse.*"

"Yes?"

"Yes," he replied, then thought a moment and gently requested an "additional consideration." A VHS videocassette of Sylvester Stallone in *Rocky II.*

"By tonight . . .," I promised.

". . . your holiness," Omri added.

Whatever the archbishop wrote in his new letter, it worked, and later that morning we were welcomed at Mar Saba.

Nowadays only six monks, all but one of them quite old, dwell in the vast complex. They showed us (and we filmed) the chapel with the skulls of forty martyrs slain in a Persian massacre in A.D. 641. In another chapel they prayed before the glass-enclosed body of their founding abbot, St. Saba. The years had left him considerably the worse for wear yet time-honored; his sightless eyes gazed upward at a string of Timex wristwatches, recent offerings. Hearing bells peal, we ran outside and saw that, to ring them, the monastery's one young monk had tied two ropes to his feet, held four more in his hands, and danced as if possessed in the belfry.

After a couple of hours we had covered even more than we had hoped to, and we lingered to have coffee with the monks who, after all, had enjoyed the interruption to their endless round of prayers, which are so all-consuming that it's been written they rarely if ever bathe. They were sorry to see us leave.

Later that afternoon back in Jerusalem, I took an hour off and wandered through the Old City, taking in its endlessly shifting sights and sounds. A gate was ajar, and beyond it in a cloistered courtyard nuns were hanging out their laundry, all white. Down the street, a shop displayed a picture of a Jesus with lenticular eyes that rolled heavenward as you walked by. Just then trumpets blared, drums rolled, and a uniformed Arab Boy Scout band rounded a corner and strode smartly by.

At the end of an unprepossessing lane, I found myself in the plaza before the Church of the Holy Sepulchre, the most revered site in Christendom. A group of German tourists emerged from its double doors. Their guide was completing an extensive dissertation on the basilica's enshrinement of the sites of Christ's sentencing, imprisonment, crucifixion, and burial. He wrapped up with "Herren und Damen, Kaffeepause! Kaffee! Kaffee! Kaffee!" As his charges went on their way with quickening step, I saw again the very monk I'd passed early in the morning ten days before. He sailed serenely through the outbound German throng and, instead of entering the main basilica, veered off and disappeared through a low door at the side of the plaza.

I hesitated for a minute, but then curiosity got the better of me, and I followed. Beyond the low door, I found myself in an empty, windowless chapel lit by a dozen flickering candles. The air was dank with age-old mold and decay, yet alive with the fragrance of smoldering frankincense. As my eyes adjusted to the darkness, I saw that beyond an iron grille, a stone staircase wound up and out of sight. Somewhere above, voices murmured.

I took the stairs, which led up to a second chapel. There the monk I had seen was pacing back and forth in front of a dozen gently swaying brothers chanting their devotions. He encouraged them with approving nods, even grins, the way a jazzman warms up the band before the sax or trumpet breaks loose.

Then, with no apparent cue, they broke into a cappella song. The words were incomprehensible to me, but seemed to be a hymn of longing for something or someone far away. It was both complex and freeform, like jazz. They sang first in unison, then antiphonally, then

with spirals of melody spinning into further spirals, echoes ringing
into echoes.

Sensing movement at the back of the chapel, I turned to see three
women who had come in after me, two dressed in white, one in in-
digo. They had fallen to their knees and were slowly, gracefully pros-
trating themselves again and again.

A backdrop to these devotions, a large canvas stretched the length
of the chapel's side wall; it depicted two clusters of people meeting
and a presentation of gifts. It looked as if it had been painted sometime in the last fifty years, for the garb of some figures was ancient, of
others modern. On the left, bearing elephant tusks, was a major-
domo in a jaunty Panama hat and a beautiful woman in a cape and
embroidered white dress. Awaiting them on the right was a clearly
important, long-haired mustachioed man accompanied by, among
others, a pair of black-hatted, forelocked *haredim*, lookalikes of the
ultra-Orthodox who daily bustle about Jerusalem.

Attendants to the beautiful woman offered the mustachioed man

In the chapel of the Ethiopian Copts

censers of incense. She was the queen of Sheba come to the court of King Solomon.

I did not then understand that this queen is held in immeasurable esteem by all Ethiopian Copts. I was also to learn that these monks were unique in their fervor and dedication, an exception to the reportedly less than spiritual fathers at the Holy Sepulchre next door. In his 1980 guidebook *The Holy Land*, Jerome Murphy-O'Connor, a Franciscan, writes: "They [the Ethiopians] live among the ruins of [an adjoining] medieval cloister . . . Silent and inward looking, the immense dignity of the tall slender men generates the atmosphere of contemplation so desperately lacking in the church."[2]

I wanted to stay until the end of the service, but I had to leave to meet my wife, Kay, who was scheduled to arrive that afternoon from California. Whenever possible, she took time off from her calling as a social worker and federal probation officer and helped out with my on-location filmmaking.

Very early the next morning, after only a few hours' sleep, we loaded our van and headed south from Jerusalem. By dawn we were driving along the shore of the Dead Sea, and at midday we turned southwest onto a dirt track that led through the ocher and charcoal mountains of the Sinai peninsula, the Old Testament's "great and terrible wilderness." Just as Jerusalem was the City of God, this was the Desert of God, where "God spoke in thunder" to the Israelites seeking their Promised Land. We crossed from Israeli into Egyptian territory, and an hour later we crested a rise to see, at sunset, the fiery red banner of Mount Sinai.

It was dark by the time we reached the most storied of desert monasteries, St. Katherine's, a massive fortress brooding in Mount Sinai's moon shadow. Drawn to the sole patch of light, we passed through a gate that angled to the left, then abruptly to the right (so defenders could waylay invaders), and entered a world a thousand years in the past. Monks carrying lanterns appeared and disappeared in a shad-

owy maze of lanes, courtyards, stairs, and rickety balconies. Buildings—living quarters, a library, storerooms, even a mosque (for the
monastery's bedouin servants)—strained for space in what was in essence an intact archaic city.

Somewhere a resonant hollow log was struck, summoning the
monks to a round of devotions that would continue through the
night. In a reversal of what we're accustomed to, the daytime hours
would then be their time of rest. We peered through great cedar-of-
Lebanon doors into a church resplendent with Greek and Russian
icons of inestimable value and seven-foot-high bronze candlesticks
cast in storied Nineveh. Greek lettering proclaimed, "In this place
the Lord said to Moses, I am the God of thy fathers, the God of Isaac,
the God of Jacob. I AM THAT I AM." Rows of opulent chandeliers
cast their soft glow upward to a dome inlaid with golden mosaics of
Jesus flanked by Moses and Elijah. Two of these three, the faithful believe, had once been *right here,* as had their God, speaking
through a Burning Bush and then handing down the Ten Commandments.

We asked to see the monastery's abbot and were told that regrettably he was away in Greece; we were directed instead to the quarters
of the senior monk at the time, Father Sephranos. Father Sephranos
had a luxuriant, unkempt gray beard and watery eyes with an indefinable glint.[3] Worldly? Mischievous? He offered us Turkish coffee,
and I sketched for him the story we hoped to capture.

Built between A.D. 530 and 565, St. Katherine's monastery, it
has been determined, is the oldest continually inhabited building
on earth, a hard-won distinction, for the monastery's architect, one
Doulas, made a serious mistake in choosing this site—serious
enough that the Christian (though not overly charitable) Emperor
Justinian had him beheaded. The most dramatic and meaningful
place to erect the monastery would have been high up on Mount Sinai, where Moses had received the Ten Commandments. But that

choice would have meant a construction nightmare. There was no water on the peak, and it was singed by sky-ripping thunder. So Doulas elected to build the monastery in a natural bowl at the base of the mountain, at a spring associated with the Burning Bush. The liability of this location was that high above the monastery, the mountain provided an endless supply of huge boulders, which the local bedouin delighted in prying loose and watching crash down to—and through—St. Katherine's walls. They would then overrun and loot the place.

After some centuries, the put-upon monks offered the bedouin a deal: if they would stop rolling down boulders—and would even *guard* the monastery—the desert fathers would forever supply them with bread. The arrangement, we had been told, continued to this day.

Father Sephranos confirmed that this was correct and that we *might* be able to film the bread being baked and distributed to the local bedouin. He did agree that we could film sequences that would illustrate how St. Katherine's, after the resolution of its bedouin depredations, had serenely survived numerous wars and waves of religious turmoil.

Over the next three days an ever more capricious Father Sephranos had the time of his life. Whatever we wanted to photograph, he said no, we couldn't photograph that. Well, maybe we could. On one occasion, Omri, Kay, and I were in the midst of earnest negotiations with him when he took a step backward, began humming to himself, reached into the pockets of his capacious cassock, and produced three shiny, bright red apples, which he skillfully juggled.

On what was to be our third and final day in the Sinai, we were up early and at the monastery, only to find that the monks, despite promises to the contrary, had already baked their weekly allotment of bread for the bedouin. As this was a key element in our story, we were disappointed, but saw that there was still hope for a sequence. The bread had not yet been distributed; the bedouin were just now arriving and lining up. We hastily set up our battery lights to catch Father Sephranos and an assistant using long wooden paddles to withdraw the last few loaves from a large, quite biblical oven. Our only regret was that its fiery glow had long since died out. With a flourish, the good father stamped the loaves with the monastery's venerable seal. Bert moved in for a close-up, glanced at me out of the corner of his eye, and gave a thumbs up.

I breathed a sigh of relief and invited Father Sephranos to see himself on our video camera's viewfinder. Bert rewound the tape and pressed PLAY. With his eye to the eyepiece, Father Sephranos at first seemed pleased, then muttered, scowled, and looked up to exclaim darkly, "No good! All wrong! You cannot use this!" We were undone and, no doubt, soon to be expelled from St. Katherine's by the mad monk.

But then Father Sephranos turned to Bert and shouted, "Lights! And what next do you say?"

"Camera?" Bert volunteered.

"Camera, yes, camera!" ordered the monk. And, as before, he withdrew a paddle of loaves from the oven. This time, as he picked one up, he uttered a startled "Hot! Hot!" and tossed the bread from hand to hand before putting it down and theatrically shaking and licking his fingers. The bread, of course, was stone cold, just as it had been on the first take.

"Better! Better!" he said. "And, and . . ."

"Cut?" Bert queried.

"Cut!" Father Sephranos exclaimed, and laughed so hard that tears streamed down his cheeks.

That was the day Kay and I, and Bert too, realized that the Middle East would be writ large in our lives. Where else do the sacred and profane so cheerfully rub elbows? Where else can you wake up in the morning and have not the faintest idea what the day will bring? Quite often it will include an unexpected glimpse of "living history" or "the living Bible." Though both phrases are clichés, they are apt in the Middle East. In the tangible remnants of the past, the spirit of the past persists. Ancient figures—both saints and sinners—exert a powerful pull, as do their ideas and aspirations.

As we doubled back across the Sinai later that day, Kay read aloud about how early anchorites and monks had been drawn to this barren, lonely land. As the hermit Onuphrios wrote in the fifth century, "He who holds intercourse with his fellow man will never be able to speak with angels."

"*Jews*," Omri noted, "can talk to each other *and* talk to angels."

"Listen to what the writer of this book says," Kay continued. "There is an innocence in Onuphrios's saying that calls forth a deep response of gentle admiration . . . Yet there is a terrible selfishness too, and I think a terrible pride. For what kind of man is it who denies men for angels, who denies his own humanity, in fact, for the inhuman, reaching for what is by definition unreachable?"[4]

"A little harsh," I ventured.

"Probably the monks have a lot of avoidance personality, schizoid even," said social worker Kay. "Did you notice how they have a hard time looking you in the eye? But they're comfortable where they are, and I say God bless them."

We agreed that monks were all right, if a little touched—*provided* that they prayed for all humanity as well as for their own souls. Though I had my doubts about the holiness/transcendence of the desert fathers we had filmed at Mar Saba and St. Katherine's, I thought again about the chant and song of the Ethiopian Copts back in Jerusalem.

Watched over by the queen of Sheba.

Having left St. Katherine's later than we should have, we reached the Egypt-Israel border crossing after dark. It was closed. We managed, though, to rouse the resident Egyptian officials, who agreed to make an exception and process us through. The only problem was that though there was a building to inspect our passports, a building to clear the van, and so on, the post had only a single working light bulb. So a little procession—Egyptian, Israeli, Dutch, and American—formed and went from building to building. In each an official would clamber up on a desk, screw in the bulb, examine and stamp passports and paperwork, then gently unscrew the light bulb and bear it back out into the starry desert night.

2

I Kings 10

ON THE FLIGHT back to Los Angeles, I leafed through my Jerusalem Bible, looking for the story of the queen of Sheba.[1] There really
wasn't all that much to it:

1 The fame of Solomon having reached the queen of Sheba . . .
2 she came to test him with difficult questions. •She brought immense riches to Jerusalem with her, camels laden with spices,
   great quantities of gold, and precious stones. On coming to Solo-
3 mon she opened her mind freely to him; •and Solomon had an
   answer for all her questions, not one of them was too obscure for
4 the king to expound. •When the queen of Sheba saw all the wis-
5 dom of Solomon, the palace he had built, •the food at his table,
   the accommodations for his officials, the organization of his staff
   and the way they were dressed, his cup-bearers, and the holocausts he offered in the Temple of Yahweh, it left her breathless,
6 •and she said to the king, "What I heard in my own country
7 about you and your wisdom was true, then! •Until I came and
   saw it with my own eyes I could not believe what they told me,
   but clearly they told me less than half: for wisdom and prosper-
8 ity you surpass the report I heard. •How happy your wives are!
   How happy are these servants of yours who wait on you always
9 and hear your wisdom! •Blessed be Yahweh your God who has
   granted you his favor, setting you on the throne of Israel! Because of Yahweh's everlasting love for Israel, he has made you

10 king to deal out law and justice." •And she presented the king
    with a hundred and twenty talents of gold and great quantities of
    spices and precious stones; no such wealth of spices ever came
    again as those given to King Solomon by the queen of Sheba.
11 •And the fleet of Hiram, which carried gold from Ophir, also
    brought great cargoes of almuggim wood and precious stones.
12 •The king made supports with the almuggim wood for the Tem-
    ple of Yahweh and for the royal palace, and lyres and harps for
    the musicians; no more of this almuggim wood has since come
13 or been seen to this day. •And King Solomon in his turn, pre-
    sented the queen of Sheba with all she expressed a wish for, be-
    sides those presents he made her out of his royal bounty. Then
    she went home, she and her servants, to her own country.

I had little idea that I would spend years puzzling over the sense
and implications of this passage.

"Good morning, folks," a flight attendant announced with forced
cheeriness, "if you look out the window you can see ice floes and,
just ahead, the Labrador coast." Our adventures of the past weeks
over, we, like the queen of Sheba, were going home from Jerusalem
to our own country.

3
Songs of Sheba

RAISED IN MISSISSIPPI AND LOUISIANA, Kay was a daughter of the South and of jazz music. From time to time, puttering about our home in Los Angeles's Laurel Canyon, watering plants or feeding the birds, she would break into song. She was fond of daffy lyrics, as in a 1920 Tin Pan Alley ditty that begins:

> In the Bronx of New York City
> Lives a girl, she's not so pretty.
> Le-na is her name . . .

As the tune lilts along to a syncopated beat, Le-na crosses the seas to Pal-es-tee-na, where

> She was fat but she got lean-er
> Pushing on her con-cer-tina.

Which sets up the chorus:

> They say that . . .
> Le-na is the queen-o' Pal-es-tee-na,
> Just because they like her con-cer-ti-na.
> She plays it day and night,
> She never gets it right.

Quirky and catchy, the song now conjured for me the image of another queen who journeyed to Palestine. I'd seen her in a dimly lit

Jerusalem painting and read about her in the Jerusalem Bible. Her name, at once regal and sensuous, was not a personal name at all but a title. The queen of Sheba. A title from what land, what country? She could easily be a creature of the imagination. Like Le-na.

> On a camel's back a-sway-in'
> You could hear Miss Le-na play-in',
> O'er the desert sand . . .

The queen of Sheba's story—set in approximately 950 B.C.—appears in I Kings 10 and is repeated, with minor changes, in II Chronicles 9. In both accounts an unnamed queen of a land called Sheba journeys to the court of wise King Solomon. She is overwhelmed by his wealth, his wisdom, and the happiness of his subjects. Her day in Solomon's court leaves her breathless—or, as the traditional King James translation has it, "There was no strength left in her." She returns home.

Until the early 1980s, biblical scholars took the account more or less at face value, unconcerned that not a shred of extrabiblical evidence backed it up. There was no mention of the queen of Sheba in the annals of Egypt or Assyria or anywhere else in the ancient world. Witness an exchange that took place on the night of November 15, 1937, in the dark-paneled rooms of Britain's Royal Geographic Society. The Arabist Harry St. John Philby had just delivered an account of a daring motorcar journey through an area of southwestern Arabia that he believed to be "the Land of Sheba." Along the way he had taken pains to copy dozens of rock-cut inscriptions, which he had submitted to an Oxford don, A. F. L. Beeston. Mr. Beeston now rose from the society's starch-collared audience to say, "I'm afraid I must begin by disappointing you, because it has to be confessed that there is not in any of the inscriptions mention of a queen of Sheba." And he meant not only Philby's inscriptions but hundreds of others, copied by explorers as far back as Joseph-Thomas Arnaud, a French apothecary who in 1843 sailed to Arabia in search of the far-famed spices of the queen of Sheba.

Even so, with the exception of the skeptical Mr. Beeston and a handful of German academics, biblical scholars at that time pretty much agreed that the queen of Sheba's appearance in I Kings and II Chronicles lent her credibility as a historical personage. Her encounter with King Solomon *must* have happened, it was argued, because as biblical tales go, it was *so dull.* She shows up; she's awed; she's crestfallen; she leaves. Nobody is led in or out of temptation, is distraught or gets killed; there is no evident moral message. The story had the earmarks of a day-in, day-out formal court record, possibly transposed from a lost *Book of the Acts of Solomon,* cryptically mentioned in I Kings 11:41. The "court record" notion is reinforced by passages immediately preceding and following the Sheba story, passages that dwell on Solomon's prowess in foreign affairs. The Jerusalem Bible titles this section of I Kings "Solomon the Trader," and, whether describing the queen's visit or the joint development of a merchant fleet with King Hiram of Tyre, the goings-on are what a court scribe would have dutifully recorded.[1]

Beyond the accounts of I Kings and II Chronicles, Sheba appears here and there in the Old Testament—but more often as a people, not a person. Sheba is thrice listed in the "begats," the rambling genealogies of Genesis, and Isaiah 45:14 speaks of "the tall men of Sheba." In Ezekiel 27:21–23 they are among the far-flung merchants offering goods to the Phoenicians:

> Arabia and even the sheikhs of Kedar were all your clients; they paid in lambs, rams and he-goats. •The merchants of Sheba and Raamah traded with you; they supplied you with the best quality spices, precious stones and gold against your goods. •Haran, Canneh and Eden, traders of Sheba, Asshur and Chilmad traded with you.

The mention of Canneh and Eden would seem to be a tip-off to where these traders of Sheba came from, for sound-alike Qana and Aden were well-known ports of ancient southern Arabia. Indeed, close by these ports there flourished a people and land known as Sheba or, more accurately, Saba. But there was a problem with this. Expert opinion held that Saba's civilization in no way could have dated back to Solomon's era, falling short by two to three hundred years.

So where else might the Old Testament's books have had in mind as the queen of Sheba's homeland? Based on one or another allusion, there has been no shortage of contenders, though some seem far-fetched — Persia, Nigeria, Zimbabwe, the Comoros Islands.

More logically, Sheban traders and their queen could have hailed from nothern Arabia. Both the German scholar Hermann von Wissman and Harry Philby (after finding that his southern Arabian inscriptions made no mention of the queen) have presented compelling arguments for this region. Or Ethiopia could have been the Shebans' land. The Roman-Jewish historian Flavius Josephus tells us it was a "queen of Egypt and Ethiopia" who "heard the virtue and prudence of Solomon, and had a great mind to see him."[2] Or the woman in question — confounding scholars — could still have come from southern Arabia.

If one combs the Bible, it may fairly be said that the identity of the queen of Sheba becomes more rather than less of a mystery — and nowhere more than in the Song of Songs, where it is just possible that she is the inspiration for the ravishing, free-spirited "loveliest of women."

Allegedly penned by King Solomon, the Song of Songs is a series of short love poems or songs exchanged by two lovers, one of whom may be Solomon. The book is unique in the Bible, for it makes no mention of God, which has led some to throw up their hands in shock and others to rub them with pleasure, for the language and images of the Song of Songs are not only passionate but erotic. Indeed, in the second century A.D., a contingent of prominent Jerusalem rabbis sought to have the book expunged from the sacred canon because it "defiled the hands" and was a favorite of lusty gatherings in local "houses of drinking." That was when the great Rabbi Akiva rose to the Song's defense. "The whole world is not worth the day on which the Song of Songs was given to Israel," he wrote, "for all the Scriptures are holy, but the Song of Songs is the Holy of Holies."

For its lyricism alone, the Song deserves a place in history. The rhyme and meter, even in translation, are subtle and complex. The images are highly evocative, transforming the barren hill country of Judea—more suitable for goats than people—into a fertile and fragrant garden of delights.

At a seminar in Los Angeles in the early 1980s the personable Jesuit scholar William Fulco presented a fresh, unexpurgated translation of the Song of Songs. A fallback position of biblical moralists, he explained, was that the love described in the poems was allegorical, symbolizing the love between God and ancient Israel or, better yet, between Christ and His Church. "Nonsense!" fulminated Fulco, as he read a verse in which the woman says, "My own vineyard I have not kept." "And guess," he queried the audience, "what the word for vineyard can *also* mean in Hebrew?"

Outside the lecture hall, a siren wailed and drew close. "Yikes! It's the Vatican police," Father Fulco exclaimed, then chortled and continued his analysis. The woman in the poems is fleetingly referred to as a "Shulamite," one of a group who lived north of Jerusalem beyond the plains of Jezreel, and Fulco, like most scholars, thought that the woman was just that. Nevertheless, some aspects of her character, by chance or by design, echoed the image of the queen of Sheba in I Kings. She introduces herself:

> I am black but beautiful,
> daughters of Jerusalem.

This suggests a woman from far-away Arabia or Africa arriving at Solomon's court and confronting his legions of wives and concubines. Later, after the man extols his love's beauty, he promises,

> Until the day breathes cool
> and the shadows flee,
> I hasten to the mount of myrrh,
> to the hill of frankincense.

This could be an allusion to the woman's possible homeland in southern Arabia, where frankincense and myrrh grew and were harvested. And here, in a flight of lyrical love poetry, is a hint of a motive for the queen of Sheba's long journey to Solomon's Jerusalem: to negotiate a trade agreement. Reflecting the variety and value of the goods she could offer, the Song sings of

> nard and saffron, spice cane and cinnamon,
> with all the trees of frankincense, myrrh and aloes,
> with the finest of spices . . .
>
> Stir, O northwind, Come, O southwind,
> waft over my garden, let its spices flow.

Most biblical scholars agree that, in the form we know it, the Song of Songs was set down in the sixth century A.D., long after Solomon and Sheba's day. Yet they can only guess at the oral tradition this collage of poems sprang from or how far back it reached.[3] How wonderful it would be if the "most beautiful of women" was the queen I had seen in the painting in the chapel of the Ethiopian Copts in Jerusalem, for it would add a passionate and quite lovely dimension to the relatively standoffish narrative of I Kings. What if it was Sheba who whispered to Solomon,

> Set me a seal upon your heart,
> as a seal upon your arm.

For love is stronger than Death,
Passion more relentless than Sheol.
Its arrows are arrows of fire,
a mighty flame ablaze.
Mighty waters cannot quench Love,
nor can torrents sweep it away.
If one were to offer all his wealth for love,
he would be laughed to scorn . . .

Now! Come! My lover!
Be a gazelle! Be the prancing buck
on the mountain of spices!

As they scrutinize and deconstruct the Song of Songs, few scholars today believe that the "loveliest of women" is the queen of Sheba. But it is generally acknowledged that the Song of Songs is a *collection*, in Goethe's words "a lovely medley of fragmentary poems written one over the other and thrown together anyway." Might not the object of affection in one fragment be a Shulamite, and in another, Sheba?

It is worth noting that from medieval times until not that long ago it was universally believed that Solomon was the hero of the Song, and Sheba was the heroine. They appear together in manuscript illuminations (many specifically for the Song of Songs), and, as in the line "I am black but beautiful," Sheba is often black. In an enchanting German example from 1403, she is a willowy, emerald green–gowned queen of the realm (see plate 4).

The very saints of the medieval Church confirmed Sheba's role in the Song of Songs, among them Bernard of Clairvaux, a man rigorously dedicated to "the true cognizance of the truth," and Thomas Aquinas, in a document that purports to be the last testament of his cloistered life.

According to his contemporaries, Thomas was a shy, lumbering, raw-boned man. (*Bos mutas!*—"Dumb ox!"—his schoolmates had taunted him.) He was often tongue-tied. Plagued by stomach ailments, he did not live to see his fiftieth year, yet when he died, witnesses reported that he died blissfully, consumed by a vision of the Song of Songs, a vision recounted in "The *Aurora* or *Aurea Hora* of Blessed Thomas Aquinas."

Scholars are at odds as to whether the text of this *Dawn or Golden Hour* was written by St. Thomas before his death, transcribed or recalled by a fellow monk who was at his side as he lay dying, or attributed to Thomas by a later admirer. The manuscript portrays the quiet monk's increasingly emotional quest for enlightenment. It begins, "All good things came to me together with her, that Wisdom of the south, who preacheth abroad, who uttereth her voice in the streets, crieth out at the head of the multitudes."[4] Thomas soon gives a name to this Wisdom, a woman:

> This is Wisdom, namely the Queen of the South [a New Testament appellation for the queen of Sheba], who is said to have come from the east, like unto the MORNING RISING, [desiring] to hear, to understand, yea and to see the wisdom of Solomon, and there was given into her hand *power, honor, strength, and dominion*, bearing on her head the crown of the kingdom shining with the rays of twelve stars, prepared as a bride adorned for her husband, and having on her garments written in golden letters in Greek, in barbarian script, and in Latin: "Reigning I will reign, and my kingdom shall have not end for all them that find me and subtly and ingeniously and constantly seek me out."

The italics are mine. Of the famed women of the Bible—such as Eve, Deborah, the Virgin Mary—*only* the queen of Sheba wields temporal dominion and power.[5]

Drawn on, entranced by Sheba, Thomas's purported vision is increasingly a rapturous stream of consciousness. A man who once found the sight of women abhorrent now glories in paraphrasing the Song of Songs. He exults, "Come, my beloved, and let us go into thy field, let us abide in the villages, let us go up early to the vineyard . . . There shalt thou give thy breasts to my mouth . . . let no flower pass by us save we crown ourselves therewith, first with lilies, then with roses, before they be withered. Let no meadow escape our riot."

In his last days Thomas Aquinas barely ate. Only with great urging did his friend Reginald of Pipero persuade him to nibble a few herrings, of which he was once fond. Sixtus of Sienna was also in attendance and reported that as dawn broke over the Romagna hills on December 6, 1273, and light flooded Thomas's spare Cistercian cell, he ecstatically urged his fellow monks to share his reverie: "Venite, dilecti filii, egredemini in hortum." ("Come, beloved sons, go forth into the garden.")[6]

These words were his last.

4
The Desert Queen

IT MAY HAVE BEEN wishful thinking to consider the woman of the Song of Songs the queen of Sheba (though I was certainly in good company). Better that I should stick with the sketchy few hundred words of I Kings, where it's clear that the queen must have been a remarkable woman—intelligent, comely, and holding her own in a male-dominated Semitic world.[1] The description intrigued storytellers to come, who found her appealing and wondrous and—they being men—intimidating and even terrifying.

After the telling of her story in the Bible, more than a millennium of relative silence would pass before she made her next major appearance in the *sura* (chapter) "The Ant" in the Koran, the holy book of emerging Islam. In the interval, what may have been a glimpse of history has become legend. The tale's cast has expanded to include a talking bird and spirits called *djinns*, supernatural creatures born of smokeless fire, known to us as genies. Sheba's mother is a djinn, and a legion of djinns is in Solomon's employ, building him a temple and a splendiferous palace such as the world has not seen. These djinns must be kept under "a watchful eye." As a commentary on the Koran explains, "When [for Solomon] they had finished a work before night, they used to spoil it if they were not employed in something else" (like kids kicking over sand castles when they head home from the beach).[2]

In the pages of the Koran, the story acquires an unmistakable tension between Solomon and Sheba, with overtones of threat and resentment. He demands that she submit to him and his single God. Wary of Solomon and preferring to worship the sun, she isn't sure she wants to go along with that. She sends him a present, but he rejects it, for it is said that "if he be merely a king, he will accept it; and if he be a prophet he will not accept it."[3] Eventually, though, the two get together and get along, which leads to a moral lesson unstated in the Old Testament: "'Lord,' she said, 'I have sinned against my own soul. Now I submit with Solomon to Allah, Lord of the Creation.'"

Validated now by both the Bible and the Koran, the queen of Sheba was to inspire a multitude of elaborations from the eighth to the thirteenth century. Throughout the Middle East, before audiences in teeming souks and in serene, azure-tiled palaces, Jewish and Arab storytellers alike recited Sheba's tale—and sought to outdo each other, Jewish *spielers* versus Arab *rawis*. It was an amiable rivalry, for no one stood to lose. As Solomon was Jewish and Sheba presumably pre-Islamic, the more luminously the one was portrayed, the more the other shone in reflected glory.

The Arabs ultimately produced the liveliest tale, for they had a license to go further—and be more outrageous—than their Jewish counterparts. The difference had to do with magic. Though at times the Bible seethes with "wizards that chirp and mutter" and necromancers who spend "nights in dark corners," these marginal practitioners are roundly condemned. The Bible bears down hard on magic. Deuteronomy 18:10–12 abjures:

> There must never be anyone among you who makes his son or daughter pass through fire, who practises divination, who is soothsayer, augur or sorcerer, •who uses charms, consults ghosts or spirits, or calls up the dead. •For the man who does these things is detestable to Yahweh your God.

The Koran, too, had its proscriptions against magic and magi-cians. The Prophet Muhammad was intolerant of *kahin*, wily desert soothsayers, and *istqam*, their divinations by the mumbling of oracles or by the casting of marked arrows. Yet the Koran condones magical lore that is suppressed in the Bible. Angels play a much greater role in day-to-day events, and, significantly, djinns are given credence. After man and beast, they are categorized as a third state of earthly being.

For Jewish chroniclers, the idea of a bird chatting with Solomon might be acceptable, but not the notion of wonder-working, mis-chief-making djinns. This somewhat cramped their style, for djinns certainly spice up a story. They can be good, bad, or very bad. They can shape-change into wolves, reptiles, monkeys, or birds. They can even assume the form of humans, and marry and mate with them. Most of all, djinns can work wonderful magic. They dive to the bot-tom of the sea to fetch Solomon pearls the size of eggs; they whisk him on a magic carpet from lunch in Baghdad to dinner in Mecca. "And [in his aerial travels] Solomon passed over no city or island that did not obey him."[4]

It was to the labors of his djinns that Solomon owed the splendors of his cities and islands. Yet he never trusted them. To keep them ever in his sight, he sipped wine from a pure crystal goblet.

With djinns loose in a story, there was no end to its possible de-lights and surprises. They certainly captivated Abu Mohammed ibn 'Abd Allah al-Kisa'i, an Egyptian storyteller of the 1100s, who mod-estly described himself as "no more than a pen that writes." The composite account that follows, though drawn from a number of Jewish and Arab sources, is most indebted to his *Qisas al-Anabiya'* (Tales of the Prophets).

Listen then to what in medieval imagination became the tale of . . .

The Queen of Sheba
and Her Visit to Solomon,
King of the World

In the name of Allah, the compassionate, the merciful.
The annals of former generations are lessons to the living.
Let us be purged of folly, let us seek wisdom.

The City of Kitor, to the East

"I dreamt of a tortoise lying on its back," the temple seeress told the king. "Also, I saw red rats standing up on their hind paws and rubbing their eyes."

King Amru at first scoffed at such omens. What harm could befall his fabled desert city of Kitor? It had been blessed ever since its first king, Abdul Shams, also called Saba, had constructed a great dam and two wide canals, which in turn fed a network of smaller canals. A hot and thirsty land bloomed and became a green "Garden of Two Paradises."[5] So numerous were Kitor's palm trees that travelers were never struck by the rays of the sun, and the air was so fresh that people lived to great ages, spared of sickness. The city prospered beyond measure. Gold was no more valuable than dust, and silver was like mud in the streets.

For many generations, Kitor was ruled by kings strong and wise. Its merchants were skilled traders in gold, gems, and all manner of incense. In fact, the name Kitor means "the smoke of incense."

Unfortunately, wise men die and are not always succeeded by equally wise men.

One who was not wise was King Amru. He cared little for his people, and, captivated by frolics in his garden with young girls, he neglected the maintenance of Kitor's waterworks, a dangerous thing, for the city's canals and dam demanded constant care and repair.

After long ignoring the ominous vision of his temple seeress, King Amru one day took pause in his pleasures and rode out to examine Kitor's great dam. To his horror, he beheld red rats, as fat as porcupines but much stronger, gnawing at the wooden beams shoring up the dam. Other giant rats were tearing out blocks of stone that fifty fit men could not budge.

Amru raged. He ordered Kitor's townspeople and slaves to reinforce the dam and even to tie hundreds of hungry cats to its beams, but to no avail. The dam sprang a leak, then another. A coward, King Amru fled to another country. The red rats dug right through the dam, and it collapsed, and its waters flooded Kitor. When the waters subsided, the city's bereft people promised one another that they would better themselves.

They rebuilt the dam, directed in their labors by a vizier (king's counselor) named al-Himyari, an extraordinarily handsome man who, wherever he rode, drew the gazes of Kitor's women. Even the daughters of djinns found him irresistible, and when he rode out into the desert to hunt, they would bound across his path in the form of a gazelle or roe deer. One of these djinns, Umaya by name, felt such a burning love for the vizier that she appeared to him in the shape of a beautiful young woman. He fell in love with her, and she bore him a daughter, radiant as the sun, whom they named Bilqis.

Soon thereafter al-Himyari felt compelled to return to the city and the court of Kitor. Then his wife, the djinn Umaya, died. Their child was left in the desert wilderness, to be succored by gazelles, raised by the djinns of the dunes, and watched over by angels.

With each passing year, young Bilqis became ever lovelier in face and form. She had the grace of a gazelle and the wits of a desert fox. Her eyes were soft and brown like a deer's, but they also glinted gold, like the eyes of a leopard of the sands.

How Bilqis Became Queen of Sheba

As she approached the age of twenty, Bilqis caught sight of an incense caravan, which she followed at a distance. It was bound for Kitor. At the outskirts of the city, fate arranged that she should meet her father, the vizier, as he returned from a hunt. Beholding her, he swelled with pride, and his companions were wide-eyed, for she was both beautiful and intelligent. She excelled at riddles.

Her father asked, "What, Bilqis, is the most beautiful thing?"

She answered, "The soul in the body."

He asked, "What is the most dreadful thing?"

She answered, "The body without the soul." She then confessed, "Father, I am unhappy living among the djinns, and so I have come to the land of the humans."

The vizier was naturally pleased to have Bilqis at his side, yet he feared for her. "My daughter," he warned her, "we humans have a tyrannical king who ravishes his people's virgins out of wrath. He levies a maiden a week. He quickly tires of them and throws them from his palace, objects of scorn and shame."

Bilqis dutifully listened to her father's words, but to his surprise and chagrin, she frequently and heedlessly left the protection of his household. She appeared willing, almost anxious, to catch the eye of this king, the wicked Sharakh ibn Sharahil.

It was only a matter of time until Sharahil glimpsed her, and in a span of seconds, nearly went mad with desire. He summoned Bilqis to his palace.

As the palace gates swung shut behind her, Sharahil beckoned Bilqis forward and up staircase after staircase until they reached the king's *mifraj*, a tower chamber overlooking Kitor. It was a nest of puffs and pillows. Sharahil bid her partake of food and wine. She did, but sipped little. She saw to it that his cup was filled and refilled.

With twisted lips, Sharakh ibn Sharahil asked, "Tell me, Bilqis, what is your heart's desire?"

"In honesty," she replied, "it is to flee, but I cannot, for you are my king."

Sharahil removed his golden crown, his curved dagger, his cloak, and his slippers. Bilqis bowed her head, as if in submission. Sharahil drained his cup and, jerking her face up to his, smiled cruelly. Her lips parted, as if in willing response. He closed his wine-weighted eyelids and moaned, in anticipation of ecstasy to come. It was then that Bilqis reached for his dagger, pulled it from its sheath, and without the least bit of hesitation ran it straight through his heart. His soul was at once dragged down to the ovens of Hell.

Led by Bilqis's fretful father, the king's viziers clattered up the stairs to the king's mifraj, and at its door were met by Bilqis, who offered them wine to cloud their minds, then calmly told them, "The king says for you to send him your wives and daughters, so that he may debase and deflower every one of them. Every last one."

They became furious and cried, "Is he not satisfied with what he has already had?"

She coldly responded, "As you will. I shall go to Sharahil and acquaint him with your wrath." And she left them alone, that they might become even angrier. Upon her return she said, "I have told him what you said, but he says he must have it so." The viziers, every one, gave vent to their rage, whereupon Bilqis offered, "Would you like me to kill him and rid you of this evil, in which case I would reign over you?" They gasped, discussed the matter, and agreed. She told them to leave her alone with the king. Trembling, they retreated down the stairs. It was then that she took a big knife from the palace kitchen, ascended to the mifraj, cut off the dead Sharakh ibn Sharahil's head, and hurled it out the window, across Kitor's main square.

The crowd gathering below was stunned, but not for long. Soon there were murmurs of "Bilqis, Bilqis" and "None but you."

She appeared at the palace gate and stamped it with her bloody hand print. The crowd rejoiced. Her father and his fellow viziers swore fealty to Bilqis and made her queen of Kitor and all its lands.

Solomon's Talking Bird

In the meantime, far from Kitor, on a particular Friday the angel Jibril (Gabriel) gave King Solomon a ring so brilliant he was hardly able to look at it.[6] The ring gave him control over the four winds, who said in a single breath, "O prophet of God, God has subdued us for you, so ride us to any place you desire." The ring gave him power over the beasts and the birds and allowed him to converse with them. The ring made him king of the djinns. With the angel Jibril driving them, as a shepherd drives a flock, the djinns swarmed to Jerusalem from every direction. There were djinns with hooves, long tails, and flapping ears; there were bodiless heads and headless bodies.

Many of these djinns were evil, but even so they were God's servants. As God willed, they tempted and terrified mortals—all except Solomon, who held sway over them with his magic ring.

Solomon set the male djinns to building a lofty palace supported by a thousand marble pillars affixed with lamps of gold. From the depths of the ocean, they brought dazzling white pearls to decorate the palace's onyx halls. All the while, the female djinns cooked. They set out meals on tables a mile long, enough to feed the djinns and all the children of Israel. (With his ring, Solomon could summon the fishes and the birds to be willingly broiled and roasted. Do not slaves die gladly for their king?)

The female djinns wove Solomon a magic carpet, one side of which was red, the other green; it was said to be twenty-seven miles long. As it pleased him, he would call up the winds and sail aloft. On his travels he was shaded by the birds of his kingdom flying in close ranks to blot out the sun. Except that one day, to his annoyance, a single ray of sunshine pierced his eye. He demanded to know how this could be and was told that Hudhud, a crested hoopoe, was missing. Accordingly, Solomon dispatched a raven who found the hoopoe and warned him, "The king is enraged, beware!" Returning, Hudhud appeared before Solomon with drooping tail and wings as a sign of submission. He pleaded, "Prophet of God, hear my tale before judging my case. I bring you news of Bilqis, queen of Saba." Solomon, who was about to pluck out the hoopoe's feathers, paused to listen.

The errant little bird had been to Kitor, had seen Bilqis's palace, and, an inveterate eavesdropper, had learned of her overthrow of wicked Sharahil and the resulting prosperity and happiness of her subjects.

The king ordered pen and paper and wrote to Bilqis, "*This is from Solomon, and is: In the name of the most merciful God, Rise not up against me; but come, and surrender yourself unto me.*"[7] Sealing his letter with musk and his ring, he gave it to the hoopoe, who flew to Bilqis's palace.

The hoopoe, finding Bilqis asleep on her couch, threw the letter onto her breast and flew up to perch in the window. The little bird marveled to itself, "What a wonder that a woman rules over this place and these people."

Awakening, Bilqis read the letter and asked, "And who is Solomon?" Hudhud the hoopoe described his king's might and power, which caused the queen to become upset. Reading the letter aloud to her viziers, she said, "*Verily kings, when they enter a city by force, waste the same, and abase the most powerful of the inhabitants thereof: and so will these do with us.*" Seeking to avoid the destruction of her city, she sent Solomon gifts, thinking aloud, "If he is one of those impious, worldly prophets, we will satisfy him with money and rid ourselves of him. If, on the other hand, he is truly a pious prophet, he will not be satisfied with anything less than submission to himself and his single God." (And she would accede to this not without regret, for she would have to abandon her worship of the sun, moon, and stars.)

When Bilqis's viziers bore her gifts to Solomon, he did indeed refuse them, proving himself a pious prophet, not just a greedy king. He kept just a single item, a small box. Even before opening it, he said to Bilqis's viziers, "You are going to ask me to guess its contents. I can tell you straightaway: it contains a pearl through which a crooked hole has been bored, and your queen believes I cannot successfully draw a thread through it. Watch now, as one of my servants does it for me." At his command, a djinn brought forth a tiny worm, which crept through the pearl's winding tunnel, trailing a thread behind. As his reward, the threadworm was given the mulberry tree to live in, for it was fond of the leaves. This, verily, is how silk was invented.

Tɧe Queen of Sɧeba Journeyɗ to Jeruɗalem

Bilqis, queen of Sheba, emerged from her palace in a cloud of frankincense. Her viziers bowed before her. As her kneeling camel arose, bearing her aloft, the assembled people of Kitor cheered and rhythmically clapped. Calming them, she said, "My viziers tell me this Solomon, by God, is a prophet, and we have no strength to resist him. Besides, I have become curious and want to meet this king and discover his true intentions." Her attendants loaded up her treasury—all except her throne, which she had locked behind seven iron doors—and she set off in Solomon's direction. From the rooftops the veiled women of Kitor shattered the air with spine-tingling cries and ululations.

Bilqis's caravan passed through deserts of thirst and death until she came in sight of Jerusalem's shining walls and towers. Entering through the Gate of Benjamin, she was ushered through a curtain of crystal bells to the presence of Solomon, King of the World. She saw that he had a moon face, black eyes, and long eyelashes. He at first said nothing, but instead pointed to a corner of the vast chamber, and there Bilqis was astonished to see her own throne, her most prized possession. After she had departed from Kitor, Solomon's djinns had tunneled into her palace and, in the twinkling of an eye, spirited her throne underground to Jerusalem. It was a magnificent throne, though some say it resembled nothing more than a huge bed (which Solomon had called up in the belief that the way to a woman's heart was through her bed). Others say that King Solomon, intending to receive Bilqis with full honor, wanted to seat her on her very own throne. Be that as it may, Bilqis's throne was dwarfed by Solomon's.

Solomon's throne was fashioned of ivory and gold and studded with pearls the size of ostrich eggs. It had seven steps, each flanked with automatons of birds and beasts. When Solomon ascended the first step, bronze eagles flapped their wings. When he ascended the second step, brass lions roared; at the third, golden bulls bellowed; and so on all the way to the top, where golden peacocks perfumed him with musk and ambergris. The entire prodigious affair was kept aloft by four invisible djinns, so that visitors swore the king and his throne floated in the air.

Solomon's throne was so awesome that when he sat in judgment, litigants and wrongdoers could tell only the truth. (Nearby a lion and a rhinoceros listened intently, and if a culprit persisted in his denials, they would attack him, because God's creatures love the truth.)

Bilqis offered salutations to Solomon and stated, "I have come, mighty king, to see for myself the splendor of your works, and to admire your grace and partake of your wisdom."

Solomon smiled and said, "Then ask me a riddle."

So she asked, "What is the water that comes neither from the earth nor from the sky?"

"The sweat of horses," he answered. "Ask me another."

She ventured:

> "A storm-wind rushes through their tops;
> It cries loudly and bitterly.
> It is praiseworthy for the free,
> Shameworthy for the poor,
> Honorable for the dead,
> Joyous to the birds,
> Grievous for the fish."

"Flax," Solomon said, smiling, hardly waiting for her to finish.[8]

Bilqis tried again. "A woman says to her son, 'Your father is my father; your grandfather is my father; you are my son and I am your sister.'"

Solomon replied, "Surely these are the two daughters of Lot."[9]

Losing heart, Bilqis bowed her head, only to look up and see Solomon descending his throne and approaching her. He took her hand and offered her the hospitality of his palace and his royal company.

In the lofty throne room's gallery, Solomon's three hundred wives and seven hundred concubines giggled. Bilqis shot them a hard look. They twittered and fled.

The Glass Floor

Bilqis remained in Jerusalem, the better to become acquainted with Solomon and learn of his all-powerful God. The king and the queen came to enjoy each other, causing Solomon's djinns to become fearful. If the two married and she bore him a boy, the djinns would never be freed from slavery. Zabwa, a djinn, advised Solomon, "O prophet of God, a son by this woman will be cruel, sharp, and hot in body and soul." Zabwa and his ilk spread rumors that Bilqis was one of their own (which in part she was) and as such had the telltale hairy legs and the foot of an ass.

To determine if there was any truth to this claim, Solomon

planned a ruse. In his private quarters he laid a glass floor with water and fish beneath it. He invited Bilqis to come join him. Mistaking the glass floor for a fishpond, she quite naturally lifted her skirts to walk through the water. When he saw what he saw, he averted his glance and admitted to her, "Lo! It is a floor, made smooth of glass."

What did Solomon see?

Solomon's courtiers were uncertain, with most agreeing that though Bilqis's feet may have been misshapen in some way, they were not hooved. Her legs, though, were hairy. This alarmed Solomon, and his enslaved and mischievous djinns rejoiced, but only briefly. The king commanded them to prepare a lotion of slaked lime and ash and so remove the troublesome hair.

Then said the queen, "O Lord, verily I have dealt unjustly with my own soul; and I resign myself, together with Solomon, unto God, the Lord of all creatures."

Bilqis married Solomon and bore him a son called Rehoboam, whose arms reached down to his knees, a sign of chieftainship.

The Worm and Solomon's Staff

In time, Bilqis felt it her obligation to return to Kitor and her people. Some say Solomon visited her there three days a month; others say he didn't.

Solomon lived a long and prosperous life. He had many wives and children, yet faraway Sheba was often on his mind. From his tower, he would gaze longingly out across the desert.

Then one day he was visited by Azra'il, the Angel of Death, the Annihilator of Men, the Shadow which ends alike all joys and sorrows. When he had taken Solomon's spirit, Azra'il left his body leaning on a staff for support. Solomon just stood there, motionless, answering no questions, but looking as wise and severe as ever. During this time, Solomon's djinns were on loan, hard at work in faraway Kitor and its lands, building palaces for Bilqis.

All things come to an end.

A tiny worm inched up into Solomon's tower and gnawed at the tip of his wooden staff, day after day, month after month, eating its way through. Solomon remained upright for a year, then crumbled to the floor and disintegrated into a cloud of dust. And so it is related: it was a tiny worm that caused the fall of King Solomon, who once ruled the world.

"O folk of the djinn!" shouted a messenger hastening south to the region of Kitor, "Solomon is dead! Stop work!" The demon djinns threw down their tools and betook themselves to two great rocks, where they recorded their labors and the end of their slavery.

"We satans fashioned with our hands Salhin and Baynun
Our sweated labor raised Bainun, Sirwah, and High Hunaida
too . . .
But no more will this land see our handiwork! Rejoice!"

And then Solomon's djinns returned to the dark corners of the world from whence they had been summoned by the angel Jibril, years before.

Thereafter Bilqis, queen of Sheba, reigned for a total of seventeen years, a protectress of virtue in her land.

This is what has been related, but God knows best.

Clearly, much has been read into the encounter between king and queen since it was set down in the Bible, and even since it was re-cited in the Koran. The tale has taken on an elliptical and quirky tone, typical of both Arab and Jewish medieval storytelling. There are long buildups and sudden, pull-out-the-rug codas—like the con-clusion, which says little of Sheba after her encounter with Solo-mon.

We learn of the curious way in which silk was invented, we are privy to the mixing of the first known depilatory, and we're there for the first major industrial strike on record, when with a "Stop work!" the djinns laboring in Saba walk off the job.

As to the story's king and queen, they are no longer the pasteboard figures of the Bible; they've acquired distinct personalities. Solomon is powerful and all-knowing; as one version of the legend elaborates, "Wisdom is in ninety parts, seventy of which are in Solomon and the other twenty in the rest of the people." But he is short on humility and somewhat of a bully. He demands Bilqis's submission to his authority and humiliates her in the presence of his court. Does this, we might ask, reveal the bias of Islamic storytellers as they portrayed an Israelite king? Not at all. Their Jewish counterparts were even harder on Solomon; in a Jewish version of the story Solomon's bird-borne letter to Bilqis includes a heavy-handed threat, causing her to "tear at her garments" in consternation:

> If you refuse [to knuckle under] and will not . . . pay homage to me, I shall send out against you kings, legions, and riders. You ask who are these kings, legions, and riders of King Solomon? Know then that the beasts in the fields are my kings, the birds of the air my riders, the djinns and ghosts my legions. They will throttle you in your bed, the beasts of the fields will slay you in the fields, and the birds of the air will consume your flesh.[10]

Not only is Solomon a bully, he's a trickster. He filches Bilqis's throne; he deceives her with his clever glass floor. He's also vain and a fusspot. (The King of the World fretting about hair on a woman's legs?)

One account admires his throne, but as for Solomon, "He was— they [prior commentators] assert—pale, corpulent, clean and hairy."[11]

Bilqis, on the other hand, is as radiant as the sun, a clear-eyed beauty. And she is wily, but for good cause, as in firmly dealing with the sexual predations of King Sharahil. When she's threatened, her eyes of a doe become the eyes of a cat. And, like a proud feline, she has little interest in submission—which makes her an anomaly in the male-dominated (then and now) society of the Middle East. She accedes to Solomon's wishes only when she perceives that behind him stands a single, all-powerful God. She had worshipped the sun, but as one account has her ask, "How powerful is the sun, when it can be blotted out by a flock of birds?" Solomon's God, on the other hand, was the creator of the sun, the birds, everything, even evil as personified by the djinns that dodge in and out of the story.

Djinns . . .

Solomon drinks only from a crystal goblet, the better to keep an eye on his demon slaves; Bilqis, on the other hand, can without concern sip from a clay cup. Though raised by the djinns of the dunes, Bilqis leaves them and thereafter achieves all that she achieves *on her own*, without their questionable aid. There is an interesting juxtaposition here, for what is Solomon without his djinns? He conspires with them to trick Bilqis, and he prevails on them to construct his throne, raise his fantastical palace, and build his many splendid cities. Take away Solomon's djinns and their works, and we're left with a minor Middle Eastern king spreading his tail feathers in a rough-hewn rural palace.

Compared to Solomon's illusory world, Bilqis's royal city of Kitor rising from the desert is a far more convincing place. Its mighty dam, canals, and sprawling gardens are man-made, not the work of djinns.

In their appraisals of the queen of Sheba legend, a number of scholars have marveled at what developed from just thirteen verses in the Bible; such is the power of myth. But there may be something else at work here: quite possibly the biblical tale was embellished, reshaped even, by one or more *traditions independent of the Bible*, traditions that might preserve fragments—artifacts, if you will—of events in the life of an actual queen of Sheba. The Bible makes no mention of Solomon's glass floor and Sheba's throne. These elements surface in the Koran and, in more detail, the *Kitab al-Tijan* (Book of Crowns) of Wahb ibn Munnabih, a seventh-century Yemeni historian intent on recording his country's past kings—and a queen. In reality, stripped of its fancifulness, the glass floor could have been a stream that the queen of Sheba crossed as she came up out of the desert and neared Jerusalem. In a Persian miniature in the British Museum, it is just that.

Sheba crosses a stream, watched by Solomon, his courtiers, and his djinns

As to a real queen of Sheba's throne, if it was like other thrones of antiquity, it was far more than furniture; it was a potent symbol of power, as in the Koran's phrase, "Allah; there is no god but Him, the Lord of the Glorious Throne." On a worldly level, the kingdom of Saba may indeed have had a finely wrought and impressive throne, the envy of even a king like Solomon. (Legend counters by making his bigger and better, if preposterous.)

Describing an era in which (as far as they knew) few queens ruled, a number of storytellers take pains to explain how Bilqis came to sit upon her throne. In Wahb ibn Munnabih's telling, she takes power upon the death of her father and acts as regent until her cousin 'Amr ibn Y'afur comes of age. Quite a number of storytellers subscribe to this version, with one identifying her as the sole queen at the end of a grand all-male genealogy: Bilqis *bint* (the daughter of) Sharahil *ibn* (the son of) Dhu Jadan ibn Ayli Sharh ibn al-Haith ibn Qays ibn Sayfi ibn Saba ibn Yashjub ibn Yar'ub ibn Qahtan.[12]

By early medieval times Bilqis had gained—or maybe she had it in the first place—a distinctive, mind-of-her-own personality, both inspiring and threatening. She bravely crossed gender boundaries. Indeed, an argument for the imprint of an authentic queen is that her legend flew in the face of the Semitic stereotype that men rule and women follow, in the palace as at home. Solomon may be a king, but he's given to bluster and bullying, dependent on his djinns, undone by a tiny worm. Not so the Desert Queen. One can imagine a storyteller such as ibn Munnabih or al-Kisa'i reciting the tale of Bilqis at considerable peril, lest a listening wife or daughter take it upon herself to reorder domestic duties—and the storyteller find himself drawing water and plucking the chicken in the kitchen corner.

Next time he'll stick to tales of Og and Magog, David and Goliath, Joseph tempted by Potiphar's slinky wife. Or he'll tell how, whatever has gone wrong with the world, it was all Eve's fault.

5
With Eyes Shining As Stars

"DO YOU SPEAK ENGLISH?"

"Non," responded the young lady, with barely a glance from her magazine.

In pursuit of the Desert Queen, I had taken the afternoon express from Paris and was now at the information kiosk of the train station of Dijon. What local train might take me somewhere near the Burgundy village of Aloxe-Corton?

"Parlez anyone Ingles . . . aqui en la gare?"

"Non, non," she repeated, flipping through her *Elle*.

I wandered out to the station platform. On "E" there were a scattering of travelers and a wheezy mustard yellow train.

"Le chemin de fer . . . Aloxe-Corton?"

In response, there were *nons*, some *ouis*, and a choice *pfft* delivered with upraised palms and heavy-lidded blink. Virtually all of the *ouis*, I noted, boarded the mustard yellow train, as did I.

If such things as signs or omens exist at all, this *had* to be the right train, for across the aisle a kindly-looking elderly lady had drawn a faded orange curtain to shield herself from the glare of the midday sun, had kicked off her stolid shoes, and was lost in the pages of a well-worn paperback novel: *La Reine de Saba*—The Queen of Sheba.

My interest in the shifting legends and stories of Sheba had reached a juncture. Questions had arisen that could no longer be put to rest in library stacks; rather, they beckoned me on irregular forays to odd corners of the United States and Europe. Here, in a swaying second-class compartment in eastern France—on an admittedly quixotic errand—I was determined to find out if there was any truth to a casual statement I had run across—an aside in a 1953 essay—that the queen of Sheba was portrayed on the label of a wine from Aloxe-Corton.[1] I'd queried wine experts in the United States; if such a wine and label existed, they assured me, they would almost certainly be aware of it. And they weren't.

The train took me to a rural station, where I engaged a taxi driver, Emile. As we drove the ten kilometers to Aloxe-Corton, Emile honed his English by rating the vineyards on either side of the road. "Just fair, the reds just here. Too damp," he confided. "And ahead, the hill you see is too dry upstairs, but in middle just right."

At the foot of the hill, a cluster of thatch-roofed houses and a story-book chateau came into view. Aloxe-Corton.

I nearly missed a wayside stone post.

"Emile, au secours, back up."

The lichen-encrusted post bore the weathered image of a jolly, rotund woman roasting a goose over an open fire. A legend read: DOMAINE LA REINE PÉDAUQUE .

A rustic stone winery nestled at the end of a gravel lane. Its vermilion-smocked workers directed us to a gracious young woman, a member of the family Gagnot. She offered Emile and me glasses of a La Reine Pédauque white and a rich, spicy red. She showed us a notice by a passing connoisseur; what we were sipping was "brooding, burnt cherry, goût de terroir." But what fascinated me was the jolly woman on the bottle's label.

Could she be la reine de Saba?

"C'est possible, c'est possible," Mlle. Gagnot allowed, though personally she thought the woman on the label was "Berthe au Gran Pied"—Bertha Big Foot, wife of Pépin le Bref and mother of Charle-

"Il n'y a à les boire
que les Dieux, nos
Dames et Nous."

"Les Dieux debout,
nos Dames assises
et Nous à genoux"

Mis en bouteilles par

CAVES DE LA REINE PÉDAUQUE
NÉGOCIANT-ÉLEVEUR A ALOXE-CORTON, CÔTE-D'OR, FRANCE

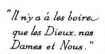

La Reine Pédauque
wine label

Detail showing the
goose feet

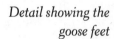

magne. "One of her foot it was big and the other it was *tres* bigger."
The winery's workers, when asked, had other ideas or no idea. An af-
fably growly retainer had his doubts about Bertha. The label, he suggested, spoke for itself.

"Si elle est Berthe au Grand Pied . . ." he began, and Emile translated, "If she Bertha Big Foot, then where, *alors*, are those big feet?"

The retainer was right. The jolly woman's feet were hard to discern, for they were tiny.

And each had three webbed toes. In a dialect of medieval France,
la reine pédauque was "the goose-footed queen."

I was invited to descend a long stone stair to see where the queen's
wine slumbered in musty darkness, deep beneath the district's sunny

vineyards. Mlle. Gagnot wiped cobwebs from a bottle dating to 1885; the winery's dank caves were far older, although no one could say exactly how old.

"La reine de Saba?" I wondered aloud.

"Peut-être . . ." If you wish it so . . .

Appreciative of the visit (and the glasses of earthy wine), I took my leave and had Emile drop me off at a rural inn. Over the next few days I sought local knowledge of la reine pédauque, walking from village to village and once, when it began to rain, hitching a ride on a farmer's wobbly tractor. I had a hard look at a gaggle of geese, and found it unnerving to imagine a woman with their scaly, reptilian feet.

I learned that images of la reine pédauque had once adorned the church of Saint-Père at Nevers and the abbey of Nesle-la-Reposte, both razed during the Terror of the French Revolution and now fallen to ruin and weeds and forgotten. At Saint-Bénigne at Dijon, a statue of her had been hammered to smithereens, yet the city's archive preserved an old engraving of it. To the right of the abbey's west portal, a crowned queen with a webbed left foot once stood in the company of David, Solomon, and Moses.[2]

This ecclesiastical, Old Testament association makes a case for the queen of Sheba as la reine pédauque—her one or two goose feet likely a Christian transmutation of the foot of the ass or hairy legs that caused Solomon such consternation in earlier Jewish-Arab mythology.[3] This identity is confirmed by an allusion in a manuscript dating to the 1150s, in which la reine pédauque is described as "a lady of Sheba and also Ethiopia, with goose-like feet and eyes shining as stars."[4]

In this and other imaginative medieval accounts, the queen of Sheba in the role of la reine pédauque is a shadowy, slightly sinister figure. Who but djinns or the Devil has a deformed foot? And the woman favors her left hand, in Latin her "sinister" hand. The tale is

A goose-footed Sheba at Dijon's Saint-Bénigne cathedral (the statues have since been destroyed)

told of la reine pédauque's journey to Jerusalem and of how, just outside the city's walls, she wades across a pond, a variation on Solomon's djinn-detecting glass floor in Jewish and Islamic legend—and is miraculously cured of her pédauqery!

> And then, by God's good will,
> Was her goose foot changed
> Into a man's like any other.[5]

But why would the queen of Sheba wade across a pond? Did her odd webbed foot or feet mean she was attracted to water? Not at all. The queen of Sheba waded because she didn't want to walk on the stout log that spanned the pond. And the reason *why* she didn't want to walk that log ties her to a biblical chronology that is inventive and amazing, for it links the queen of Sheba to the Garden of Eden — and to the cross of Christ.

And, beyond that, to the Last Judgment.

For Jacobus de Voragine, archbishop of Genoa in the middle 1200s, an affinity for the queen of Sheba came with his investiture, for one of the treasures of his Cathedral of San Lorenzo was a green glass bowl inscribed with a star of David. Brought from the Holy Land by Crusaders, it was revered as a sacred bowl three times over, for it was believed to have been given to Solomon by the queen of Sheba, then used by Jesus Christ during the Last Supper, then used by Nicodemus to collect Christ's blood after the Crucifixion.

Jacobus de Voragine loved such connections, for they exemplified how the mechanisms of the world were created, ordered, and ruled by the providence of a detail-driven God. The archbishop believed that everything — the roles of men and of beasts, even of inanimate objects — had been fitted together with an intricate and marvelous precision, and he set out to illustrate this in his *Legenda Aurea*, his "Golden Legend." In this rambling discourse on Christian saints and symbols, he offered a key role to the queen of Sheba.

Jacobus's narrative tells us that as Adam lay dying, his son Seth went to the Archangel Michael to beg for a drop of oil from heaven's Tree of Mercy. Michael refused, instead offering Seth a twig of the earthly Tree of Knowledge, the tree whose fruit gave his parents (and all humankind) both wisdom and grief. Twig in hand, Seth returned to his father, only to discover that Adam had died. The best he could do was to plant the twig on Adam's grave, where it shot upward to become a resilient and long-lived tree.

Many generations later, this tree caught King Solomon's eye, and he cut it down, intending to use it in the construction of his temple. But the tree confounded his carpenters, slyly shifting in shape and size when their backs were turned: "Sometimes it appeared to be too long, and at other times too short, and when the builders tried to cut it to the length desired, they discovered that they had cut off too much. Thereupon they became impatient with the tree." Solomon ordered it dragged from the temple and thrown across a nearby pond. Useless as lintel or pillar, it could at least serve as a footbridge.

Shortly thereafter, nearing Jerusalem, the queen of Sheba came to the bank of that pond and was about to set foot on the log that spanned it, when she had a vision that the Savior of Mankind would one day hang from that very tree, so instead she knelt and adored it. And then, rather than risk desecrating the tree, she waded across the pond—and in those few watery steps was cured of her goose-footed-ness.

Jesus' cross, Jacobus tells us, was later made from the wood of that tree. And the saga continues with the holy wood being hidden underground until Helena, mother of the first Christian emperor, Constantine, recovers it and provides the great cathedrals of Europe with splinters of the True Cross—splinters, Jacobus reveals to the faithful, that had sprung from the Garden of Eden soon after Creation and had once been venerated by the queen of Sheba.[6]

Jacobus de Voragine's tale appealed to the credulous—and to artists, who were awarded a host of commissions to interpret it.[7] Cycles of paintings incorporating the dying Adam, a devout Sheba, and the True Cross appeared on the walls of Santa Croce in Florence and a dozen other northern Italian churches. In Arezzo, the city's Franciscan fathers encouraged the merchant Giovanni Bacci to underwrite the decoration of their Capella Majore, perhaps playing on the fact that he, like Sheba, had prospered in the spice trade.

In 1452 or shortly thereafter, Bacci and a (then) little-known artist paced the church's choir. The painter, Piero della Francesca, found the wall space a little cramped but thought the problem could be solved by an unusual arrangement of the story's tableaux. The project would take him twelve years, on and off, to complete.

In the fresco's third panel (see plates 6–7), a pale dawn illuminates a hilly Jerusalem landscape, and the beautiful queen of Sheba, simply dressed, kneels before the wood of the tree that had sprouted from Adam's grave. The pond in the story has been reduced to a puddle, but it is there. Nearby, two of her grooms idly chat, oblivious to what is happening. A horse whinnies in the morning chill. These distractions aside, there is a sense of solemn ritual, for this is the miraculous moment when Sheba has the premonition that the wood will become the cross of Christ. Her ladies-in-waiting look on in somber silence.

Next in della Francesca's pantomime, beyond a Corinthian column symbolic of Solomon's Temple, Sheba and Solomon meet in a high-ceilinged hall. His courtiers are opulent, swathed in robes of Renaissance silks and brocades (Solomon's is the showiest). Because the angle of view is slightly lowered, the fresco's figures are imposing and graceful, even a portly red-robed courtier to the left (likely a rendering of Piero's patron, Giovanni Bacci).

In an artist's trick, one of Sheba's ladies-in-waiting gazes out at the viewer, as if to invite us into the picture. But, we might ask, for what? It is a joyless scene. Sheba—in profile, her head bowed—is subordinate to Solomon and apparently not at all enjoying the encounter. Though Solomon grasps her hand, her expression is of measured and icy reserve. Her eyes gaze inward. As for Solomon, he has been described as "a brave and noble figure" and "a man of moving dignity," yet look closely at his expression, and you see a world-worn man, his left eye almost closed by a drooping lid. Here, as in virtually all medieval and Renaissance art, Solomon looks as if he would rather be anywhere else. Why couldn't it have been his biblical compatriot Hiram of Tyre who had come calling; why did it have to be a queen, and this particular queen?

An explanation for this glum and dispirited Solomon may be found in the text that guided Piero, the *Legenda Aurea*. In Jacobus's account, the queen had one thing only to tell Solomon, and it stunned him. Referring to the log outside his palace, she said [to Solomon] the Savior of all the world should be hanged thereon, by whom the realm of the Jews shall be defaced and cease.[8]

(A cleric who saw no place in the world for any religion but his own, Jacobus de Voragine bears responsibility for this mean-spirited sentiment, which he unfairly ascribes to the queen of Sheba.)

Was it the artist's intention to freeze in time this remark? The one person who would know is the black-capped, thin-faced figure standing next to the red-robed courtier in the fresco. He is believed to be Piero della Francesca, in a rare self-portrait.

The queen of Sheba appears a strange choice to proclaim the coming of Christianity, unless you look—as almost certainly Jacobus de Voragine did—to two passages in the Gospels. In almost identical language, they foretell that this queen—also known as the queen of the South—is destined to reappear on earth on a future fateful day.[9]

On Judgment day the Queen of the South will rise up with this generation and condemn it, because she came from the ends of the earth to hear the wisdom of Solomon, and there is something greater than Solomon here. (Matthew 12:42, repeated with slight variation in Luke 11:31)

Joining Sheba on Judgment Day, the "something greater than Solomon," of course, is none other than Jesus Christ. If this passage is to be taken literally (or even metaphorically), both Sheba and Jesus would pass judgment, dividing the duties. Sheba's concern would be "this generation" and Jesus would weigh the virtues and vices of all mankind.[10] By "this generation" Matthew pointedly meant the Pharisees who questioned Jesus' legitimacy and scoffed at his teachings. Elsewhere in that Gospel, Jesus rails at them as "hypocrites!" "a brood of vipers," "fit for hell." And it falls to Sheba, Queen of the South, to dispatch them there.

The idea of the queen of Sheba in the company of Jesus was to furnish grist for the mystic mills of medieval Christianity. A remote Old Testament queen, more idea than flesh, came to be seen as symbolizing the Church eager to know and stand with Christ, in accordance with a decree by Abbot Suger of Saint-Denis that "the Old Testament should give access to the New." And this was just the beginning of the theological baggage the queen of Sheba would be asked to bear. In their diverse cloisters, Isadore of Seville and England's Venerable Bede independently uncovered what they believed to be a hidden biblical reference to her and Jesus as co-rulers of a kingdom to come. In Psalm 45, a line addressed to a messiah-king proclaims: "On your right hand stands the queen, in gold from Ophir." That queen, the two theologians believed, was Sheba. Elaborating on this notion, Isadore considered her to be the mystic Bride of Christ. And, not to be outdone, the widely read Honorius of Autun saw Jesus and Sheba as a single holy entity, noting in his *Speculum de Mysteriis:* "The Queen of the South gave her body and blood to the disciples."

Add to this a popular medieval tradition that identified the queen of Sheba with the Blessed Virgin Mary.

Begone reason and logic! *The Queen of the South is identified not only with the Church but with the mother of Jesus, Jesus' bride and Jesus himself.*

Contradictory as this may seem to us, it hardly troubled the medieval mind. Scholars call such cross-identifications and mergers *conflations* and point out that they appealed to the masses as well as the monks. Consider, for instance, what conflation does for the Virgin Mary. After Jesus' birth, the Gospels say little of her, aside from the times when Jesus gets angry at her. Mary is a relatively colorless, relatively powerless figure. But fuse her with Sheba, and you have at once an earthly Queen of the South and a transcendent Queen of Heaven, a queen of both Old and New Testaments.[11]

Woodcut of Solomon and goose-footed Sheba (Ulm, 1492)

Between the *Legenda Aurea* and the Gospels of Matthew and Luke, Sheba is woven into a tapestry of the beginning of time and the End Times—which makes it all the more curious that in the medieval and Renaissance world, she is often regarded with a distinct and palpable sense of unease. She may be a theological insider, but she's also an outsider, never wholly embraced by mainstream tradition. In a woodcut popular along European pilgrimage routes, Solomon regards her as reevers, millers, merchants, and knights regarded her: at arm's length, suspiciously.

What was so troublesome about this queen? The goose foot certainly was a factor. But that aside, here was an Old Testament figure recruited (coopted even) for service in the New—and when all was said and done, that wasn't where she belonged.

And she was shunned. Though she should have been accorded

the glories of a saint, she was excluded from their company. In Europe's cathedrals and abbeys, no candles flickered at her feet.

What was it about her? Was it that she was a pagan, though a "righteous pagan" (lacking in her day the option of choosing Christ as her savior)? Was it something else?

Bells pealed and tolled, as I walked in the footsteps of medieval wayfarers through England's Canterbury town to its great cathedral—and, in a rondel of stained glass, found as good an answer as I could expect for the feelings of discomfort prompted by the queen of Sheba. Directed by an understanding verger ("I'd like to sit near Solomon and Sheba." "I believe that's possible."), I took my place in the cathedral's choir, where locals and visitors were quietly gathering for Sunday Evensong. As the organ rumbled and a procession of acolytes, clergy, and choristers filed in, I had a good view of the cathedral's glass *Biblia Pauperum*, or "Poor Man's Bible," whose figures against a field of vivid blue once told largely illiterate pilgrims of the Old Testament's major characters and happenings. High and to the left, I spied the queen of Sheba come to Solomon (see plate 5). And by no means meekly. Or in awe. Or breathless. It looked for all the world as if she, her tense and edgy aides (biblical Secret Service agents?), and two camels had just burst unceremoniously through the doors of Solomon's palace. And she is clearly intimidating him. Her demeanor is take-charge, here's-the-deal. Solomon is cowering on his throne, and if stained glass could animate he'd be quaking as well.[12]

Canterbury's choristers soared in angelic descant, a contrast to the near-raucus scene up in the rondel. And there, I realized, was the crux of what so deeply bothered the medieval clergy and laity (though perhaps not the window's bemused glazier) about the queen of Sheba. Here was a woman wielding *power and dominion*. Sheba is no docile Blessed Virgin Mary. She is the antithesis of an eye-rolling, long-suffering martyr. The Bible's sole female monarch, she can be—and here is—headstrong and aggressive, a threat to what was widely perceived as nature's equilibrium and even God's design. Dread be it for a woman to usurp a man's role. She's queen of her realm—and Solomon's too, if he doesn't watch out.

The service drew to a close, and the echo of a last anthem reverberated in Canterbury's soaring and now shadowy vaults. I watched as the last rays of the sun glinted on the irregular glass of the Biblia Pauperum and darkness overtook the great window. I thanked the verger who had shown me to the queen; he was a bit distracted as he looked about for Thomas, an orange marmalade cathedral cat. "Has to be thrown out as many as six times a service, that one. But wouldn't you know, nowhere in sight when time comes to close up. Did you enjoy Evensong?"

"I did. Very much."

"I find it calming. I don't find cats calming. Well, good night, then."

The last to leave, I made my way out of the cathedral's twilit close, appreciative that Canterbury preserved a collage of colored glass as telling as any manuscript in its expression of the queen of Sheba's power and dominion. And if these attributes troubled medieval folk—or if Solomon himself once shuddered—that was their worry, not hers (I told myself).

No matter how suspect or resented, she was ever radiant, she "of goose foot and eyes shining as stars."

6

Touched By the Queen

As the enlightenment of the Renaissance swept Europe, the bubble that was the *Legenda Aurea*, shimmering with tales of the queen of Sheba and scores of saints, was pricked by skeptical scholarship and burst. The once revered Jacobus de Voragine was condemned as barbaric, superstitious, even immoral; he was dismissed as typical of "those who love to hear or tell of feign'd Miracles and strange lyes, and are never weary of any Tale . . . and the more do they tickle their itching ears." Quite suddenly, the queen of Sheba was of little import to the theology and teachings of the Church. There would be no more paintings—or even mention—of her discovery of the True Cross. She was distanced from Jesus, and who would remember her role in the Last Judgment?

Yet over the years she would touch the lives of a collection of both obscure and renowned painters (including Raphael, Tintoretto, and Veronese) and composers. She captivated a New England man of letters. A noted Hollywood director followed her star, fatally so, as did a Death Valley fortune seeker.

They were an odd lot, and their stories odder yet.

IN MUSIC . . .

Courtly and formal were the airs of George Frideric Handel's 1749 oratorio *Solomon*.[1] Act III is a stately masque staged by Solomon to impress visiting Sheba. King and chorus poetically sing of (but hardly exhibit) the passions of blind fury, a tortured soul, and final calm. Sheba is awed, presents Judah's chosen king with treasure, and takes her leave, saying

> May peace in Salem ever dwell!
> Illustrious Solomon, farewell.

Premiered by the Paris Opera a century later, Charles Gounod's *La Reine de Saba* failed to excite audiences, even though in Act II the chorus reached a pitch of vocal frenzy as volcanoes erupted off-stage and furnaces exploded onstage. It wasn't until Karl Goldmark's 1875 opera, *Die Königin von Saba*, that the full operatic (that is, brimming with love, deceit, and death) potential of the story was realized.

Mendelssohn, Schubert, and Brahms were the toast of Vienna in the mid-nineteenth century; Karl Goldmark was not. A frayed-collar, hapless piano teacher, he "existed one winter simply on potatoes, without any bread, the following summer on curds and raw cucumbers."[2] The only light of his life was the all-too-rare promising student, such as seven-year-old Karoline Bettelheim. "She had a clear mind," he recalled, "and little hands of steel."

In the often long hours between lessons, Goldmark composed music, and by his own admission he wasn't very good at it. Aware of the achievements of Viennese prodigies from Mozart on, he confessed, "I am overcome with grief . . . For me the whole flower of youth with its brimming imagination and its passionate emotion was lost, lost through misery and want, but even more through lack of any kind of instruction." In his early thirties he destroyed all that he had written. He did get a steady job, though, as a violinist in a Viennese variety theater. His glissades and trills accompanied Klischnigg's monkey act; Pepita, the sensuous but technically disastrous Spanish dancer; and Miss Ella, the trick rider, who repeatedly and alarmingly bloodied herself as she jumped from her galloping horse onto a springboard—and missed.

It was then that his ex-student Karoline Bettelheim, barely fifteen years old, made her debut as a soprano with Vienna's Imperial Court Opera. Her one-time piano teacher, watching from the wings, heard the stage manager say, "Look at the girl! The face! The very image of the queen of Sheba!"

This chance observation inspired luckless Karl Goldmark to give his all to *Die Königin von Saba* and to submit the completed score to the principal stage director of the Court Opera, who looked at what the variety theater violinist had written and declared, "It was out of the question to produce the opera because all the laws of harmony had been ignored and there were discords throughout." A sad Goldmark accepted his plight; his thank-you-anyway note to the Court Opera's patron, Prince von Hohenlohe, began, "I have had the great misfortune to compose an opera."

To Goldmark's surprise, the prince responded by regally paying him two hundred florins for his work. That wasn't even enough to cover the cost of copying, but Goldmark didn't mind, for the prince promised to set straight the Court Opera's snippy stage director. Declared von Hohenlohe: "I will break his neck if he does not produce the opera."

Rehearsals went badly. The whole affair was impossibly leaden. The chorus hissed the composer. Goldmark was forced to patch together his own sets. He fainted dead away. He repaired to a late-night café and sought solace from his acquaintance Johannes Brahms. "Ah, well," said Brahms of the coming performance, "it is customary to drown the first litter."

For the premiere, the queen of Sheba was sung not by Goldmark's protégé and inspiration, Karoline, but by the popular Amalie Materna, dark-eyed, long-haired, and plump, a condition not altogether successfully masked by row upon row of pearls. Listening to the sole recording of the opera and following its libretto, one wonders what could have gone on between Karl and Karoline and what Karoline ("with little hands of steel") was really like, for Goldmark's queen is a scheming temptress "with her mouth trembling between a smile and seduction." She dominates the action, taking Solomon for granted and pursuing with unholy energy a Jewish nobleman named Assad, paying no heed that he's betrothed to Solomon's daughter. Assad is doomed when he spies Sheba bathing in a forest in Lebanon:

> From crystal waves a swan-like body rises,
> It is a woman of celestial beauty! . . .
> She throws her lily arms around my neck!
> She draws me to her softly swelling bosom,
> Confused and half unconscious I kneel down
> Upon my knees before the fair enchantress.

To bend events to her will, Sheba seduces, prevaricates, attacks, and makes bellicose demands—and transforms a series of set-piece scenes into an operatically searing drama, all to music that incorporates both Wagnerian thunder and delicate Oriental motifs, some sung hauntingly a cappella. The opera takes on a hallucinatory character. "Is't delusion? Am I dreaming?" Assad asks before demanding of Sheba, "Demon, with thy glance bewitching . . . Go, and accursed be!" With a spine-chilling shriek she in turn seals his fate:

> Then fare thee well, joy and contentment.
> Shadows of night, engulf your prey!

Assad dies in the throes of an Arabian sandstorm, and Solomon himself barely succeeds in breaking Sheba's demonic power. Curtain, Act IV.

As Goldmark bravely recalled, Vienna's critics were unanimous in their "ridicule, lies, contempt!" Nevertheless, the opera was an immediate popular success, packing the Court Opera throughout the 1876 winter season. In the years to follow, Strauss and Mahler conducted *Die Königin von Saba*, as did the tempestuous Carlo Pedrotti, who on an opening night in Turin brought his orchestra to a dead stop when a gentleman in the front row objected to Goldmark's Oriental sonorities with an audible "Why, that is all wrong." Pedrotti whirled around to exclaim, "That is not true! You do not understand anything!" With great passion he plunged on, failing to catch an error in his score, a passage marked *andante* instead of *largo*. His tempo became so furious that the kettledrums could not keep up, so Pedrotti took over by loudly beating his brass music stand with his baton, forcing the winds to skip all but the most essential notes. Goldmark recalled, "I was standing behind the curtain wringing my hands in expectation of hisses and cat calls, but the effect was quite different. The audience jumped to their feet, applauded and shouted *encore* like mad."

Karl Goldmark's great and only major success is of historical interest in that its "highly spiced" music—as well as Sheba's exotic, dark character—advanced the cause of "Orientalism" in the arts, a movement that glorified the sultry and mysterious East. In studios tricked up to resemble seraglios, painters turned out images of fierce bedouin bristling with knives and muskets and dwelt on the ripe delights of concubines cavorting in harem pools. Non-artistes caught up in the craze were moved to add "Turkish rooms" to their houses, cluttered with hookahs, poufs, and ornamental screens.

Musically, Richard Strauss gave Orientalism a boost with his opera *Salome*, as did Ottorino Respighi with his exotic, lavish, and thunderous ballet *Belkis, Regina di Saba*.[3]

Across the seas in America, denizens of Tin Pan Alley—including Irving Berlin—had their own take on the alluring East. Songs like "In My Harem" and "Behind Your Silken Veil" told of "lonely des-ert lands filled with beau-ties rare, flash-ing eyes of par-a-dise." These songs, called "Oriental Novelties," beckoned bumpkins and bankers to witness gauzy hootchy-cootchy delights in sawdust-floored tents of rural fairs and carnivals. "Inside! An ancient harem dance of bondage!" barkers promised. "Sinful!" ministers railed, running many a show out of town. Nevertheless, cheeky girls answered ads promising twenty-two dollars a week to shake and shimmy for "four minutes and kick only when the piano plays or you fail to receive your salary." They became Marie Beyrooty (the Dervish whirler), Sultry Salome (of the Seven Veils), and Betty from Babylon,

> With Arabia in her dreamy eyes—
> and naughty sighs.

Assuming that the queen of Sheba would also have been a carnival figure, I sought her in the memories of tent show veterans. My questions drew a blank. "Which is surprising," girlie-show impresario Al Stencil mused. "We gave everything a try. Coney Island even had Fatima, the cootch-dancing bear. No Sheba, though. Nope, not that I ever heard. Too biblical, I suppose. Too *good* biblical. Never did nothing bad . . . or did she?"

Sheba's "goodness," however, made her precisely the person to elevate hootchy-cootch from behind the midway to Main Street. The rationale was this: the Bible tells us that Sheba and her attendants, most if not all female, came calling. And if they danced? It was biblical! Why, Solomon could have dancers, too, and a circus could show off its exotic livestock and wild animals in a crowd-pleasing spectacle. As the *Atlanta Constitution* noted of a "spec" (short for "spectacle") featuring the queen of Sheba, a "reputedly immoral ballet was clothed in religious respectability, allowing the audience to catch a glimpse of rounded thighs and at the same time improve their minds." Clergymen might grumble, but they couldn't object.

Sheba joined the circus and rode America's rails. On tour from 1891 to 1896, John Robinson's Great World Exposition featured "the

Queen of Sheba girls" sashaying from gaily painted Pullmans to the Big Top, where they participated in a twenty- to thirty-minute pageant culminating in a "GRAND BALLET. The most beautiful and chaste Terpsichorean Divertissement . . . entrancing poses, posturings and changes." Or, as a San Jose reporter appraised, "a hip rumble." He went on to carp that the scenery was shoddy and the costumes threadbare.

This was hardly a charge leveled at Barnum and Bailey's all-out 1903–04 *Tribute of Balkis*.[4] The spec's impresario, Hungarian émigré Bolossy Kiralfy, delighted in marshaling supernumeraries into kaleidoscopic patterns, rippling kick lines, living pyramids, and endless processions. His friend, actor Otis Skinner, recalls him stroking his waxed mustache and rehearsing, "Von-two-tree! No! No! Stop! Vots de matter mit de back line? No, please—Ladies, LADIES!"

As a poster colorfully recorded, Kiralfy's queen of Sheba was trailed by "countless dancing girls in magnificent costumes . . . as far as the eye could see" (see plate 8). If that wasn't enough, the circus's cook-house men played Hebrew soldiers wielding battle-axes, and roustabouts doubled as masons and slaves. A huge, specially built stage overflowed with incense bearers, coryphées, horses and camels, necromancers, figurants, and Persian elephants.

Not to be outdone, in 1915 the rival Ringling Brothers circus mounted a spectacle that incorporated, if we are to believe a newspaper ad, "1250 characters, 300 dancing girls, chorus of 400 voices, orchestra of 90 & 735 horses." And swelling in accompaniment was a "Grand triple pneumatic Cathedral Pipe organ, the Most Magnificent Musical Instrument Ever Constructed." Faded photographs confirm that the production was wonderful—and hardly wicked. The cast of fresh-faced young men and women was recruited in and around the Ringling Brothers hometown of Baraboo, Wisconsin. Sheba was portrayed by a demure Mrs. Bartik. How excited these prairie innocents must have been as they traveled the nation, steaming across high trestles and clickety-clacking past barns pasted with six-sheet posters:

PULSATING IN WEALTH OF WONDROUS COLOR THE DAYS OF SOLOMON AND THE BEAUTIFUL QUEEN OF SHEBA FLASH FORTH FROM THE DIMNESS OF THE AGES.

In the show-business argot of the day, the queen of Sheba was the acme of hotta-stuffa.

IN MINING . . .

In 1908 in the heart of Death Valley, the thrill of the circus was a world away as thirty-five-year-old Chester Pray tended his campfire at Salt Springs. For company he had "Old John" Lemoigne and the asthmatic W. A. "Whispering" Kelly. The fire was for cooking, not warmth: it was summer, and temperatures hovered at 120 degrees Fahrenheit in the shade, if you could find any. To get to where they were, you had to descend from the Funeral Mountains into Death Valley, make your way to Badwater and then strike out across the Devil's Golf Course.

Over their bread and beans, the three men talked of women, but not all that much. The fair sex generally made desert rats uncomfortable (the doves du prairie behind Robinson's store over at Ballarat excepted). As his companions later recalled, Chester would allude to a fiancée down in Los Angeles, then veer off into flighty mining talk.[5] One by one the prospectors would go over to the springs to soak their sheets, then wrap themselves in the cool wet cloth and fitfully doze. The relentless heat might drop a few degrees by midnight.

In the next blazing days the group split up to work the foothills of the Panamint Range, and there Chester Pray found a vein breaking the surface that would assay at 15 percent lead with a bonus of five ounces of silver and a trace of gold per ton. He named his claim the

Carbonate and spent the next five years trying to make a go of it. The ore was good, but transporting it to a smelter was prohibitively costly.

Then things began to look up. The price of lead rose, and speculation was rife that lead would become a bonanza metal.

It was then that the well-known Death Valley promoter Jack Salsberry took an interest in Chester Pray's operation, and the two filed partnership papers in early April of 1913. Either he or Chester decided that if the mine was to become a world-beater, it needed a better name, a name that would outshine the surrounding desert's Silver Queen, Gold Crown, and King Solomon.

They renamed the workings the Queen of Sheba, perhaps recalling a touring circus or perhaps just taken by the airy and beautiful sound of the name.

The nearest town of consequence was Goldfield, Nevada, and in the early summer of 1913 its *Tribune* reported Jack Salsberry looking after business interests in San Francisco while Chester Pray supervised a crew cutting a serviceable wagon road from the Queen of Sheba mine to the nearest siding of the Tonopah and Tidewater Railroad. On Saturday, June 7, they were at the halfway mark, about to cross Jubilee Pass. The hell of the valley's salt flats was behind them, and Chester was in good spirits. "Yes, sir, he acted jolly and cutting up the same as ever," road worker Jack Gallagher later testified.

Chester Pray's future was bright, so it was a shock when just before dawn the next day some two to five shots rang out, and Chester was found a few hundred yards down the road from camp with one or possibly two bullets in his head.[6] His crew packed him onto a burro for the journey to the railroad town of Tecopa, where a hastily convened coroner's jury pronounced the death a suicide, a case of "mental derangement" brought on by sunstroke suffered years before. There was little doubt that Chester Pray had his demons; as a child he had been committed to an asylum. His aunt recalled, "He frequently said he knew he was not like other people."

At a simple service in Goldfield, members of the Elks Lodge

placed little sprays of forget-me-nots on Pray's zinc-lined casket, and he was laid to rest. Jack Salsberry covered the costs.

Curious about the case, I tracked down surviving copies of the Goldfield *Tribune* from 1913. On Thursday, June 5—two days before Chester Pray lay dead in Death Valley—the paper's innocuous "Personal Mention" column reported: "John Salsberry came down from Reno this morning on his way to a mineral property in which he is interested over the line in California." That property could only be the Queen of Sheba. Salsberry was *not* in San Francisco at the time of the killing, as was reported elsewhere; he and parties unknown were heading for the mine and a rendezvous with Chester Pray.

Journalists in both California and Nevada were unsure: was it suicide or murder? Had Pray possibly been killed by Indians?[7]

That fall, Jack Salsberry enjoyed the riches of what was now his mine. When World War I broke out, the price of lead tripled, and the mine, "looming up as the latest sensation of the Western mining world . . . a desert metropolis," produced forty tons a week.[8] Of Death Valley's hundreds of claims and strikes, none equaled the Queen of Sheba, staked by poor Chester Pray.

IN THE MOVIES . . .

In the years when Chester Pray was pursuing his Death Valley dream, stage director J. Gordon Edwards was writing a queen of Sheba play. He worked on it a little at a time in bars and hotels as his touring company moved from city to city. When fortune offered Edwards a Hollywood movie director's megaphone, Sheba was not forgotten; Edwards rewrote his play as a photoplay and convinced mogul William Fox to put it on his studio's slate for 1921.

The hope of a hundred musty hotel rooms and twenty years of writing became a spectacular reality. The alluring Betty Blythe was cast in the title role, and in nouveau Babylonian style, Sheba's exotic city arose on Fox's Western Avenue lot, complete with a coliseum in which oater star Tom Mix would stage a thrilling chariot race between Sheba (and her four white horses) and the villainess Vashti (and her four black horses). Thousands of extras were gotten up in burlap robes and awning material, and the featured costumes were fantastic: exotic dancers wore peacock-plume headdresses several yards square, and Betty wore hardly anything at all. "I wear twenty-eight costumes," she confided to a reporter, "and if I put them on all at once, I couldn't keep warm" (see plates 10–12).[9]

For inspiration, a five-piece orchestra was on hand when the cameras rolled. According to those who saw it, the film was often quite moving. Near the end, Sheba must forever take leave of her child by Solomon. As the scene was shot, Betty Blythe related, "I put my arm around the child. I didn't look at him. I just looked into the ages I would have to spend without this great love. Mr. Edwards had his handkerchief out [and said] as he wiped his eyes, 'That can never again be made like that. Cut. Everyone go home.' Everyone went home. It was three in the afternoon."

The Queen of Sheba was a hit. Not only did it tug at the heartstrings, but it appealed to the religious, it dignified hootchy-cootch, and it was action-packed. As Miss Blythe recalled, "Bodies were flying through the air like popcorn . . . The audiences in New York stood up with excitement." *Motion Picture News* added, "One instinctively grasps the arms of the seat as the chariots come tearing straight toward the camera. And Sheba wins." On the basis of his success, the director was sent off to Europe to scout locations for a whole series of biblical epics.

Then, as Betty Blythe sadly remembered, "Mr. Edwards returned to this country and his whole flash of genius just went to ashes. I don't know the details, except the blame lay with Fox. Now I just carry in my heart the love of this beautiful thing—*The Queen of Sheba*."

J. Gordon Edwards was about to check out of his New York hotel room and try for a Hollywood comeback when he died on Christmas

Day, 1925. Reported *Photoplay,* "He was 58 and jobless. A broken heart. They called it pneumonia." What is sadder yet is that not one of Edwards's films survives. Not a foot of film remains of the love of his life as an artist, *The Queen of Sheba.*[10]

So star-crossed was a man in her thrall.[11]

IN LITERATURE . . .

Sheba was featured in the first printed treatise on women, *De Mulieribus Claris* ("Concerning Famous Women," 1362) by Giovanni Boccaccio, he of the adroitly risqué. His telling of her tale is actually quite chaste, hewing to the biblical line. He found her "the more worthy of remembrance in that, being born among uncivilized people, she shone the more brightly for her good conduct." Thereafter, though, writers saw her as they wished to see her, a creature of their imagining. Sheba is often a metaphor for how regal, beautiful, and sometimes haughty a woman can be; as Professor Henry Higgins tells Eliza Doolittle in *My Fair Lady,* "Why, I could pass you off as the queen of Sheba!" Just as readily, she could be lurid, dazzlingly so, as in her bravura turn in Gustave Flaubert's *The Temptation of St. Antony.* As if the demon-plagued Desert Father doesn't have enough to contend with, Sheba materializes on the beach by his Red Sea cave. She's clad in rippling golden brocade accented by falbalas of pearl, jet, and sapphire; nestled between her breasts a diamond scorpion sticks out its tongue. Poor Antony is dumbstruck as she vamps.

> Ah! Fine hermit! Fine hermit! My heart swoons! I've fidgeted so impatiently I've got calluses on my feet and I've broken one of my nails! I love you! Oh! yes! very much!
>
> [Stage direction] *Antony stays quite still, stiff as a rod, and as pale as death. She takes Saint Antony by both cheeks; he pushes her off at arm's length. She performs a pirouette.*

I am not a woman, but a world. My clothes need only fall away for you to discover in my person one continuous mystery!

Antony's teeth are chattering.

If you laid your finger on my shoulder, it would affect you like fire running through your veins. The possession of the least place on my body will give you sharper joy than the conquest of an empire. Offer your lips!

Antony crosses himself.

You scorn me! Such a beautiful woman!

You'll regret it, fine hermit, you'll be sorry! And bored! But I don't care! La! la! la! oh! oh! oh!

As the queen of Sheba withdraws, a monkey lifts up her robe to reveal a deformed foot. She lets out a sort of convulsive hiccup, not unlike a sob or a snigger.[12]

In other literary appearances, Sheba is an enigma, a riddle within a riddle, as in the highly personal philosophizing of Robert Browning, William Butler Yeats, and Bertrand Russell. Whimsically, a poem by Rudyard Kipling tells us:

> There never was a Queen like Balkis,
> From here to the wide world's end;
> But Balkis talked to a butterfly
> As you would talk to a friend.

The most affecting literary Sheba I encountered wasn't Sheba at all but a woman who thought she was. For the better part of a week, I had been methodically checking out entry after queen of Sheba entry in the New York Public Library. The volume at hand, titled *The Queen of Sheba*, was written by Thomas B. Aldrich in 1876. Aldrich, I later learned, had a decade earlier quit his job as a clerk in his uncle's New York bank and moved to Boston so that he might walk in the footsteps of Ralph Waldo Emerson, Nathaniel Hawthorne, and Henry James, all of whom he revered. At the time, his fiction was commended for its technical skill and charm but faulted for its superficiality. Sniped a critic, "He will not challenge the masters for a place on the heights."

Rain splattered the windows of the library reading room as I turned to page one and saw that the book was a romance of nineteenth-century New England and had nothing to do with a historical queen of Sheba. Nevertheless, warm and dry in my pool of green-shaded library light, I read on.

It seems that "in search of the picturesque and peculiar," a clerk, Edward Lynde, has chosen to tramp the hill country of New Hampshire on his vacation. Down the trail, he spies a young woman.

> As she drew nearer, Lynde was conscious of being dazzled by a pair of heavily fringed black eyes, large and lustrous, set in an oval face of exquisite pallor. The girl held a dandelion in one hand, twirling it by the end of its long, snake-like stem as she approached. She was close upon him now; for an instant he caught wind of the flower as it swiftly described a circle within an inch of his cheek. The girl paused in front of him, and drawing herself up to her full height said haughtily,
> "I am the Queen of Sheba."[13]

Lynde is both taken aback and entranced. As she passes by, he confesses to himself, "I never saw a girl at once so—so audacious and modest, or so lovely. I didn't know there was any thing on earth so lovely as that girl."

Years go by and events take Lynde to the Continent, where he sees the very same woman, gathers the courage to introduce himself to her, and is crestfallen when she informs him she has no recollection of ever having seen him, and, though from America, she has never been to New Hampshire.

But, oh, she *had* been there, committed to a private asylum for the deranged and insane—and Lynde had passed her on the morning she escaped!

The story goes on from there, but I would rather not give it away, on the off chance that a reader might want to blow the dust from Aldrich's wonderful book, still to be found in town and country libraries established in the 1800s. Suffice it to say, he weaves an engaging story that has some very moving moments played against finely crafted set pieces, including a near-fatal picnic at the edge of a Swiss glacier. Neglecting a long list of books I had intended to check, I read *The Queen of Sheba* straight through until the rain stopped, the street lights came on, and I took my leave of the New York Public Library, bidding good night to its guardian lions.

What I admired about the book was that (contrary to accusations of its superficiality) it caught what it is about women that attracts men—and hopelessly and forever perplexes them. On his journey to the Continent, Edward Lynde tries to appraise afresh the woman who, in an earlier delusional state, announced herself as the Queen of Sheba.

> She is very self-possessed, with just a suspicion of haughtiness; personally, tall, slight, a sort of dusky Eastern beauty, with the clear warm colors of a New England September twilight . . . I say she is a girl to flirt with, and yet, with that sensitive-cut mouth and those deep eyes, she could do awful things in the way of tenderness if she had a mind to. She's a puzzle, with her dove's innocence and her serpent's wisdom. All women are problems. I suppose every married man of us goes down to his grave with his particular problem not quite solved.

The clerk Edward Lynde's life would never be the same and would be forever unsettled.

And what do we conclude about a grand opera acclaimed in its time yet thereafter plunged into obscurity, a suicide—or murder—in Death Valley, the career of a prominent movie director turned to ashes? When the queen of Sheba is around, things don't seem to go so well, yet it is hard to say why. The curse of an ancient queen? That would be melodramatic—that is, if this queen ever existed. Rather, Karl Goldmark, Chester Pray, J. Gordon Edwards, and Edward Lynde may simply have been stricken by life's random heartbreak, heightened by the fact that when Sheba is the subject, expectations rise and passions flare.

Liken her to a starburst in an ancient night sky, exploding overhead in a kaleidoscope of fire and color, captivating some, frightening others. And her embers still fall to earth. Subtly, she can be found in the fabric of contemporary life. She may not have the following accorded a popular singer or politician—or any following at all—but most of us are at least hazily aware of her. We've all remarked or heard, "Who does she think she is, the Queen of Sheba?"

In her preface to *The Boston Cooking School Cook Book* Fannie Farmer quotes Ruskin: "Cookery means the knowledge of Medea and of Circe and of Helen and of the Queen of Sheba." Sheba is an icon for the perfume Aqaba, marketed by Manhattan's upscale Henri Bendel. A consumer survey determined "Sheba" the best possible name for a cat food. In "A Thing Called Love," country singer Bonnie Raitt demurs, "Baby, you know I ain't no queen of Sheba."

She is there for the right man, at least in a recent personal ad in the Los Angeles *New Times:*

> SHEBA SEEKS SOLOMON
> Straight BF, 31, professional stu-
> dent, 5′9″, 140 lbs, gorgeous, no
> makeup, light lemony colored
> skin, black hair, brown eyes,
> unique expensive taste, articu-
> late, seeks best friend in male
> counter part. Prefer 40+; good
> looking Jewish men a plus.

In Which
We Seek Solomon and Sheba
in the Holy Land

7
O Jerusalem!

EARLY ON A THURSDAY morning in May 1997, I motored into the Holy Land wedged into the sprung back seat of a sandblasted Palestinian *sherut*. I'd flown to Jordan from the United States the day before and taken a bus to the Allenby Bridge. Once across the bridge, I had cleared Israeli Customs and was wondering how best to proceed to Jerusalem, when the sherut's driver had solicited, "I am friend Inglesi!"

"But I'm American."

"I friend Americans more!" he assured me, packing my luggage into his sagging Peugeot. I joined a stone-faced Palestinian matriarch, a French water-pump salesman, and, up front, two chain-smoking brothers hotheadedly shouting at each other and the driver in Arabic. The *Brothers Intifada*, I thought. Their problem, it developed, was that they had an audiocassette of al-Fayrouz, the renowned Lebanese songstress, and the Peugeot's tape player didn't want to deal with it. "Have to kiss, have to kiss," intervened the driver as he reached over and gently wiggled the cassette to coax al-Fayrouz to sing for us.

"It's nice," said the water-pump salesman, surveying the overgrazed landscape. "I sell to all this, the whole area. And water pumps is nice because they pump water. Of course they pump water. What I mean to say is that nobody they blow up each other with water pumps." He pointed out a benefit of traveling in green-license-plate

Palestinian vehicles: "Is nice, because no people with clothing over faces throw rocks at you."

For my part, the time had come to seriously seek a historical queen of Sheba. I was well aware that I was on an uncertain road. At the moment it was two lanes and paved, curving up through the Judean Hills, but at any time it could become a track too faint to follow.

The sherut's driver slowed down, then chose to speed up and bang on the horn to scatter pedestrians crossing the road from market to mosque on the outskirts of Jerusalem. Jerusalem, a city visited by the queen of Sheba. Jerusalem, a lodestar for her legend. What about her reality?

Our woman passenger—who throughout the journey had said not a word, staring grimly ahead—disembarked at a muffler shop. Then, rather than proceed directly into the city, we labored up the back side of the Mount of Olives to drop the pump salesman at his favorite hotel ("nobody stays there; nobody bother you"). A little farther, and we crested the mount and looked across to the walled Old City, undulating with domes and shot with spires. Over there Solomon held court, Muhammad spurred his magic horse, Baraq, to heaven, and Jesus rode through the streets on a lowly donkey. I spied Jerusalem's walled-up Golden Gate—which, it's believed, will open when Jesus returns to offer mercy and demand penance on Judgment Day. And, if the Evangelists Matthew and Luke are to be taken literally, he will have at his side Sheba, queen of the South.

As the sherut braked and shuddered down the Mount of Olives, I penciled some impressions of the Old City that when I later reviewed them made little or no sense. The truth is, I didn't know what to feel, though I had several options. I could have been struck with awe that what I beheld was the mystical mirror of an unseen, heavenly Jerusalem, St. Augustine's City of God. Or I could have taken the darker view found in the Jerusalem journal of Herman Melville.

After he completed *Moby Dick*—whose White Whale was in part a metaphor for God, by turns elusive and angry—the author's fits of nervous temper prompted his family to send him abroad for his health. They chose the Levant, believing that there he might find peace with God. But instead he was appalled by Jerusalem's spiritual and physical decay. "No country will more quickly dissipate romantic expectations than Palestine," he wrote, "particularly Jerusalem. To some the disappointment is heart sickening. Is the desolation of the land the result of the fatal embrace of the Deity? Hapless are the favorites of heaven."[1]

The Brothers Intifada ejected their tape and got out at the Damascus Gate. The sherut circled the Old City's walls to the Jaffa Gate, honked its way through urchins and their elders peddling chewing gum and misinformation, and dropped me off at Christ Church Hospice.

"Mr. Bill Clinton," assured the driver, "he okay."

With a fine Gothic façade and a freshly whitewashed interior, the hospice was a welcoming, slightly quirky place (as Anglican enterprises are wont to be). Though this was a pilgrim's inn, there was no requirement to show up for services; you could join in prayer or not, as you wished. Leaving my luggage, I set off on foot down nearby David Street, passed the long-shuttered Mediterranean Hotel (where Herman Melville had stayed and sulked), and zigzagged over to the plaza in front of the Church of the Holy Sepulchre.

The worn wooden door was off to the side, just as I remembered it. No one was about. Passing two familiar Ethiopian Coptic chapels, I ascended a twisting flight of stone stairs. Ahead, sunshine streamed through a low door. "Tizahair al harosh!" a voice warned. "Bitte, kopf runter!" I bumped my head on the jamb as I looked up to see, on the roof of the Holy Sepulchre, a monk perched on a wooden stool. "Ha, ha," he said, now switching to English. "Ha, I simple monk may not know much, but I know to say 'Please to mind the head' in eight languages."

Where the monk sat, the flat roof supported a cluster of African-looking domed huts, originally mud, now cemented over. The story of their presence here reaches back to the days of early Christianity, when Ethiopia had a major stake in the operation of the Church of the Holy Sepulchre. This lasted until 1838, when a smallpox epidemic ravaged the Holy City and killed off its Ethiopian monks. It was then that the five remaining sects sharing the church negotiated an arrangement known as the Status Quo. They divided the place up, determining who could worship when and in what chapel, even who could light and snuff the church's every candle. The intent was to end centuries of incessant squabbling. An all-too-human result was that the Ethiopians, absent from the Status Quo negotiations, were elbowed out of Christianity's holiest shrine. When replacement monks arrived from Africa, the best they could do was to camp out on the Holy Sepulchre's roof and eventually lay claim to two small chapels in an adjoining building.

Here and there on the roof, monks were absorbed in prayer books, murmuring to themselves in Ge'ez, Ethiopia's ancient ritual language. An older monk beckoned me into a low-roofed refectory, where he offered me Ritz crackers and a tin cup of pungent coffee.

"The queen of Sheba . . ." I ventured.

"Sheba. Ah, ah. No Inglesi."

"Anybody speak Inglesi?" I asked, looking out across the monk-speckled rooftop.

He gestured to the monk I'd first encountered, who had dozed off in the afternoon sun. I nodded thank you, and walked over to him. The stones beneath my feet resonated with a Latin hymn being sung below in the Chapel of St. Helena, by whatever sect was marking its territory at the time.

"Oh, whatcha looking for?" asked the monk, blinking awake.

I described my quest for Sheba; he smiled and nodded. "Yea-ahs, yea-ahs." Sighing a sigh for ancient times, he said, "She was a great queen. She have her royal city in Aksum in Abyssinia. That was old name for Ethiopia. She was black like me. Yea-ahs! Then she heard of Jerusalem, and she decided to see Jerusalem for herself. So she come to Ga-za, then she come over here with presents for King Solomon. She stayed months. She keep her camels at Ga-za, but she herself live right here, right at this place where we talk. And Solomon he see how much she like it here, he give her gift of this land, and land in Ga-za too."

"And the two of them they rest, yea-ahs, together. And King Solomon he give Sheba another gift. I give you a hint. It was a mysterious gift she only found out about when she was on her way home to Aksum. Boss, you guess it?"

Before I could answer, he grinned and exclaimed, "Menelik, their son, he born." Then, quite abruptly, he lowered his gaze to his prayer book and softly chanted. I stood there a minute, puzzled, then guessed that he could spare only so much time before returning to his devotions. To learn about Menelik, son of the queen of Sheba and Solomon, I would have to return another day.

I left the roof and retraced my steps to the plaza in front of the Holy Sepulchre, where a stubble-chinned man wearing a ski cap implored me to rent one of his eight-foot crosses and drag it along the Via Dolorosa. I thanked him but chose instead to enter the church. I was to visit it frequently in the next week or so. It was like returning, again and again, to the lobby of a very old and cavernous and gloomy hotel where you have a vaguely perceived spiritual room. At the Gothic-arched entryway, a rat-faced, ponytailed monk was pulling his shift as God's doorman. Inside, empty Coke cans and Evian bottles had been left on stone ledges; rotting paintings sagged from the walls; candles guttered and dripped so much wax that I had to watch my step to avoid slipping and cracking an elbow. "One looks for luminous light," writes Father Murphy-O'Connor in *The Holy Land: An Archaeological Guide*. "One desires holiness only to encounter a jealous possessiveness . . . The frailty of man is nowhere more apparent than here; it epitomizes the human condition. The empty who come to be filled will leave desolate."[2] I wandered through a warren of passageways, stairs, and chapels and paused by a Crusader-graffitied pillar facing the Edicule, the incense- and smoke-stained stone structure guarding Christ's tomb. Father Murphy-O'Connor calls it "hideously ugly." At once it towers and sags; iron bands have been added to keep it from imploding.

"Two lines into the tomb," a monk intoned. "En deux lignes . . . zwei reihen." I watched as a woman in black entered the Edicule, crossing herself and kissing everything she could—railings, masonry, candlesticks. Behind her a Slav of some sort was having trouble with his flash. Then came two American teenagers. "So I hear Alisha became a cheerleader," prattled one. "Alisha! Her? I don't believe it!" The other girl hardly heard as she spread her arms in supplication, trembling and prayerful, overwhelmed by where she was and what it meant to her. She passed into Jesus' last place on earth, a cramped chamber containing a marble slab, lit by a constellation of sacred lamps.

The Edicule figures in many a spiritual odyssey and rarely for the best. Melville's journal laments the "dingy light—a sort of plague-stricken splendor—All is glitter and nothing gold." Not that long ago, at the end of a five-year spiritual quest, a computer technician from New York got to this point and broke out shouting to those around him, "Pagans! You adore idols! You are all pagans!" and had to be taken to the hospital on the hill of Kfar Shaul. This afternoon a group of Scandinavian pilgrims were unnerved as they made their uncertain way through the labyrinthine church, singing hymns of home, hymns reminiscent of white wooden churches in snowy fields. What a shock it must be to find Christianity's greatest shrine so dark and derelict, all but defying their bravely flickering lights of faith.

It is enough to unhinge people—and it does. There are some two hundred cases a year of what has been identified as the "Jerusalem Syndrome."

The next morning I made my way across the city to Kfar Shaul, the mental hospital that handles what happens when the spiritual becomes the psychotic. It was a cheerful place, a series of cottages climbing a grassy hill. It was ecumenical, though with a preponderance of *haredim*, the devotedly Orthodox Jews who, in their shawls and fur hats are forever bustling through Jerusalem—except that here at Kfar Shaul they've lost their direction, and now spin in circles like broken wind-up toys. Climbing an outside staircase to a second-floor administrative center, I was shown into the sunny book- and file-cluttered office of the director, Dr. Yiir Bar-El, a jolly bear of a man who relished running his meshuggeneh hospital (his words).

"At the outset," he said, "you must understand that Jerusalem is a city of the past, but not a normal city of the past. It is a gate to another world, a world of God, angels, and eternity. A lot of people believe this." From recent experience, he spoke of a teacher from Denmark who could see and talk to Jesus—but *only* in Jerusalem. And the English lady who every afternoon set tea for Jesus on the Mount of Olives, though he never came. These people had symptoms of the Jerusalem Syndrome: they either imagined themselves in contact with religious figures or they *assumed the identity of these figures.*

He recalled a time when Kfar Shaul had three Marys at once, all believing themselves pregnant and on the verge of delivering the next Jesus. And the tumult when two Moseses were inadvertently housed in the same cottage.

Dr. Bar-El had studied and analyzed the syndrome and compiled statistics. Most of his patients, as one might expect, had prior histories of mental illness, and it didn't take much to set them off. But in a significant number of cases there was no hint of a problem, other than that these pilgrims and tourists, mostly Protestant, were from families in which the Bible was the major, sometimes the only, book in the house. In areas of rural Scandinavia, he'd learned, when family disputes arose it was not uncommon for the youngest child to randomly open the Bible to a passage that was then interpreted to provide an answer for whatever was at issue. In the Holy Land, where the importance of the Bible is intensified, more than a few visitors experienced a seven-step progression of symptoms.

1. Feeling anxious
2. Wanting to be alone and to make one's own tour
3. Practicing purification rites—cutting nails, showering incessantly
4. Wearing white—often a hotel sheet
5. Singing biblical songs
6. Making personal pilgrimages to holy places
7. Making inordinate demands on tour group

Around the third step, there was often a degree of psychotic break. When brought to Kfar Shaul, victims were frequently quite aware of this, felt ashamed, and didn't want to talk about their condition. This was all right, for it typically passed in five to seven days.

A good-natured nurse joined us and spoke of the pull to identify—to become one—with a particular biblical figure. A Samson had cooled off here (after assaulting the masonry of the Western Wall), as had kings David (with harp and crown) and Solomon. Of women, as well as many Marys, there had been a Deborah, an alarming Jael (who in the book of Judges hammered a tent peg through the head of a sleeping guest)—and a queen of the Nile, one of the titles attributed to the queen of Sheba.[3] She had been brought in after shedding her clothes and circling the Old City's walls, singing and dancing that the desert might bloom.

I hesitated to ask for more details of the lady who imagined herself Sheba; her psychosis was transient, and as Dr. Bar-El had stated when I initially phoned him, he was bound to respect a patient's identity and offer only the sketchiest of details.

As we parted, Dr. Bar-El allowed that he wasn't looking forward to the millennium. Already, three large U.S. congregations had announced their plans to sell all their material possessions and move to Jerusalem. Lord knows how many patients he'd have on his hands. But it must be said that Dr. Bar-El was the right man in the right place. In English, his name was "Yiir, Son of God."

At Christ Church Hospice, I listened as breakfasting pilgrims compared notes. A stout, gray-bobbed British Midlands lady announced that in Jerusalem she "had been filled with the spirit of God." All right. Then there was a fragment of conversation that ended as a wide-eyed young woman, American I think, said, "And then God took me and showed me His wonderful throne." He did? I admired Dr. Bar-El's efforts to make a distinction between fervent faith and the Jerusalem Syndrome. Perhaps the difference began when the sheets came off the bed and imagining became acting out.

"And what brings you here, lad?" I was asked. I of course was no lad, but he was a Scotsman, and that's how they talk. Thinking he might find my queen of Sheba quest peculiar, I said something about researching the beliefs of the Ethiopian Copts.

"Ah, yes, I've been there, to their rooftop accommodations. I call them the *Keystone Kopts*, as they are always skittering about and peeking at you, waggling their ears at you, then it's back with their noses in the prayer book. I was over to the Sepulchre a day or two ago, and they had come down for some devotions at the Lord's tomb, when the Franciscans spied them and rushed up and drowned them out by thundering away on their bloody loud organ." He added, "A fine display of Christian charity."

After breakfast I went over to the monastery of the Ethiopian Copts to look for my English-speaking storyteller. He wasn't there. A fellow monk indicated he would be back later in the day.

As I walked through the Old City's Christian and Arab quarters, it struck me that this wasn't a city where people just happened to work and play and otherwise live out their lives. It was as if everyone had a role—from supernumerary to leading player—in whatever scene was now being played in a long-running drama. Street sweepers, merchants, mullahs, rabbis, and prelates were all part of the story. Visitors, pious or scoffing, could join in. The plot was difficult to divine, other than having something to do with the nature and presence of God. Its outcome was yet to be revealed.

Later in the day I joined the Ethiopian Copts for their afternoon service, which had so impressed me years before and was still a wonderful occasion, with its soul-of-Africa improvisational song. My storytelling monk was there, and afterward, by twilight up on the church's roof, he continued where he had left off the day before. "Yea-ahs," he exclaimed approvingly, "in Abyssinia, baby Menelik he was born of Solomon and Sheba, and when he grow up he return to Jerusalem with a ring his father had given his mother, so as Solomon would know who he was. But it was no necessary. He was a photocopy of his father. He spent three years here learning the king's know-how, then went home with twelve thousand specialists, where he became number one of the dynasty of Abyssinian kings that lasted and lasted many, many centuries, right up to the lately Haile Selassie."

"And all that time, there were Ethiopians here in Jerusalem, right here. It was bad with the plague [smallpox in 1838], but our people didn't stop coming on foots and animal back. And do you know why? You know why? It's because Sheba she promised Solomon to come back herself or send people bearing gifts. Every year. Every year. To today."

"You please to come back Easter week. We put up big tent like Sheba's tent, and praise God. We here because she here." He let the words hang in the air to make sure I understood, then excused himself and hastened off across the roof.

"Night, boss," he said over his shoulder, and ducked into his cell.

Descending the stairs from the roof to the now shadowy plaza before the Holy Sepulchre, I was surprised to see rival monks—in this case, Greek and Armenian—stealing smokes and amicably chatting. Their break over, they went inside to hold steady rickety stepladders, as one, then another, climbed up, licked his fingers, and extinguished the candles prior to locking up for the night.

The tourists and pilgrims were back in their hotels and hospices. The great hulk of a church was nearly empty—and no longer as grim as it had appeared when I first arrived. It was the creation of man reaching out for something—and perhaps failing miserably, but reaching out nonetheless. Perched on his stepladder, a wick-pinching monk waved as I went back out into the night.

A cool breeze blew through the shuttered streets as it did every night at this time, no matter how warm or stifling the day. Here and there, in cavelike stalls, merchants were counting their day's take in the glare of dangling, unshaded bulbs. I walked home to my hospice through the Old City's square mile of faith, mendacity, blood, and peace.

8

Looking for Solomon

FROM MY THIRD-FLOOR HOSPICE window I looked out on a moonlit wall splashed with red Arabic graffiti and on sacks of cement stored on a rooftop next to a broken television antenna. Not much of a view, but the sounds of Jerusalem's night filled it out: an unseen donkey cart creaking by below, footsteps ringing on cobblestones, and from time to time indistinct fragments of song. Hymns, possibly, or closing time at the Armenian Tavern down the way.

The city out there was once the city of Solomon, and that ancient reality was why I was here. A perspective on this celebrated biblical king—and the archaeology of his era—could nudge Sheba out of the realm of fantasy and into a documented historical framework. The context would be the United Monarchy, the period when, under David and his son, Solomon, the tribes of Israel held sway over an empire said to stretch from Egypt to the river Euphrates.

I knew before coming to Jerusalem that I would have a difficult time with this.

For as long as I had asked biblical scholars and archaeologists about this period, I had sensed an indefinable unease. Casual, seemingly innocent queries led to long, awkward pauses and sudden changes of subject. "So how would Solomon be addressed?" I'd curiously ask. "Your majesty? My Lord?"

"Probably not," I'd be told, "as those forms would be reserved for Yahweh."

"Well, what, then?"

I was puzzled, for I never got a straight answer to this and other such questions. Just shrugs and evasion . . . that is, until an academic with Ph.D.s in both archaeology and theology blurted, "How on earth can we know how Solomon was addressed when we don't even know if he was a real person?"

In the late 1640s, Bishop James Ussher, Anglican primate of all Ireland, totaled the consecutive life spans of the Bible's genealogical "begats" and determined that the earth and everything upon it was created at noon on October 23, 4004 B.C. And that was that. The Bible was God's Holy Word, nothing less—and any questioning of the historicity of the Word was heresy, an invitation to a beheading. Cloistered scholars dared not point out that some passages in Genesis clearly contradicted others and that it was unlikely that Moses wrote the first five books of the Bible, since the narrative included a report of his death. It was only in 1753 that Jean Astruk, a French physician with an interest in textual analysis, respectfully suggested that the early books of the Bible might have certain mythical elements. In 1905 a turning point came when the German academic Julius Wellhausen wrote, "Freilich über die Patriarchen ist hier kein historisches Wissen zu gewinnen, sondern nur über die Zeit, in welcher die Erzählungen über sie im israelitschen Volke entstanden." The sentence was considered notorious, for it said: "Ah, well, about the Patriarchs there is no historical knowledge to be gained here. Just only about the period in which their [later] stories originated among the Hebrew people."[1] Wellhausen and a number of disciples thereupon debated the Bible's historicity, but gently so and not in public; their exchanges were limited to the pages of arcane journals. They ventured that whoever wrote the Bible was not writing history; rather, they were writing, on the one hand, to glorify Israel's past and, on the other, to understand why God did what he did, particularly when he was angry (which he often was in Old Testament times). They raised some questions about patriarchal figures and when they actually lived—not *if* they lived.

That was to come.

In recent years, Philip Davies of the University of Sheffield in England and Thomas Thompson and Niels Peter Lemche of the University of Copenhagen, among others, further explored—and promoted—Wellhausen's thesis. They contended that the Bible's writers and editors (several of whom could now be stylistically identified) didn't abide by modern distinctions between history and myth, between nonfiction and fiction. Fiction, they pointed out, did not then exist as a genre or a term and, accordingly, about the best that could be said of the Bible was that it was *literature*, rich in storytelling and moral messages. Given the absence of extrabiblical records of the early Israelites, these scholars allowed that the Bible might present the best image we could obtain of these people but went on to point out that this in no way qualified the Bible as a reliable or useful historical source.

They raised brash questions in articles with such titles as "Was King David No More Historical Than King Arthur?" and "Solomon and the Wizard of Oz." One by one, the familiar figures framed on Sunday School walls were declared to be of dubious reality. The first to come under fire was Abraham. Then Moses was dismissed as a stereotypical Middle Eastern mythological figure. It was pointed out that as a baby he had been abandoned in the bulrushes—but so had infants from Sargon II to Romulus and Remus, and all were credited with founding great nations. And if Moses had led forty thousand Israelites across the Sinai Desert, where were the archaeological remains of their forty years of campground litter, the B.C. equivalent of discarded tires and pop bottles?

For the most part, mainstream scholars ignored these contentions, though a few privately admitted that they had their doubts about his-

torical figures whose existence was not supported either by archaeology or by sources beyond the Bible.

Then David and Solomon and their United Monarchy came under attack.

Traditionalists now raised their voices in ire, though not very
loudly and well away from the public eye and ear. Davies, Thompson, Lemche, and company were labeled "Minimalists," an appellation not of their choosing. If anything, they responded, they were
"Maximalists," trying to extract as much history as possible from the
Bible, at best a shaky source. Just possibly, they allowed, King David
was a real person; their rationale was that, in spite of the need to cast
him as a heroic figure, the Bible relates that he committed a number
of less-than-laudable deeds. Some ten instances of David's bad behavior were cited: he was an exhibitionist, adulterer, murderer, pro-
tector of a rapist, and a depraved old man. His most often cited failing was his lust for Bathsheba, which prompted him to callously
dispatch her husband on a suicidal military mission.

But Solomon, born of David and Bathsheba—*he* was mythical.
The Bible records some questionable things—he tolerated and even
worshipped pagan gods—but nothing nasty enough to certify that he
was all too human and therefore historical. As the Minimalists appraised Solomon's mythological aura—and his vaunted wealth and
wisdom, as well as his city- and nation-building—a term was coined:
"Le mirage solomoniein." It was doubted that he had built a great
palace and temple or had unified twelve fractious Israelite tribes under a United Monarchy.

Traditionalists said what they had said all along, only louder: the
Bible is to be trusted, accepted as a matter of faith.

I had to admit that I felt the Minimalists were on to something in
the idea that biblical storytelling didn't necessarily abide by a later
distinction between fiction and nonfiction, which was not clearly
made until the 1500s.[2] Until then history was considered a branch of

rhetoric, "in which," says Cicero, "a region is described or a battle narrated in ornate language, and speeches and harangues are inserted." He adds that "it is permitted to rhetors to falsify somewhat in their histories, in order to make their point more forcibly." If I read this correctly, Cicero was saying *yes* to embroidery, but strongly implying *no* to weaving out of whole cloth. A region had to have existed; a battle had to have been fought. So the story of Solomon—and Sheba—must have had some underlying truth.

Mustn't it?

At breakfast at the hospice the next morning, I pored over a *Survey of Israel* map of the Old City and its surroundings, which delineated every lane, every house. My plan for the day was to follow on foot, as best I could, the path that the queen of Sheba might have taken as she entered and made her way through Solomon's city. From her perspective, I could get a sense of the city in the tenth century B.C.

"Not going there, are you?" questioned the Scotsman I had chatted with a few days back. My finger was resting on Haceldama, deep in the Hinnom Valley south of Jerusalem.

"A place of dark feelings," he said, "save for a Glasgow pub I'd as soon not remember."

"A feeling of?"

"Old, old terror."

Haceldama means "field of blood," and an hour later I was trudging across that field. Here was where Judas hanged himself, and where the Old Testament's Canaanites cast their first-born into the fiery furnace of the god Moloch. Dusty and litter-strewn, its half-alive trees stunted and eerily twisted, Haceldama had yet to cast off its curses. If Jerusalem was a heavenly city, I suppose a hell was necessary too. But it wasn't the place's drear that drew me; what interested me was that caravans from the east and south would have passed this way as they made their way from desert wilderness to the

Ophel, a ridge rising northward from Haceldama. The roughly ten-acre Ophel is generally considered to be the site of the city of David and then Solomon.

Prior to exploring sites I've never visited, I run and rerun in my mind what I expect to see—and even feel—based on what I've read and heard. The exercise is quite useful. Spooling my mental movie, I find many a "scene missing" that sends me hastening off for further research. As I headed north from Haceldama, here is what I projected. Passing the place where a gate of Benjamin once stood, I

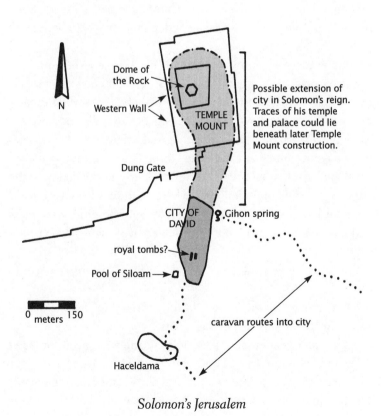

Solomon's Jerusalem

would have a sense of entering a king's garden, the garden of spices and rarest fruits evoked in the Song of Songs. As I neared the pool of Siloam (if it wasn't too much to ask), sunlight would pierce the leaden sky. If only in my mind, I'd be back in biblical times, with old Jerusalem before me.

This scenario was not to be.

There was not a trace of Solomon's city wall, let alone a gate of Benjamin. Dogged by a one-eared dog, I came upon the pool of Siloam, its still waters clogged with trash. Newspapers, broken glass, a sodden army boot. The masonry-lined pool deserved better, for it truly was biblical, though it had been built three centuries after Solomon. Just possibly a nearby irrigation ditch might date to Solomon's century. Nobody could say.

I climbed a worn "stairway of David" (maybe so, maybe not), then zigzagged upward on a path through a neighborhood of strangely lifeless Arab homes to the crest of the Ophel. Here several excavations by several teams had laid bare evidence of walls and towers—which proved to have been built either well before or well after Solomon's reign. I came upon and poked through several caves—alleged "royal tombs"—that had been cleared of debris. In the depths of the largest, I paced off an indentation where an impressive sarcophagus may once have rested. Four by seven feet. But whose? David's, Solomon's, or a latter-day rich but forgettable Jewish nobleman or merchant?

The Ophel was a ridge of ifs and maybes. The sun was yet to shine.

A tour group trundled down from a parking lot farther up the ridge. The theme was "In Biblical Footsteps."

"Ladies and gentlemen, please to now enter the royal tombs of David and Solomon. As we know from the Bible . . ."

The rapt group conversed in hushed voices as they ran their hands along the rough walls of the caves. A few crossed themselves. And, as there really wasn't much to see, they were soon on their way to the Gihon spring, where Solomon was anointed and crowned king.

With the Bible in hand, it is indeed all here—the site of the royal gardens, the Gihon spring, the royal tombs. But put the Bible aside and Solomon's Jerusalem vanishes. Still, there was hope for *some* hint of his city and even of the queen of Sheba coming this way. From the end of the Ophel, she would have ridden or walked a few hundred feet farther to Solomon's palace on the shoulder of Mount Moriah, and then on to his Temple of Yahweh; both figure in the account of I Kings 10. The queen of Sheba was dazzled by what she saw, and left breathless.

Ahead, where palace and temple once rose, the view was obscured and the way completely blocked by a massive wall. Though Solomon had had no hand in erecting this wall, its inspiration dated to his era.

On Mount Moriah's summit, the Bible recounts, Solomon spent seven years building his great temple, which then served the Israelites from the 900s until 586 B.C., when it was destroyed by the besieging forces of the Babylonian Nebuchadnezzar II. Another temple took its place and was torn down—but not vindictively—by Herod the Great shortly before the time of Christ. His intent was to crown Mount Moriah with a vast platform. Its walls were upward of two hundred feet high, with single ashlars weighing as much as four hundred tons. The platform supported enormous galleries and courts of assembly, and at its heart was a rebuilt Temple of Yahweh, faithful to the dimensions of Solomon's original temple as painstakingly recorded in the Book of Kings.

In A.D. 70, invading Romans razed this rebuilt temple but left Herod's massive platform more or less intact—as it looms today. It is surmounted by the gold-clad Dome of the Rock, which is, after Mecca and Medina, Islam's third holiest shrine.

The Temple Mount is controlled by an Arab *waqf* (council),

which disconcerts some Israelis, but not as much as one might imagine. Though they are free to do so, Orthodox Jews abstain from setting foot upon the platform, for fear that they might inadvertently step on the site of the Holy of Holies of Solomon's temple, the inner sanctum wherein the *Shekinah*, God's divine presence, once dwelt. There are theories but no agreement as to exactly where the inner sanctum was located.

Instead, the Orthodox—and all religious Jews—flock to the Temple Mount's Western Wall, where they believe the Shekinah still hovers.

I entered the Old City through its Dung Gate (named for the refuse once cast down toward Haceldama) and was stopped at an Israeli Defense Force command post, not for a security check, but to be handed a paper *kippah* to cover my head. I crossed a spacious plaza and walked slowly to the Western Wall. Assembled haredim were lost in prayer, their forelocks swinging back and forth. An old man sat on a white plastic patio chair, a worn hand spread on the stone, his face buried in the crook of his elbow. Parents and hyperkinetic children made preparations for a bar mitzvah.

"You look lost," said an ample, seventyish lady, pausing on her way to the Wall's segregated women's section. Introducing herself as Hilda Nussbaum, she told me she had grown up and had lived in Brooklyn until two years earlier, when her husband passed away. Then, though she knew her children would miss her, she had moved to the Jewish quarter, overlooking the Western Wall plaza, so that every day she could wake up and be as close as possible to God.

"I ask you, what more in this life could I want?"

Friends and, indeed, anyone back in Brooklyn or the Bronx were invited to share the blessing that God had offered her. If they wrote their hopes and pleas on pieces of paper—"little pieces, I told them" —she would take them to the Western Wall and, with an appropriate prayer, tuck them into its crevices.

"Here is as close as you can come to Solomon's holy temple," she said, and with a kindly *shalom* she went on her way to deliver the day's clutch of messages.

As I paced to the far end of the Western Wall, then back again, a dank day gave way to rain. Worshippers scattered, except for a hardy few who pulled plastic ponchos over their black striped shawls, and continued to pray. For them, this was where God's kingdom touched the earth.

I retreated across the plaza to the stairs leading up into the Jewish quarter, where I found shelter in the lee of a Crusader arch. Lightning flashed off in the Judean hills. I had a sweeping view of both the Wall and the length of Herod's enormous Temple Mount, built to honor Solomon's temple, but now with the Dome of the Rock as its centerpiece.

No other place in Jerusalem is so spiritually compelling and so mysterious—for what lies beneath the Mount's thirty-five-acre platform?

If archaeologists could gain access and be given a reasonably free hand, they could use ground-penetrating radar to map the underlying contours and features of Mount Moriah, then selectively probe for foundations and artifacts dating to Solomon's day. They could continue the work begun by the Palestine Exploration Fund in the 1860s but then broken off in 1909.[3] The fund's Royal Engineers found the Mount honeycombed with passages, shafts, chambers, and cisterns. The largest cistern, the Great Sea, which possibly consolidated several earlier reservoirs, had a capacity of ten million gallons, enough to sustain all Jerusalem. The much smaller Well of the Pomegranate, it was thought, might have functioned as a drain for blood sacrifices.

Beneath the Temple Mount's pavement there might be evidence not only of Solomon's temple but of his palace and other royal buildings. The finds would probably be quite homely—tenth-century masonry reused by Herod's workmen or *ostraca*, communications scratched on bits of broken pottery.

It would be a new leaf for Jerusalem if talented Arab archaeologists—and there are many—could conduct a state-of-the-art survey of the Temple Mount or, better yet, if this could be a joint Palestinian-Israeli project. I looked to the plaza below, where scattered IDF soldiers cradled their Uzis. Not in my lifetime, I thought. On the other hand, handshakes, reason, and constructive self-interest might yet prevail in the Middle East.

The rain let up, and I was on my way, only to be caught in a renewed downpour. I hopscotched rivulets and dodged overhead drains and was thoroughly soaked when I reached my hospice.

The next day I left the Old City through the Damascus Gate, looking for I wasn't sure what. Reassurance that the Bible was to be believed? Evidence that it wasn't? Past the East Jerusalem bus station I walked up a long street buzzing with sheruts and motor scooters and turned into an oasis of shady calm, the venerable Albright Institute, where I had an appointment with a prominent scholar. He was remarkably tanned and sported a double-breasted navy blazer accented by a pointy powder blue handkerchief. With a knowing smile and dismissive nod, he told me that no one he knew of took biblical Minimalists seriously, though he could see that their ideas might alarm a neophite to biblical archaeology. The Minimalists were out on a limb, so far out that their ideas were not worth debating.

"But by now, shouldn't more biblical history have been confirmed archaeologically?"

"Read the reports," he advised, waving his hand at a wall of them. An answer that wasn't an answer. He then changed the subject. I don't remember anything of what he had to say, but he said it very well.

A few blocks away, I rang the bell next to a heavy door set in the outer wall of the Ecole Biblique et Archéologique Française, the institute that under the late Roland de Vaux had produced the landmark Jerusalem Bible. A father opened the door, but only far enough to tell me in excellent English that regretfully nobody was about who would have anything to say that would shed light on the queen of Sheba.

"Perhaps someone knowledgeable about Solomon? That would be all right."

"No, no one here," he said, adjusting the fit of his sunglasses. "There might be one person, but he's away. Perhaps you could come back later. In a few months, yes?"

On I went to the Rockefeller Museum, a fusty, depressing place, I had been told. True, there were no splashy graphics or anything hands-on—just gallery after excellent gallery illuminating every aspect of life in the biblical world. I was welcomed by Joe Zias, curator of archaeology and anthropology for the Israel Antiquities Authority, who led me down a back stair to his office, tucked in a corner of the museum's artifact-jammed basement. Something here should speak of Solomon, if not of Sheba.

"You like Turkish coffee?" he asked, igniting a propane camp stove. "Leaded?"

Lean, no-nonsense Joe Zias looked as though he had just come in from the field (not from his tailor) and would just as soon be back out there. I opened with a roundabout question, phrased to ease into the what's-going-on-with-Solomon controversy.

"The Minimalists, that's what you're getting at?"

"Yes."

"Well, they're arrogant, but they keep us honest." He sipped his coffee, then added, "It used to be that we would dig and worry about *when* biblical figures existed, not *if* they existed."

He filled me in on some recent developments, relating how the Minimalist-Traditionalist row had broken out of academic journals and onto the Internet, where it was becoming a free-for-all. The Minimalists had vehemently protested their name, which they considered a "sneering epithet." Traditionalists used it all the more, especially when rubbing in the discovery of a seal inscribed *u . . . k byd dwd*, "King of the House of David" (exactly which king is unknown). The inscription was probably a fake salted in a dig, the Minimalists intimated. A Traditionalist counterattack demoted the Minimalists to "Biblical Nihilists" and dismissed their ideas as "postmodernist piffle."

Zias underscored that most of the combatants were historians versed in ancient languages and literature rather than archaeologists—and that he and his colleagues, Israeli and foreign, were more bemused than upset by the dispute. Archaeologists deal in tangible remains—stones and bones—and are reluctant to ascend ivory towers or fall to Internet squabbling. Yet, whether it be the next year or sometime in the twenty-first century, they would be the only ones who could either quell or validate the Minimalist uprising. On an academic level, about all that could be said had been said. Only new discoveries in the field could tilt the balance in the direction of either a real or a mythical Solomon (plus or minus forebears).

I described my trek up the Ophel ridge to the Temple Mount, and Zias allowed that, though archaeologically rich in other periods, Jerusalem was a blank when it came to Solomon's reign. Yes, it was true, he admitted, not a single potsherd could be definitively dated to the tenth century B.C. There were, though, reasons for this dearth. Over time the Ophel's masonry had been pillaged and recycled into other structures, which had themselves been torn apart, notably by construction-crazed King Herod. If this hadn't sufficiently confused the site, Herod quarried away a good part of the ridge, as did later Romans.

For this there is an archaeological axiom: absence of evidence is not evidence of absence.

"In any case, there is a lot that can tell us of Israel in that period. A lot of new ways of looking at things. Like pig bones."

"Pig bones?"

Joe explained that his country's search for archaeological solutions was taking an anthropological turn, with imaginative questions being posed as to how people lived and how groups of people interrelated. The focus was on the Israelites versus the Canaanites. The former had vanquished the latter, but how? Was it by invasion, with biblical trumpets blaring and walls tumbling? Or, less melodramatically, had the Israelites emerged from Canaanite stock? In puzzling this out site by site, one way to identify Israelite settlements was to rummage through ancient garbage. If the pig-bone pickings were slim, it meant that eating the animal was probably taboo—and the local abstainers were Jewish.

After two more cups of Turkish coffee, I had a fresh perspective on Israeli archaeology and a recommendation to check up on the research of Tel Aviv University's Israel Finkelstein. Joe thought well of his work, though he took issue with some of his colleague's conclusions. In reinterpreting the evidence from hundreds of sites, Finkelstein saw the Israelites not as wanderers striving to reach their Promised Land but as an indigenous culture. He was skeptical about those forty years in the wilderness; he felt that the Israelites were here all along. "The Israelites weren't a unique phenomenon," Finkelstein maintained in an interview. "The Israelite *schleppers* and the Canaanite *schleppers* are turning out to be much more alike than we've ever thought before."

Like it or not, this was a fresh perspective, backed by considerable archaeological data. And Finkelstein had another shoe to drop.

In his site surveys he had been unable to find evidence of the building boom that the Bible ascribes to Solomon. No such evidence had been uncovered in Jerusalem, and he doubted that a boom could be shown to have occurred in Solomon's "chariot cities" of Gezer, Hazor, and Megiddo (settlements with major garrisons, as reported in I Kings 9:19). The upshot was that, intentionally or not, Finkelstein was adding fuel to the Minimalist fires, for the existence of the chariot cities had long been taken as convincing evidence that Solomon had actually ruled and had done what the Bible said he had.

"So what do you think?" I asked Joe.

"Maybe it's old-fashioned, but for now, I'm sticking with the Bible." He gestured to his bulletin board and a hard-shell bumper sticker given him as a joke. It proclaimed:

GOD SAID IT

I BELIEVE IT

THAT SETTLES IT

"No, no, not that extreme, of course," he was quick to say. "But I think the Bible can be trusted in giving us the big picture, if not the details. And let me tell you why . . ." With his fingers he ticked off three points that were the most compelling of any I had heard or read.

"One. We know from the Dead Sea Scrolls that the Bible changed very little across the centuries. So, regarding Solomon and your Sheba, the account in Kings may be essentially the same as a lost account written hundreds of years earlier or even an account memorized and passed down orally.[4]

"Two. Unlike a lot of Middle Eastern texts, the Bible has its feet very much on the ground. Sure, its characters have visions and dreams, but they stay clear of magic. It's from magic that myths arise—and serious misinformation.

"And three. The Bible is quirky and human—and so, I think, it is believable."

We discussed the quirkiness part. It included the character of God Himself, who is fickle, vain, petty, given to outbursts of temper and

worse—as in the troubling passage where God tells Moses, after killing the firstborn of Egypt, "I will make mine arrows drunk with
blood, and My sword shall devour flesh." The fact that this murderous boast was not censored or even watered down testifies to generations of storytellers and scribes compelled to stick to the original
story, no matter how onerous.[5]

"You know, it's curious," concluded Joe. "An inscription turns
up—Mesopotamian, Egyptian, Phoenician, from wherever—and
whatever it says, we agree, that's it, the truth. But with the Bible, it
is becoming prove it or lose it. Well, I guess that's what keeps us
honest."

I thanked him for his time and the coffee. He walked me from the
basement to the Rockefeller's extensive library; I was welcome to
spend the next day or so reading up on what we had discussed. I soon
had a stack of new books and journals that touched on Solomon—or
was it "le mirage solomoniein"?

And then I left Jerusalem.

At the Latrun interchange—named for a monastery where monks
live out their lives speaking not a word to each other—I turned off
the main Jerusalem–Tel Aviv highway. On my mind was: How is
God served by silence? Why are rental cars painted strange colors?
Where was Solomon's chariot city of Gezer? Directed by Murphy-
O'Connor's *The Holy Land*, I followed an ever-worsening track
through fallow farmland and parched vineyards. The father's direc-
tions were noncommittal as to which of several forks to take and gave
no warning of padlocked gates or of boulders scraping the oil pan.
Reluctantly, I turned back.

Had I made it to Tel Gezer, I would have walked through the remains of a six-chambered gate, a passageway flanked by three alcoves
on each side, giving guards three opportunities to fall upon invaders.
Here the village elders passed the time of day, and a king on his royal

rounds dispensed justice. I knew I would see near-identical gates to the north; they were the signature feature of Solomon's chariot cities, which the Bible says he fortified to defend the United Monarchy.

Driving north past Tel Aviv, I swung east through fields of golden wheat and orchards climbing gentle hills. Streams were lined with cypress, crocuses, and flowering nettles. And unseen, as in the Song of Songs, there were surely little foxes in their dens. After staying overnight at the friendly kibbutz Ayelet Hashachar, I got up early to hike, while the day was cool and damp, to nearby Tel Hazor and examine its six-chambered gate.

Massive and sullen, it was impressive: impervious to fire and buttressed against any battering a siege and its machinery might inflict. And woe to attackers on foot. They would be forced into a cramped, narrow defile that thwarted the use of bows and arrows and spears. They'd be up against defenders to the left, right, and frontally. Here was a brilliant yet simple work of military architecture.

The sun was high in the sky and the day hot enough to silence the buzz of cicadas when I reached Megiddo, the final chariot city—and the Armageddon of the New Testament, the site of a final battle between the forces of good and evil at the end of days. At the moment, though, the contest was over who had ruled in the days of the site's six-chambered gate.

"Solomonic" gate
at Gezer

Hazor gate

Megiddo gate

This gate, like those at Gezer and Hazor, was long considered to have been "built by Solomon's architects from identical blueprints, with minor changes in each case, made necessary by the terrain."[6] That was a worthy idea—until in recent years additional six-chambered gates had been unearthed along the Mediterranean coast and east across Israel into southern Jordan.

No longer could the gates at Gezer, Hazor, and Megiddo be considered identifiably Solomonic or even Israelite. And carbon-14 dating—with its considerable plus-or-minus error factor that far back—hadn't been able to resolve the issue. Other methods would be needed to determine who built the gates and when. At Megiddo, efforts are under way to firmly date its gate's stratum VA-IVB by a highly technical comparison of Megiddo's pottery shards with pottery from other sites. The news so far was not good, at least for Solomon.

Another oft-cited structure at Megiddo is known as "Solomon's stables." But as Murphy-O'Connor notes, "If they were stables, they must have housed very small, house-broken ponies. It is more probable that they were storehouses built by Omri or Ahab as at Hazor." Omri, one of the most despised kings in the Bible? Ahab, for whom Melville's hell-bent whaler was named? The idea may not be welcome, but one or the other king—reigning a century after Solomon—stands to displace him as the master builder of the northern cities with the six-chambered gates. Omri (who ruled 882–871 B.C.), incidentally, is the earliest of the Old Testament's patriarchs or kings to be corroborated by external evidence; two foreign inscriptions bear his name.

I regretted that Megiddo's current excavator—Israel Finkelstein— was not at the site. I had caught up on his work at the Rockefeller Museum, and a few months later I would meet him at a Los Angeles seminar. I found him charming, well spoken, and almost (but not quite) apologetic about putting a sizable dent in Solomon's reputation. His bottom line was that he had yet to see any evidence of Israelites creating an identifiable state until the ninth century B.C. and thus that the glory of the chariot cities should be reassigned to that century. Although his findings abetted the biblical Minimalists, Finkelstein was careful to distance himself from their pronouncements. He was, indeed, quite willing to be proven wrong; he allowed that *if* his dating assumptions were incorrect, there would be "no difficulty in demonstrating that in the tenth century there was a strong, well-developed and well-organized state stretching over most of the territory of western Palestine."[7] But the more he dug, the less likely that seemed.

Nevertheless, in reflective moments Finkelstein still believed that David and Solomon were historical personages. He saw them, father and son, as successive hill-country chieftains holding forth on Jerusalem's Ophel ridge and uniting, if briefly, a dozen surrounding tribes as far away as one or more of the so-called chariot cities. And even if Solomon's architectural achievements prove to be illusory, Finkelstein saw him as an astute and resourceful leader, a force for change, a harbinger of transition from tribalism to statehood.[8]

Here, at least, was a possible (though, to many, unpalatable) middle ground between the stances taken by the biblical Minimalists and the Traditionalists. And it raised an interesting possibility for the queen of Sheba. If the biblical narrative made more sense scaled down—with Solomon a chieftain rather than a great king—she might have come from no farther away than a neighboring tribe.

From Megiddo I headed south to the Negev Desert, to look for her.

9
Zabibi and Samsi

THE BUGS of all Israel were drawn to my lime green car. At a concrete-block gas station just before the Judean hills give way to the
sweep of the Negev Desert, I scraped away at the carcasses on the
windshield, gnats to grasshoppers. Having gotten off to an early start,
I soon would have driven all the way "from Dan to Beersheba," the
Bible's description of the north-south extent of Solomon's kingdom.

It was past noon when I pulled into the gravelly parking lot at the
foot of Tel Beersheba.[1] I exchanged shaloms with a young couple
packing away picnic gear and little kids topped with blue Negev hats.
Their VW van rumbled away, and I was alone at the site. I walked
uphill through what was left of a two-chambered gate and into a
compact, workaday—and storied—Israelite town. Here, the Bible
tells us, Abraham dwelt, and in the heat of the day sat beneath his favorite tamarisk tree, gazing out across the Negev, a bleached, shimmering wilderness stretching to the far horizon.

Abraham was watchful, as were his seed.

And the day would come when a plume of dust drew closer and
closer, the caravan of the queen of Sheba.

Had she come from far or near? If from somewhere nearby, she
might have been an Amalekite (the Bible's catchall term for the
Arabs who hectored Israel's borders). At Beersheba they were apparently not much of a threat and from time to time may have been
allies of the Israelites. The settlement's well was *outside* its walls,
which suggests that keeping the town square free of thirsty livestock

was more important than making sure the water supply was secure in the event of a siege.

Over the next several days I roamed the land of the Amalekites south of Beersheba. I'd follow a track up a wadi, then get out and walk for hours, slipping, sliding, and scrambling. I was intrigued by an arc of twenty structures said to be "fortlets." Many were oval, others square or rectangular. Crude casemate walls enclosed open-to-the-sky areas the size, typically, of a modest house lot. They may have been Amalekite refuges. Or Israelite outposts of frontier Beersheba, the equivalent of the sandbagged IDF posts that today dot the Negev (as it says in Ecclesiastes: "What was will be again; what has been done will be done again; and there is nothing new under the sun"). The Negev's fortlets were apparently short-lived, used for just a few dozen years before coming to a shared sorry end marked by a layer of ash. Just possibly those years were during the reign of Solomon and the ash is evidence of the invasion of Palestine by Pharaoh Sheshonq I (Sheshak in the Bible) a few years after Solomon's death. If this dating could be proved, the fortlets might be an indication that the domain of Solomon the hill-country chieftain, as he may have been, reached south to exact tolls from caravans following the Bible's Way of Shur and Way of Spies.

In my search for fortlets and caravan routes, I became reacquainted with the desert's timeless cycle: a cool and golden dawn, so full of promise, then that promise dashed by the glare and harsh heat of midday, when small animals take to their burrows and songbirds cease to sing. Sunset brings respite, and evenings are balmy in all but the hottest months. And it will be the same again tomorrow.

Evading the high noon sun, I hiked 1,000-foot-deep Ein Avdat canyon. Its dark recesses sheltered a spring flowing into a string of ponds croaking with tiny frogs. An Amalekite lair? Possibly, though the more I sought the Amalekites, the more they appeared to be a seminomadic population scraping out a living herding sheep and goats and harvesting marginal gardens. They were hardly a people to

give rise to a queen as memorable as Sheba. They may have ma-
rauded caravans, but how—why?—would they organize caravans?
What goods did the Amalekites have that others lacked? That's an
important question, for the possession of such goods—often exotic—
is the rationale for trade that reaches beyond local markets to distant
lands.

The overall sense of the Negev—and of a larger arc of desert
sweeping from Jordan's Wadi Rum across into Egypt's Sinai—is that
this was a place of passage, a landscape where caravans hastened
from spring to seep to well and left little behind but graffiti. Variations on "Yazkar was here" can be seen scratched in ancient scripts,
and processions of camels make their way across slabs of desert-
varnished rock. A frazzled little figure in one petroglyph looks as
though he has had enough of dust and heat and camels at the end of
a very long day.

Though the queen of Sheba and her people may not have come
from the Negev, might she not have come from beyond the next
range of hazy blue-black mountains, or the next? That has been the
surmise of the majority of scholars who have taken it upon themselves to seek her homeland, from Harry Philby in the 1930s to contemporary Israeli, Arab, and European archaeologists. In the land
that the Bible calls Midian, they point out, a scattering of oases gave
rise to a series of ancient trading centers. Sheba might have been
queen of one or all of them.[2]

A vexed caravaneer

In Midian, it was written, there was gold, which would be reason enough for biblical caravans.

How I would have loved to explore Midian, a day away across the Gulf of Aqaba. But I doubted that I ever could. This ancient land is almost entirely within the borders of Saudi Arabia, which I understood to be off the map for archaeologically curious outsiders, professionals and amateurs alike. Dispiritedly, I hiked the rim of a crater where a primordial meteor had once smashed into the Negev. The view to the east was inspiring—of where I couldn't go. For any insights into Midian, I'd have to surmise what I could from Philby's memoirs and a brief survey by a team from the University of London in the 1970s.

Haplessly, I perched on a boulder and watched as the sinking sun painted the mountains of Midian in shades of orange, rust, and red. And night fell, quickly, as it does in the desert.

Months later.

A dog barked in the night. A distant faint chanting rose from the desert. A single resonant voice. Then another and another, rising and falling. Arabic harmonies interwove, went their own ways, then swelled together like waves lapping on sand. From a dozen minarets, the day's first call to prayer proclaimed, "Allah Akhbar! Allah Akhbar!" God is great.

The dog stopped barking. A line of gray edged the horizon. A little after five, my wife, Kay, whispered in the dark, "Oh, my, we're here. What do you think?"

"Shukran . . . [thanks] . . ."

"Afwan . . . [you're welcome] . . ."

It was our first morning in the land of Midian. Kay had encouraged me to apply and reapply to visit Saudi Arabia, and a few weeks before, an itinerary had been approved for a modest archaeological survey. The kingdom was cautiously opening its doors to interested Westerners.

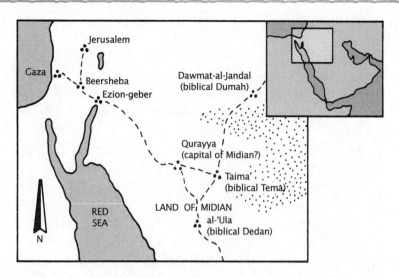

Ancient oasis cities of northwest Arabia

The sky brightened, and we joined our informal team at the local hotel's breakfast of boiled eggs, pita bread and hummus, fruit, and the first of the day's innumerable glasses of *chai* (tea) and small ceramic cups of coffee. We numbered ten, a mix of amateur archaeologists and three professionals: the kingdom's Abdullah Saud al-Saud and Hussein Ali Abul al-Hasan, and Martha Joukowsky of Brown University's Center for Old World Art and Archaeology.[3] (I had attended Brown with Martha and her husband, Arte.) As with any calling, there is a spectrum of archaeologists. Some keep to themselves, accumulate mind-numbing data, draw not too many conclusions, and raise an eyebrow at those who do. At the other extreme there is Martha. She comes upon a site exclaiming, "Okay, what was going on here? What's this place all about?"—all but challenging the stones and bones to ante up the answers. While she enjoys analyzing flints and shards, she relishes excavating and restoring palaces and temples; she prefers a crane to a dental pick.

And there was Kay. Having retired as a federal probation officer, she had recently begun to specialize in the defense of capital cases. To facilitate this work, she had become licensed as a California private investigator—a PI—and was acquiring a reputation for turning up evidence that others passed by. "I go fishing," she put it. "I fish and I fish, and I never know what I'll catch." In Arabia she could apply her skills to archaeology, which when it's fun is a detective story, replete with telling clues, false leads, evolving scenarios, and fascinating and elusive characters—at present, the queen of Sheba.

In deference to Saudi custom, Kay had swathed herself in a head scarf and a long, black, flapping *abayya*—her "raven suit," she called it—but she soon discovered that she could wear whatever she comfortably pleased underneath and stuff the abayya into a backpack when we were sufficiently far from town.

The northern Arabian landscape, our maps told us, was vast. But Kay and I had not imagined how scenic it was, with majestic sandstone formations rising from beige, salmon, and deep rust dunes. Or how populated, both past and present. No matter how far from the highway our two Chevy Suburbans took us, we were rarely out of sight of black goat-hair bedouin tents, and rarely was there a good place to camp that didn't have petroglyphs pecked by passing caravaneers . . . .

Mimmanat and Rabib drove [animals] along quickly.
Nathal loves Maslyt.
Yafia' son of 'Aarsham. He is dumb.
'Arab loves Nashaf passionately.

We drove up shady Eknah canyon, its walls so crowded with rock drawings and inscriptions that Hussein al-Hasan had devoted his Ph.D. thesis to this single site. "Look over here—inscriptions not incised but excised, carved in bas-relief," he said, gesturing. "And look around at the languages. Aramaic here, Greek there. And Nabatean, Safiatic, Lihyanite, Thamudic, Sabean."

Many people of many tribes had traveled through the land of Midian and left their passing marks. Judging from the devotional content of the inscriptions, Eknah canyon may have been known as a place where the gods hovered and could bless and reward caravans laden with incense and exotic goods; a common inscriptional word is ٩١Υ𐩠, "perfume" or "incense." As well, Hussein told us that many of the inscriptions contained evidence of nearby sedentary settlements. High on a wall blackened with desert varnish, he pointed out what looked to be a repeated abstract rectangular pattern.

"They are harps," clarified Hussein. "You see, with five strings?"

"And those figures by them. Dancers?"

"Yes, dancers."

It was conceivable that a caravan might pack a harp and that someone could play it, but five harps and seven dancers conjured an image of something more.

"City nights?" Kay wondered. "A banquet. A palace?"

We knew from the University of London survey that such a palace might be no more than a few miles away in the extensive ruins of al-'Ula. And could such a palace be the queen of Sheba's? It could be — in the event that this was her land. The possibility that it *was* her land is bolstered by a further, remarkable series of inscriptions, not

Petroglyph of harps and dancers

scratched on boulders but formally chiseled on tablets. And not from here but from Assyria, off to the northeast (in what now is Iraq). Pieced together, their texts reveal that a dynasty of queens once roamed and ruled Midian.

Hellion queens.

The earliest known is Zabibi, a queen of the "Aribi"—the very first written mention of Arabs. She's mentioned in a long list of independent rulers subjugated by the Assyrian monarch Tiglath-pileser III and forced to offer him tribute in 738 B.C. Though this was two centuries after the era of the queen of Sheba, it seems unlikely that the Aribi one day decided, "Enough of kings! How about some queens?" Rather, it is likely that the Aribi had had many prior queens.

Zabibi, with only a single inscriptional mention, was succeeded by Samsi, who appears four times—twice as a thorn in the side of the Assyrian empire. She initially sent tribute to mighty Tiglath-pileser III, but in 733 B.C. enough was apparently enough, and she broke her oath of allegiance, even though it was sworn to Shammash, the god of the sun (and her namesake). The Aribi would rue her action. Their settlements were attacked and pillaged, and Samsi was forced to flee into the desert: "She set her face to the desert, an arid place, like a wild she ass." There she was cornered and captured, but she was neither executed nor imprisoned. Satisfied that "she bowed to my yoke," Tiglath-pileser III allowed her to retain her throne, though to assure her good behavior he dispatched an overseer to her court.

In the end, Samsi outlived Tiglath-pileser III by at least twelve years, having wished upon "the king of all four rims of the earth" her share of mischief.

What is intriguing is the enduring nature of Samsi's rule—despite the mess she made of the Aribi's relationship with the Assyrians, despite the rout, humiliation, and loss of face suffered by her people. And she would not be the only queen given to misadventures yet not deposed by the Aribi (and replaced with a king). Iali'e, next in line,

PLATE 1. The queen of Sheba in a 1590 Persian miniature. Perched on a branch to the right, a tiny bird — a hoopoe — bears a message from Solomon.

PLATE 2. If you look closely at Sheba's gown, you will see a bird, then the heads of several animals, hints of her ancestry in the world of the djinns.

PLATE 3. An Ethiopian animal-skin painting of Sheba traveling to Jerusalem, dining with Solomon, and reaching for a fateful drink of water.

PLATE 4. "I am black, but beautiful." Sheba in a medieval German manuscript.

PLATE 5. Sheba intimidates Solomon in Canterbury Cathedral's *Biblia Pauperum*.

PLATE 6. Scenes of Sheba come to Jerusalem in a 1452 fresco by Piero della Francesca.

Sheba   Pond   Solomon and Sheba

Wood of the Holy Cross   Piero della Francesca?

PLATE 7.
Detail of
Solomon and
Sheba.

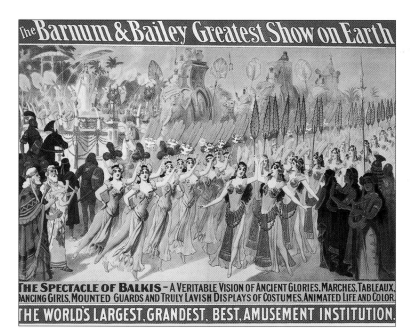

PLATE 8. A poster for the 1903–1904 Barnum and Bailey pageant *A Tribute to Balkis.* The queen's dancing girls gave hootchy-cootch a newfound respectability.

PLATE 9. A poster for Ringling Brothers' 1915 spectacle *Solomon and the Queen of Sheba.*

PLATES 10–12. Betty Blythe stars in the 1921 Fox film *The Queen of Sheba.*

PLATE 13. In the Jebel Saber region of Yemen, a present-day trader, a woman to be reckoned with.

IN SEARCH OF SHEBA

PLATES 14 AND 15.
Early morning in Jerusalem, 1980.
A chance pass-by of an Ethiopian
Coptic monk was to trigger a
twenty-year quest.

Plates 16 and 17. Palmyra, Syria. A sandstorm sweeps through the temple of Bel. Was this the queen of Sheba's tomb?

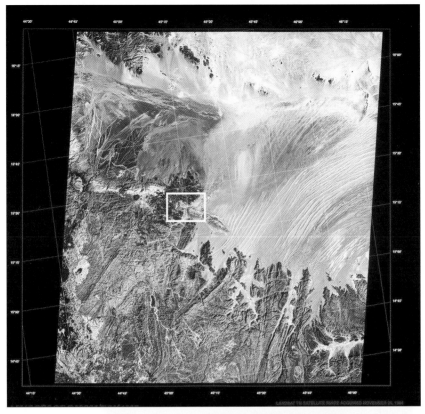

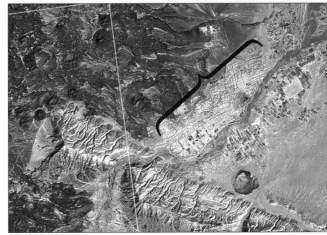

PLATE 18. A
Landsat 5 image
of the Ramlat
Sabateyn, a sector
of Arabia's
"Empty Quarter."

PLATE 19.
Detail of the area
surrounding
Ma'rib. A network
of Sabean irriga-
tion canals is
clearly visible.

PLATE 20. In the Ramlat Sabateyn. We rest after a satisfying lunch of grilled goat and locusts. Our desert guide Ali al-Sharif is to the right.

PLATE 21. Driver "Desert Hussein" al-Ajlan.

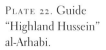

PLATE 22. Guide "Highland Hussein" al-Arhabi.

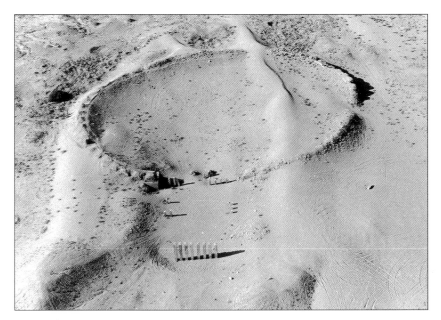

PLATES 23 AND 24. At Ma'rib, the Mahram Bilqis — the Moon Temple of the Queen of Sheba.

PLATE 25. The sunken church of St. George in Lalibela, Ethiopia.

PLATE 26. Ethiopian monks chant and dance to the accompaniment of drums and sistrums.

PLATE 27. Docked at Djibouti on the Indian Ocean, the dhow *Fatah Alkyar* ("Bringer of Good Things") prepares to cast off for Yemen.

PLATE 29. The first mate's foot.

PLATE 28. The first mate.

PLATE 30. At Sirwah, Yemen. The curved east wall of the remarkably well preserved Temple of 'Ilumqah. Mana al-Nasirah, standing to the right, shows the scale.

PLATE 31. A Sabean woman gazes from a funerary stela recently unearthed at Ma'rib's Mahram Bilqis.

also rebelled against the Assyrians (unsuccessfully), as did the later Te'lkhunu, who was dragged off to exile in Nineveh. Two subsequent hit-and-run Aribi queens, Baslu of Ikhilu and Iapa' of Dikhani, were subdued, predictably and wearily, by the Assyrians.

After Iapa' there is no further evidence, inscriptional or otherwise, of Zabibi's dynasty of queens, a dynasty that at its inception may have included a queen of Sheba.

Powerful Arab queens, I learned, were by no means rare. Beyond Zabibi and Samsi's desert shores, some forty-two additional female Arab monarchs are recorded, and historians have estimated that an equal number are unrecorded. Several were quaintly profiled in *De Mulieribus Claris*, Boccaccio's (1362) compilation of biographies of famous women. In this first-ever work of its kind, Boccaccio wavers in what to make of Arab queens, as he does of all women. He paints some as demonic, some divine, many both: "The sacred and cursed are confused, and mercy, overwhelmed by great sins, is changed into blood . . . O marvelous road to the throne!" He was particularly taken by Semiramis, an Assyrian answer to Zabibi and Samsi:

> One day, after she had pacified her domains and was resting at lei-sure, she was having her maids comb her hair with feminine care into braids as was the custom of the country. Her hair was only half combed when the news that Babylon had rebelled was brought to her. This so angered her that she threw aside her comb and imme-diately abandoned her womanly pursuits. She arose in anger, took up arms, and . . . did not finish combing her hair until she had forced that mighty city to surrender.

At your peril, Babylonians, disturb a woman having her hair done.

Back to Zabibi and Samsi.

These are the queens whom most scholars cite as providing com-pelling evidence for a queen of Sheba from northern Arabia. But did their dynasty reach back to Solomon's time? And, more important, were there viable trading cities in northern Arabia in the tenth century B.C.? We'd look for answers to these questions as we explored the mysteries of the region's major and minor sites.

The first site was al-'Ula—called, in the Bible, Dedan.

"What a mess! What a mess! And it's wonderful! How wonderful!" exclaimed Martha as we slowed to a halt and spilled out of our Suburbans. What she meant was that al-'Ula's tumbled stone structures were hard to define and that there were a lot of them—acre upon acre. She complimented Abdullah al-Saud on the fact that the government had securely fenced the site in preparation for excavation and restoration. Like other cities of the desert, al-'Ula may have been sacked and looted in the past, but not now.

Many archaeological teams are highly organized. The cadre dons neatly pressed khaki uniforms, takes bearings, and moves through a site with quasi-military precision. Not ours. At al-'Ula and elsewhere, we were all, invariably and independently, off on our own. See you later. Martha, for one, would start by puzzling over a site's orientation and layout. "Abdullah, what do we have here, going all the way over there. See the line of the wall? A temple? A residence? What do you think?"

As Abdullah offered his opinion, Martha's husband, Arte, would set off looking for the best angles and light to take pictures, for archaeology poses a never-ending photographic challenge: how to make shattered and tumbled masonry look like more than shattered and tumbled masonry. Meanwhile the Joukowskys' daughter Nina and nine-year-old granddaughter, Suraya (who was entranced by archaeology), would scamper to the site's highest point. Hussein would be keeping an eye out for inscriptions. And John and Diane Peavey, who in real life were Idaho ranchers, would seek out the settlement's water supply and trace its path as it was channeled through dams and canals; we would then have at least a rough idea of the amount of surrounding land under cultivation and its carrying capacity. This was a vastly different land from the Negev. The ruined cities here were large in scale, able to sustain populations of thousands. And somewhere in their sand-blown rubble there had to be evidence of Zabibi and Samsi.

And Sheba?

For an hour I would wander back and forth between our scattered searchers to get a sense of a site, for no two were alike. Then, if Kay hadn't already found it, I would help her locate what long ago was the municipal garbage dump, which now, with everything else long since rotted away, was the pottery dump. The dump's location could be elusive, and in the case of very old or worn material, it was difficult to discern what was pottery and what wasn't.

"What about these?" Kay would ask Martha, offering a handful of shards.

"*Malesh* [never mind] . . .," she evaluated the first, tossing it aside. The others were eggshell thin. Northern Arabians had a knack for firing ware no thicker than the cover of a hardback book.

Martha examined them. No decoration. She rubbed them between her fingers. "Tough call, Kay. I'm not sure. Feels like bone, warm, slick. Pottery is colder, and generally has more texture. Stone is colder yet. You may have pieces of an ostrich egg."

The ostrich, Kay knew, was a desert bird. "Around here?"

I was able to fill in the blank, for I'd caught sight of two ostriches — orange-on-black petroglyph ostriches — trotting along the face of a rock outcropping a few feet away.

Once focused on a site's dump, Kay's PI determination netted dozens and dozens of shards that could be classified on the basis of their decoration — painted? incised? — and other charcteristics. The shards could then be compared with pottery assemblages — and dates — that had been published for sites in Egypt and the Sinai, Israel, and across into Mesopotamia.

When you're only looking, not digging, you can deduce more

about a site from a surface collection of shards than from just about anything else. For this, our key site was Qurayya, a candidate for the principal city of the biblical Midianites.

Qurayya's pottery was colorful and inventive, with well over a dozen identifiable styles in the period 1750–1050 B.C., when the desert city served as a link between New Kingdom Egypt and Mesopotamia (and could even have been where Moses sojourned and took as his wife Zipporah, daughter of the Midianite priest Jethro). But after the decline of these great empires, there was a fallow period in Qurayya's pottery sequence. And this occurred, unfortunately, a century before the queen of Sheba's appearance on the biblical stage, which more or less ruled out Qurayya as her city. Only several centuries later did the city rebound and again flourish.

The news was no more encouraging at the other sites we visited, all of which had a weak or an entirely missing tenth century. Solomon's century, Sheba's century.

And beyond the chronological problem, there was the question of the goods that the queen delivered to Solomon. Could they be from here? I Kings tells us that "she brought immense riches to Jerusalem . . . And she presented the king with a hundred and twenty talents of gold and great quantities of spices; no such wealth of spices ever came again as those given to King Solomon by the queen of Sheba."

Other than a scattering of desert herbs, no spices grow in northern Arabia. As for gold, adventurer-scholars from Sir Richard Burton to Harry St. John Philby had evoked "the gold of Midian." But where was it?

At Qurayya, still hopeful of finding some tenth-century evidence, I located what had been reported as a cluster kiln for firing pottery, and rounded up the others for a look.

"These may be kilns all right," Martha said, picking up a greenish-black porous rock, "but not for firing pottery. This is slag. What was going on here was smelting. They packed the ore between layers of charcoal, which they ignited and fanned with animal-skin bellows."

"Gold?" I asked expectantly.

"Copper. Add ten percent tin and you have bronze."

"But no gold? Here we are in Midian, and no gold?"

Hussein al-Hassan was helpful with this. Barring some startling new discovery, he told us, the gold of Midian was a myth. "There's gold in Arabia, plenty of it south of Medina and down toward Yemen. But not here." Recent extensive geological surveys had confirmed this.

"No gold, no spices . . ."

And Martha confirmed that in the tenth century the production and quality of pottery were at a low ebb.

"Doesn't look so good," Kay said with a sidelong glance, toeing copper slag with her boot, "for your queen of Sheba."

I had to agree.

(Though with a reservation: in the tenth century most of the sites we visited could have functioned as caravansaries—welcome respite and resupply points—for caravans in transit from other distant lands.)

As the shadows lengthened and the sun slipped behind mountains to the west, such was our enthusiasm that we continued to stray and wander. Amused, Abdullah and Hussein looked on as one, then another, of the unruly Americans drifted back to our Suburbans, thought of a last something to investigate, ricocheted off, and became dots in the desert.

"Like shoveling frogs into a wheelbarrow," rancher John Peavey wryly noted. "Three in, two out."

Each night I went over my notes and asked and asked again: were we missing something? Were there key sites yet to be discovered? Doubtful. Early explorers, geological surveys, and the bedouin—

still a major presence in the landscape—had crisscrossed Midian, and they had had little reason to withhold what they had found or seen.

Furthermore, I was impressed by the extent to which the Old Testament had been aware of—and had filled in—the land of Midian (see map, page 113). The oasis of al-'Ula was the Bible's Dedan, Taima' was its Tema, and Dawmat al-Jandal its Dumah; Qurayya was probably Midian's principal city. So complete, in fact, was the Bible's geography that there was little room to squeeze in a queen of Sheba and Saba, her land.

If Solomon's visitor were from here, wouldn't she have been the Queen of Midian (or of Dedan or Tema or Dumah), not the Queen of Sheba?

Setting thoughts of Sheba aside, we enjoyed our passage through Midian. True to its bedouin roots, Saudi hospitality was unfailing. One night we would be invited for dinner in a grand country villa; the next night, in a modest mud-brick home. On the last day of our journey, we crossed the border from the kingdom of Saudi Arabia into the kingdom of Jordan and spent the evening with the leader of the Bedul tribe, Dakhilallah ibn Qublan, his son Haroun, and their extended family. (For years they had worked with Arte and Martha Joukowsky in digging and then rebuilding the Great Temple of Petra, dating to the first century A.D.) As in more and more Arabian households, segregation by age and sex had been cheerfully abandoned. Kids careened about Dakhilallah's mifraj; his wife and Haroun's joined in the conversation.

After dinner came the time for storytelling, the common thread being tales of love. Lamps were turned low, the stars shone brightly, and all was hushed as John Peavey asked his wife, Diane, to tell of a love letter mailed in an Idaho spring when snowmelt gave way to south-slope grasses, and antelope ran free. Dakhilallah's clan, who spoke and understood English, delighted in the cascade and imagery of Diane's tale.

Haroun ibn Dakhilallah next told how he had met his wife, Layla. Theirs was hardly an arranged marriage. On a college semester abroad from Spain, she had visited Petra. He had guided her through the ruins and won her heart. Their pride was their spirited daughter, Dunia, age three, who spoke Castilian to her mother, Arabic to her father, and English to us. The world grows smaller.

The last guest to recite a tale was Wyche Fowler, America's ambassador to Saudi Arabia, who had learned of our journey and had asked if he could join us for a few days. He had promised that he would be no problem; if called away on matters of state (as he was), he would catch the next bus to the nearest big city (as he did).

He told of an elderly Saudi prince he had known. As a young man of fourteen, the prince had roamed the desert, sleeping alone, taking care of himself. He was proud to be a man. Late one afternoon, he caught sight of a beautiful girl, agile and graceful, tending her family's flock on the far side of a remote valley. When he approached to ask her name, she backed away and refused to speak to him. He persisted. She picked up a rock and hurled it as hard as she could, hitting him squarely in the forehead.

Dakhilallah's family edged forward. What could he expect for being so presumptuous? But brave.

Shocked and hurt, the prince left the valley, but he couldn't banish the shepherdess's face from his mind. Three years went by, and he found his way back to her valley, sought her family's encampment, and without hesitation went right to the women's tent.

The Bedul were startled, then laughed. The prince did *that?*

Prince or not, he was thrown out. But then the young woman stepped from the tent and exclaimed, "It's you!"

The smitten prince apologized. "I didn't mean to make you angry . . . but I loved you the moment I saw you, and I love you now." Hesitantly, she nodded, then asked her father's permission to talk to this stranger, which he granted.

The prince asked the beautiful shepherdess to marry him.

She looked into his eyes and said, "I will."

On the day they were joined, the valley echoed with festive gunshots and cries of joy. In the months that followed, they were the two happiest people in the desert.

A year later she died.

Wyche paused. There was a stunned silence—of disbelief, then resignation.

And at the age of eighty-four, Wyche concluded, the prince confided to him that not a day had gone by that he didn't wake up in the morning and touch a sixty-year-old knot on his forehead and say to himself, "I love you still."

III

In a
Desert Oasis,
an Unexpected Sheba

10

Further Suspects

IN THE MIDDLE EAST, days and nights can be frenetic. Or time can stand still, as it does at airports and border crossings when you don't have quite the right paperwork. The best strategy is to patiently wait it out, a mote in officials' eyes as they sip their tiny cups of coffee. Eventually, the time will come for them to go home, and they'll mutter, thrash your passport with rubber stamps, and dismissively wave you through. In the meantime, I've found it helpful to have along a good detective story to while away the hours as the overhead fluorescents flicker and buzz and the sad-faced man in the tattered blue jumpsuit mops the floor.

Mysteries are excellent company, too, on interminable airplane flights and in lonely hotel rooms. I have to confess that I am forever duped. On page 161 I'll be convinced that I'm one up on Navajo detective Jim Chee or my hometown sleuths Lew Archer and Philip Marlowe, and I turn down the corner of that page so I can show Kay, the PI, how soon and brilliantly I have solved the mystery. By page 361, inevitably, I discover that I'm wrong.

As things were panning out, my search for the queen of Sheba was no exception.

The case shouldn't have been all that complicated: a missing person and a missing land. I had investigated Sheba's known associate King Solomon and found that he appeared to have been a hill-country chieftain rather than a mighty monarch, though this in no way diminished his biblical repute as a man of faith and wisdom. It then stood to reason that Sheba would have been from a neighboring tribe, from no farther away than Midian in northern Arabia. Yet we had found no trace of her there, or of a state that could have been the source of the goods and wealth she spread on the floor of Solomon's palace. Had the Bible wildly exaggerated her resources and role? I didn't think so.[1]

So where did the mystery stand?

1. There are those who maintain Sheba *nevertheless* could have been a northern Arabian queen, a forerunner of Zabibi, Samsi, and their dynasty.

2. Sheba's homeland may have been farther south in Arabia, where a kingdom of Saba (or Sheba) once flourished. Yet there was longstanding evidence that this kingdom significantly post-dated Solomon's era. Harry Philby, among others, had been there and wrestled his motorcar from ruin to ruin and had sought and copied inscriptions that, in his words, "date back to about 460 B.C. . . . The genealogical details which these and others give [us] enable the details of the first Sabean dynasty to be traced back to about 500 B.C., leaving a blank of some three and a half centuries between then and the earlier time of Solomon."[2]

   Be this as it may, the pendulum of opinion as to the queen's origins had recently begun to swing from northern to southern Arabia. Inevitably, I would be drawn there—to Yemen—which is as far south as south can be in the biblical world.[3]

   But if Philby and others were correct in ruling out a southern Arabian queen, what then?

3. She might have been a queen of Ethiopia, as the Coptic monks I'd met in Jerusalem passionately believed. I looked forward to researching the history of Ethiopia and tracking down knowledgeable archaeologists.

4. In a new wrinkle, I had come across an account that, wherever the queen's homeland was hidden, at the end of her days she was laid to rest in the Syrian oasis of Palmyra. By good fortune, an opportunity had come up for me to travel now to Syria and look into this.

And if I turned over every stone, dogged every clue, and found not a trace of the queen of Sheba or her civilization?

I would be reluctantly persuaded that she was a creature of the imagination. She would join the purring, seductive, fictional noir ladies of the detective stories I so enjoyed.

11

The Caliph's Command

KAY WASN'T ABLE to come along for the next chapter in the quest, but—as a measure of family tolerance for quixotic behavior—she was spelled by our daughter Cristina. Both Cristina and her sister, Jennifer, enjoyed the Middle East. Jenny studied medieval Islam at Cairo's American University and spoke presentable Arabic. Cristina was fascinated by the region's pop culture: Day-Glo hands of Fatima, "Imagine" played on the oud.

Cristina and I joined a dozen archaeologist friends for a busman's holiday in Syria, with a first stop in Damascus, a Russian-engineered concrete sprawl that has obliterated what once was a fabled garden city.[1] Even so, Damascus's ancient heart—its walled Old City and vaulted medieval souk—is intact, fragrant with whiffs of cardamom-flavored coffee, honey pastries, and sacks spilling over with all the spices of the East. A maze of twisting lanes leads to the Great Mosque, built in the early 700s A.D. and surely the most splendid in Islam. Its minarets soar to the heavens and look down upon a vast open courtyard where savants once gathered and kept alive mathematics, medicine, and all learning after Rome fell and Europe was plunged into darkness. These learned men were robed in Damascene brocade and topped with enormous red and yellow turbans. It was said that the larger the turban, the wiser the wearer. To the south of the courtyard, a hundred silver chandeliers still illuminated the mosque's richly carpeted prayer hall. Here caliphs and slaves alike praised and thanked Allah and paid their respects to a reliquary enshrining the head of John the Baptist. Another prophet claimed by Damascus was Suleiman—Solomon. The medieval historian al-Tha'labi credited him with building not only the city but, off in the desert to the east, in the oasis of Tadmor, later known as Palmyra, a pleasure palace for the queen of Sheba. There, al-Tha'labi and others attest, the queen lived out her life, and there she died, and was buried.

And was raised from the dead, though still of the dead. In the eighth century A.D., the Umayyad caliph of Damascus, Hisham ibn 'Abd al-Malik, wearer of the largest turban of all, received a report that bedouin had discovered the mortal remains of the queen of Sheba in the desert ruins of Palmyra. Born and raised nearby, 'Abd al-Malik took an interest in this. He believed that as Islam had risen from the sands of Arabia, so had the queen of Sheba. It was his wish that she receive a fitting Islamic reinterment—and as one would expect, his wish was his command. Whether 'Abd al-Malik himself journeyed to Palmyra is unknown.

Our bus, having cleared Damascus's fuming and honking traffic, was on its way to Palmyra. Treeless, baked hills stretched away to the heat-hazed horizon. There was a sudden scream, a Syrian air force Mirage skimming low over the desert highway. A lone jet was a frequent sight in the Middle East, a display of military might on a budget, Cristina and I speculated, wherein after breakfast a pilot would go looping around his country demonstrating who was in charge, at least of the skies.

Three hours east of Damascus, we crested a rise and, quite suddenly, saw before us the temples, amphitheater, and thousand gleaming columns of Palmyra. Though some columns had fallen, most still stood, converging on a splendid *tetrapylon*, a cluster of massive pillars supporting a decorative architrave. These pillars, of the finest granite, had been quarried in upper Egypt, floated down the Nile and across the Mediterranean, then dragged hundreds of miles across the desert.

Though now in ruins, Palmyra had once bloomed as a great city of the Arabs, a wondrous stone flower set against the green of ten thousand palms.

"Like Vegas," Cristina mused.

"What?"

"Las Vegas."

"You mean this is an oasis and Las Vegas is an oasis?"

"More than that, I think. It's what they built here."

The remark was irreverent, but as further observation would prove, quite appropriate. What struck Cristina was that two cities in two deserts had taken established architectural styles and pushed them over the top. The look of Palmyra was classical Greek or Roman, but where the Greeks or Romans would have lined a thoroughfare with a single row of columns on each side, the Palmyrans erected three rows on each side and halfway up each column affixed statues of themselves. Judging from what remains of them, the statues were artistically hit or miss. Some were beautifully rendered, others had outsize eyes and curiously flattened triangular noses. Who knows what vivid colors the Palmyrans had used in painting their statues and pillars and buildings, all now bone white.

Sometime between A.D. 724 and 738 a party dispatched by Caliph 'Abd al-Malik had come this way. The party included masons and artisans, for his intent was to inter the queen of Sheba's alleged remains in a mausoleum worthy of her role in the holy Koran. The caliph's men would have seen Palmyra quite as we saw it, in ruins. The city had centuries before been devastated by the vainglory of its Arab queen, Bat Zabbai, better known as Zenobia. In the tradition of the earlier queens Zabibi and Samsi, Zenobia was strong yet given to folly.[2] She challenged a great power—Rome—and lost disastrously. Conquered and then pillaged by legionaries under the personal command of the emperor Aurelian, Palmyra became a backwater first of the Roman, then of the Islamic Umayyad empire.

(It may well be that Caliph 'Abd al-Malik had to some degree confused Sheba with Zenobia. By coincidence, Zenobia's name in Arabic, Bat Zabbai, meant "the hairy one," an epithet that was taken to refer to her legs—and it was Sheba's hairy legs that in legend so upset Solomon.)

In ruined Palmyra the caliph's men reportedly found a woman's body in a perfect state of preservation! Where exactly they found her is not recorded, though a possibility is one of the tower tombs just west of the city proper. The tombs ring a low hill called the Umm al-Balqis, the "Mother of Balqis" (Balqis, it may be recalled, is a proper name for the queen of Sheba).

The logical place for the reinterment of this Sheba would have been in a mosque set in what previously had been a sacred precinct dedicated to Bel, the principal deity of the pagan Palmyrans.

A sudden gust of wind swept Palmyra. To the west, small dark clouds bunched in the desert sky as Cristina and I entered the realm of Bel, the "Master of the Universe" revered in one form or another throughout the ancient Middle East. His precinct, properly known as a *tenemos*, was an artificially leveled nine-acre quadrangle lined by a colonnade of nearly three hundred pillars.

Here the Palmyrans assembled to witness elaborate blood offerings to Bel. We saw where the priests purified themselves at a water-filled stone basin before proceeding to an open-air altar to sacrifice camels, bulls, and rams. Beyond the altar, in the center of the quadrangle, was the towering temple of Bel, at whose whim, the Palmyrans believed, they would either prosper or perish.

I remembered from Sunday School that Bel had shared billing

with a dragon in a story in the Apocrypha. What it was about I didn't recall, but I had the impression that the Bible's Bel and Milcom and Chemosh were small-time pagan gods, "abominations" tucked away in caves and ravines in the backwaters of the Holy Land. Crude clay idols, tempting to the foolish. Not so, not by the evidence at Palmyra. The scale of Bel's temple spoke of a powerful rival to the Old Testament's Yahweh.

The elaborate ceilings of the temple's north and south *adytons*, its interior sanctuaries, were inlaid with intricately carved stone thistles and rosettes. Each adyton once held an effigy of Bel—images long gone, either carted off, melted down, or wrathfully destroyed. After Palmyra's fall, the temple of Bel was used as a church and then as a mosque.

Yet neither Christianity nor Islam had been able to erase the temple's pagan grandeur. The only evidence of those faiths was an inscription in Archaic Cufic (a very early Arabic script) on the back wall of the empty north adyton. It read: "May God take pity on Abd as-Samad, son of Obeid, and on Muhammad, son of Yazid, and forgive them their sins, old and recent; written in the year 110. May God take pity on anyone who says after reading this: Amen."

Here was a dramatic coincidence. The Islamic year 110 corresponds to the Christian A.D. 728–729—when Caliph Hisham ibn 'Abd al-Malik was said to have ordered the queen of Sheba reinterred! Could the two penitents in the inscription have been involved in the burial? Might the queen of Sheba's mausoleum have been the sanctuary where we now stood? The only answer, I told Cristina, was the phrase Islam's early historians invoked at the conclusion of their flights of fact and fancy: "but God knows best."

"A good story: 'The Caliph and the Dead Queen,'" she said. "That's the extent of it?"

"That's it, except . . ."

Woven into the 576th night of *A Thousand Nights and a Night* is a scene that I'll wager was inspired by 'Abd al-Malik's wish and his command and by what may or may not have happened where we stood in Bel's temple. The tale is "The City of Brass," and in it Emir Musa (read Caliph 'Abd al-Malik) journeys across a great desert to an imposing abandoned city. Its gates are locked. The emir requests a ladder. He climbs over its wall, wanders its streets, and enters a vast, sepulchral palace. At its heart is a domed chamber containing

> a canopy of brocade reposing on pillars of red gold . . . and on the couch [beneath it] lay a damsel, as if she were the lucindent sun, eyes never saw a fairer . . . And it seemed as if she gazed on them to the right and to the left . . . [Above her head] a golden plaque was inscribed 'O thou, if thou know me not, I will acquaint thee with my name: I am Tadmurah, daughter of the Kings of the Amalekites, of those who held dominion over the lands in equity and brought low the necks of humanity.'[3]

Translating this passage, the nineteenth-century *savant terrible* Sir Richard Burton was convinced that the woman was none other than the queen of Sheba. And "Tadmurah" fixes the location, for the name means "woman of Tadmor," and Tadmor is an older name for Palmyra.

The Emir Musa steps forward to greet this queen of Sheba, only to have one of his men point out:

> "Allah preserve thee, O Emir, verily this damsel is dead and there is no life in her; so how shall she return thy salaam?"; adding, "Indeed, she is but a corpse embalmed with exceeding art; her eyes were taken out after her death and quicksilver set under them, after which they were restored to their sockets. Wherefore they glisten and when the air moveth the lashes, she seemeth to wink and it appeareth to the beholder as though she looked at him, for all she is dead."

A chilling scene.

And a thrill it was to run this fragment of *A Thousand Nights and a Night* to its likely source, following in the footsteps of the fictional Emir Musa and the real Caliph 'Abd al-Malik. Perhaps, as the tale would indicate, the caliph indeed journeyed to Palmyra to honor a woman he was convinced was the queen of Sheba.

That should have been all there was to Palmyra's role in Sheba's story. But it was not.

After a last look around, Cristina and I left Bel's temple and rejoined our group, which was examining a relief of three veiled women, evidence that veiling predated the rise of Islam. The practice was not religious; the intent was to spare women of childbearing age from leering looks and lewd gestures and to set them apart from slaves, servants, and harlots.[4]

Temple of Bel:
three veiled women

A few steps away was a second image, difficult to see. A slab of masonry had long ago pitched to earth from the upper reaches of Bel's temple and now rested on two smaller slabs. If you weren't claustrophobic, you could lie down on your back and wriggle underneath to view an extraordinarily pristine relief, sheltered from the elements. I waited until everyone else had taken a turn, then scooted under the slab. Just inches beyond my nose I beheld a statuesque woman in a diaphanous gown (as diaphanous as stone can suggest). Her face was unveiled, as was a breast. What a contrast to the shrouded women out in the sunlight just a few feet away. Was she a slave, servant, or harlot? No, for she was winged. An angel? Her left hand grasped a snakelike vine—or was it a vinelike snake? And she wore what appeared to be a helmet. A warrior? And what was wrong with her right hand? Where there should have been fingers there was a hoof. I fumbled for my camera and squirmed to fit it with a fisheye lens that could cover a wide field at close range.

"Dad . . . time to move it along."

As I laid the camera on its back and guessed at the composition, I became aware of a commotion: running footsteps, muffled exclamations, an eerie whirring.

"Dad, out from under there! Now!"

I took my picture and slid out from under. The sun was dimmed. A towering cyclonic cloud, brown with sand and debris, was bearing down on the temple. Everyone was hastening to reach the shelter of the precinct's west gate. Most of the group made it, but not Cristina and I. Sand stung our eyes, gritted our hair, poured down our necks. But the tornado's vortex was not as scary as it had seemed. Crazed corkscrew winds, but not enough to spiral us skyward. I managed to shoot a few pictures (see plates 16–17).

For several minutes the cloud swirled around the enclosure, then it was gone, twisting off across the desert to the east. The rest of the day was overcast, the air heavy with hanging dust and the smell of vegetation torn up by the tornado.

Temple of Bel:
Nike-Astarte

It wasn't until I returned to California and had my film processed that I thought about the woman under the rock, and then I thought about her a lot.

Tom Parker, an archaeologist on the excursion, had suggested that she might be a Nike, a local version of Greece's Winged Victory, and he was right. In pose and dress she was derived from a famous Nike of Pantos. Yet there was more to this woman. The vine or snake in her left hand was a symbol of fertility; her hooflike right hand was the mark of a demon. The woman under the rock appeared to be a conflation of Nike and . . . who else I wasn't sure, until I discovered more about Astarte, the omnipresent goddess of Palmyra.[5]

Like helmeted Nike, Astarte loved battle and descended from the heavens to offer victory to those she deemed worthy. Like a mysterious flashing gemstone, she had many and shifting facets. She had aspects of a fertility goddess and a goddess of love. She was Fortune. Under the name Beltu ("Lady"), she was consort to Bel ("Lord"). She was the brightest of all stars, the evening star. She was the moon. She was the queen of heaven. She belonged to no one culture; she was queen to them all. She was Ishtar to the Babylonians,

Allat or Attar to the Arabians, and Ashtoreth to the Canaanites and Israelites.

And according to some, Astarte was the queen of Sheba.

Wary of complex hypothetical theories, I was at first skeptical of
what the German scholar Erich Zehren had to say about the queen
of Sheba. He proposed that a clue to her identity can be found if you
read the I Kings account of her appearance before Solomon, then
turn the page to where Solomon drifts away from Yahweh and wor-
ships competing gods. I Kings 11:5 relates, "Solomon became a fol-
lower of Astarte, the goddess of the Sidonians." (Sidon, a city in
Syria, predated the rise of Palmyra.) In Astarte's honor Solomon
raised pillars on the summit of a hill south of the Mount of Olives,
opposite Jerusalem.

Zehren sees this line as reciprocal to the prior visit of the queen of
Sheba—who, he suggests, is *an incarnation of Astarte*, rung into the
text of I Kings to glorify Solomon. By praising Solomon, Sheba—
read Astarte—validates his identity as a mighty and wise king and, as
well, validates Yahweh, ascendant as the supreme god of the Israelites. In Sheba's guise, Astarte is lavish in her paean, "How happy
your wives are! How happy are these servants of yours who wait on
you always and hear your wisdom! Blessed be Yahweh your God who
has granted you his favor, setting you on the throne of Israel!"

In the tenth century B.C., Solomon and Yahweh needed all the
help they could muster. The Israelites were emerging from a Canaanite culture yet were reluctant to turn their backs on powerful
Canaanite gods. What better way to break their hold than to have
one of these gods—Astarte—admire Solomon's wisdom and his
God? A recurrent theme in Middle Eastern and classical mythology
is that *the goddess intervenes on behalf of the hero. And when she does,
she assumes human form.* In Homer's *Odyssey*, Athena appears on
the beach to aid Odysseus; so Astarte appears before Solomon.

As myth-infused as this characterization of Sheba might seem, it
made sense to me. And even if I could discover an entirely earthly

Sheba, an overtone of Astarte would, in my mind at least, reverberate in the story. She was there to help Yahweh compete with powerful neighboring nature gods—herself included—that regularly filled people's hearts with fear by calling down plague and famine, stirring up storms, and unleashing awesome displays of lightning and thunder. Even as the Israelites praised Yahweh, they felt a near overwhelming urge to acknowledge and placate long-standing pagan deities. In the end, Solomon himself could not resist their pull, nor could subsequent generations. Some four hundred years later the prophet Jeremiah wrote that in a vision Yahweh complained: "Cannot you see what they are doing in the towns of Judah and in the streets of Jerusalem? The children collect the wood, the fathers light the fire, the women knead the dough, to make cakes for the Queen of Heaven . . ."

Astarte, the queen of heaven.

All afternoon the sky had been dark, the heavens agitated. Fitful raindrops had splattered stonework and thirsty sand. At dusk our bus took us up a twisting track for a panoramic view of Palmyra from the battlements of a ruined fort on the summit of a nearby mountain. We watched, saying little, as darkness engulfed the spectral glory spread below us. Palmyra and its ghosts: a city under the spell of Zenobia, Sheba, and Astarte, queen of heaven.

There was a rumble of thunder and a buzzing, a static in the air. At first almost imperceptible, then louder. With an edge of "I'm not nervous about this, but what do you think?" Cristina suggested I look down to see if I saw what she saw.

All around my hiking boots, the sand was vibrating. Small pebbles leapt in the air. Lightning flashed. I looked up. Cristina's hair, everyone's, swirled upward and stood on end. It began to rain, blurring my glasses.

"Dad, maybe there are better places to be than on top of a fort on top of a mountain just now," Cristina suggested.

In Which
We Venture to a Land
of Incense and Spices

12

To Far Arabia

"IN YEMEN," confided the airline clerk, "many little Balqis. It is most often name for girls." With a flourish he handed me my Yemenia airline ticket and wished, "Grand travel, sir!"

I was accumulating Shebas: a Sheba from northwestern Arabia, a Sheba in haunted Palmyra. The first was questionable but not entirely to be ruled out. The second was convincing but mythical, Astarte come to earth.

Later in the day, the rest of an expedition—to Yemen now, in search of Sheba—flew into Amman, Jordan, from California and Brazil. Two individuals: David Meltzer and Ricardo de Monte Rosa. Cristina would have loved to join us, but in a few days she was due back at work in Los Angeles.

I'd known David Meltzer for almost thirty years. A craggy-faced Beverly Hills psychoanalyst, he was, I'm sure, insightful and quietly reassuring during his fifty-minute hours. But as our family well knew, he was given to wild enthusiasms: ripping around on his racing bicycle, recording life's joys and sadnesses with his classic Leica and two years earlier, venturing with Kay and me across Arabian sands. He loved the desert—dancing at a rural wedding, target shooting with the bedouin. Whenever he got a chance, he conscientiously phoned his patients; one worried that he might never return home.

Hearing of David's enthusiasm for Arabia, his old friend Ricardo de Monte Rosa asked to be counted in on further adventures, exactly where or why didn't matter. If it was chasing after a distant queen, that was fine. Never having met the fellow, I was not sure how he would fare in you-never-know-what's-going-to-happen-next-and-it-might-be-scary Yemen. A jovial man with twinkling eyes set in steel-framed spectacles, it may be fairly said that Ricardo was a bon vivant. He typically had a fine Cuban cigar in one hand and a libation in the other—if all else failed it would be a glass drawn from his reserve silver flask of Brazilian *cachaca*. That was by night; by day he wielded a Global Positioning System navigation device. He was to prove expert at charting our uncertain course. "Jungles, deserts, wine, women—to deal with them is an art," he was to comment. "And I am an artist."

David and Ricardo had cheerfully agreed to my one condition as to the adventure before us: no complaints—about heat, sand, bugs, food, uncertainties, or dangers.

And now, as explorers are supposed to, we trained by hiking in southern Jordan, in a landscape of convoluted beige and rose-red sandstone outcroppings rent by sudden, shadowy canyons. Cristina accompanied us on this three-day exercise and was a frequent voice of reason, suggesting, "Wouldn't it be preferable to go around rather than jump across and break your neck?" We acclimated to 100-plus degrees Fahrenheit and developed a routine for working with map, compass, and our GPS units. Well, to an extent. At one point it was not satellites but Cristina who instinctively led us out of a brush-choked blind canyon.

Picnicking in a grassy vale, we sampled what were to be our emergency rations: peanut butter, dried apricots, and Laughing Cow cheese.

"So why this search?" Cristina asked. "Isn't it strange for three grown men to . . ."

"Life is strange," David interrupted.

"And life is women," anted Ricardo.

"Because . . ." I began to answer, but found myself at a loss for words.

"Well, when you figure out the why," offered Cristina good-naturedly, "let me know and I'll tell everyone else, including your wife."

The next day Cristina saw us off on an all-smoking Yemenia flight. As we pulled away from the gate, flight attendants rushed up and down the aisle, waving their hands to clear a path through the blue smoke and shouting, as if to naughty children, "La tdakhin! La, la, la!" No smoking! No! The man in front of me slyly slipped his cigarette under his fez; others put theirs out, only to reignite them after the attendants had buckled up for take-off.

For the next few hours, I divided my time between watching the fez bobbing in the seat ahead—it appeared to have a life of its own, tilting this way and that at impossible angles—and gazing out the window at the hazy, harsh deserts of Saudi Arabia, streaming by endlessly and hypnotically below. What an achievement it would have been for a queen of Sheba—or anyone—to survive a crossing from far-off Yemen. Yet thousands and thousands of caravaneers and heavily laden camels had long ago made the fourteen-hundred-mile trek to Jerusalem and other cities of the classical world. And this was but half of their journey, for they would race the rising heat of the desert spring to return home the same year.

Their route—the Incense Road—would define our coming journey.

Frankincense, the finest of incenses, was no more than the sap of a humble tree found on the desert side of the Dhofar Mountains, in what is today the Sultanate of Oman. A tree's bark was slashed; its sap bubbled to the surface and, exposed to air, soon crystallized and was scraped into reed baskets. In ancient times frankincense had little inherent value—until it made its way north, where it was in demand for use in temples to please the gods and for use in homes to freshen the air. In Rome, frankincense was as valued as gold.[1]

Our plan in Yemen was to follow, as best we could, the Incense

Road's first few hundred miles. We would pass through three city-state kingdoms that had long ago prospered as they dispatched caravans laden not only with incense but with gold, spices, and precious stones. The kingdoms were Hadramaut, Qataban, and Saba, and the greatest of these was Saba, or Sheba. Though fierce rivals and chronically at each other's throats, they shared a common architecture, script, and religion, that of the dominant Sabeans.[2]

To track our journey we had the benefit of space imagery created by good friends and Jet Propulsion Lab scientists Ron Blom and Bob Crippen. I had color-copied their master image onto a dozen pages, which I now studied, as I had many times, tracing where the Incense Road might have threaded its way from one Arabian city state to the next.

Bumpy skies, though, put this task on hold. The fez in front of me canted to the left, should have catapulted off its owner's head and gone rolling on down the aisle, but didn't. Out the window, the beige desert was giving way to the green of farmed foothills and then rugged mountains. We had crossed from Saudi Arabia into Yemen—and into the realm covered by our space imagery. Comparing a landscape captured from four hundred miles above the earth with that of four miles up, I was able to track our approach and descent to the capital city of Sana'a.

The airport's arrival hall was mobbed with wildly gesticulating passengers claiming enormous, contents-spilling cardboard boxes, crated kitchen appliances, and tractor tires. Heavily armed militia, garbed in a variety of homemade uniforms, looked on with glazed indifference, their cheeks bulging with the drug *qat*. Eyeing our gear, a man with enormous crimson epaulets officiously commanded David, Ricardo, and me, "Open it! Open them! Open them all!" We began to unlatch and unzip, only to have him become bored and shout, "Ha! Ha! Close it! Close it! Close them all!" I shared an observation from a once-classified U.S. State Department manual; its opening page was blank but for the words "The Yemenis have a genius for chaos."

Ahead, above a seething crowd, a hand waved; it belonged to a handsome, luxuriantly mustachioed, hawk-faced man who introduced himself as Hussein al-Arhabi, our guide for the weeks ahead. He was a debonair fellow swathed in an immaculate beige robe and an orange-and-brown turban, with a curved, silver-sheathed dagger at his belt.

On the ride into Sana'a, Hussein pointed out a flurry of new construction, though progress was having its problems. A sizable commercial block, though finished, had yet to be occupied. In laying the foundation, the contractor had skipped precautionary ceremonies—and djinns, ever present with the Yemenis and up to no good, had moved in. If you entered the building you were at risk of being hurled from room to room or even out the window by invisible hands.

Down the street, past the Sheba supermarket and Sheba Neon, we dropped off our luggage at the Taj Sheba Hotel and headed for Sana'a's walled Old City, and life as it was in *A Thousand Nights and a Night*. Men with red henna-dyed beards and wildflowers tucked into their turbans . . . women veiled head to toe in black . . . beggars, maimed and covered with oozing sores. Guided by Hussein, we joined a throng surging through a maze of more than fourteen thousand fancifully decorated cut-stone tower houses, six to ten stories high. This was a very old city, founded, it is said, soon after the Flood by Shem, son of Noah.

We passed a blindfolded camel circling endlessly to power a mill that ground sesame seeds for oil; if the camel was allowed to see what he was doing, Hussein said, he would go crazy, realizing that he had gone no farther than when he had started years ago. A few steps away, a beady-eyed medicine man squatted by a wheelbarrow piled with bottles and ampules of drugs long past their "use by" dates. When

Hussein pointed out the steaming domes of a *hammam*, a Turkish bath dating to the fourteenth century, we decided to venture into its gloomy passageways and chambers. It was a set for a sepulchral bad dream, except that the faces in the mist, the bath's regulars, were polite and cheery. We returned to the street and agreed that even though we'd been inside for only a few minutes, fully clothed, we were remarkably refreshed. We turned into a cramped, twisting alley, its walls caked with soot. In tiny niches, ashen gray men sat cross-legged, beating molten iron and steel into scissors and daggers, lit by the glow of their furnaces and showers of sparks.

Dark clouds stole what little sunlight filtered into the Old City. It began to rain. Rooftop waterspouts gushed; lanes flooded. I looked up as a flash of lightning illuminated the face of a somber little girl, gazing expressionless from a window outlined with whitewash to keep djinns from riding in on the damp air of the coming night.

As quickly as it came, the rain squall swept off across the Yemeni highlands; it would dwindle and die in the desert to the east.

We negotiated for a battered canister of butane and bought a case of Kit Kat candy bars and a camelhair rug to spread in the sand. David and Ricardo wanted to dress as the bedouin do, so Hussein found a tailor to stitch up robes by the light of a gas lantern. Waiting on the shop's stone threshold, I watched, across an irregular square, a wizened old man sitting in a pool of light in an open doorway, leafing through the pages of an enormous tome and periodically drawing smoke from a bubbling hookah.

David and Ricardo did Lawrence of Arabia turns in their desert robes. The tailor turned off his gas lamp and dumped his garbage in the street, fodder for the herds of goats that by night would be driven through the city.

Early the next morning, guide Hussein rendezvoused with us at the Taj Sheba Hotel. And a familiar, formidable figure strode across the lobby. "Neek-holas! Daoud!" (Big smiles and hugs.) "How are you?" He was Hussein al-Ajlan, our driver on a previous journey through Yemen. He had the legs-apart stance and shoulder hunch of a sumo wrestler, and like them he could move with the speed and agility of a cat. His eyes flashed to Ricardo: "And you?"

"I am Ricardo."

"Ree-car-e-do. You are Eye-tal-iano?"

"Brazilian."

"Ah, better. All people from Eye-tal-iano they speak smooth but very small." Switching to a tiny voice: "Ah-lora. Mul-ti bene. Graz-z-z-ia." Back to a bigger voice: "Now come see Ibn al-Qad, all fixed up."

He led us out to "the Son of the Camel," his desert-worn Toyota Land Cruiser. Since last we'd ridden with Hussein, he had relined the brakes and installed a little velvet curtain to keep the sand out of a newly installed cassette player.

"But, God forbid, Hussein, we're not squandering any money on tires," commented David, eyeing a suggestion of treads.

"Same-same as last time," Hussein said with a nod. "But they get us through. Enshallah."

A fellow carrying two large white plastic sacks joined us. Until now I'd known him only via fax: Mohammed Osman. He had recruited the Husseins, guide and driver, for us, and now handed over enough rial banknotes to fill an entire backpack. He'd changed them from traveler's checks we'd yesterday given guide Hussein. Without Mohammed's enterprise, the adventure that lay ahead would have been impossible; only two months before, he had cleared the way for us to follow Arabia's Incense Road. With typographic élan, he had faxed:

Mr. Naser Zaied (the king of the desert—as I used to name him) **PROMISED** to accompany you personally to visit the requested places!!! THOUGH/STILL these places are **NOT open for regu-**

lar/ordinary tourists!!!!! I think we may need to PAY Mr. Naser
EXTRA!!! I do not have any idea right now how much, but I will
practice any possible pressure to minimize this extra!!!!

This very afternoon, we would meet Sheik/Mr. Naser Zaied, the
king of the desert. Moreover, Mohammed announced he had already and favorably settled what was needed to PAY Mr. Naser EX-
TRA!!!

We stowed our gear in the Land Cruiser and were soon on our way
out of Sana'a and across a highland plateau. We debated how to ad-
dress our dual Husseins. After some discussion, we settled on different tones of voice, a querying "Hussein?" (guide) versus a declarative
"Hussein!" (driver). As well, we identified the two by where they
came from: highland Hussein al-Arhabi as opposed to desert Hussein
al-Ajlan.

Before long we came to the first of what were to be dozens of road-
blocks. An Askari, a ragtag local militiaman, advised us to "stay here
you are" and not proceed until a convoy of desert-bound vehicles
could be formed. The next hundred or so kilometers were subject to
the depredations of renegade sheiks and their followers, capable, if
they chose, of shutting down the highway with armored vehicles, as
they had recently done for three months. A quarter-ton truck fitted
with a .50-caliber machine gun pulled ahead of us; it was packed
with a dozen armed Askaris. Several vehicles back, a second truck
sported a double-barreled ack-ack gun, not aimed at the sky but leveled to deal with overland attack. Desert Hussein slid his Kalashnikov out from under the seat, snapped in a magazine, and then
checked the clip in his .45 automatic. For intimate encounters, two
daggers, one ceremonial and one practical, were tucked into his belt.
("Arsenal" is an Arabic word.) Hussein stretched and smiled and
eased up on the clutch. The convoy moved out and soon was switch-
backing down a dramatic escarpment to the desert floor, 8,000 feet
below.

Yemenis, whether in the highlands or the desert, heed landmarks that Westerners would hardly notice—a streak of quartz in an out-cropping, say, or a grayish patch of sand. Often a landmark is no more than where something happened, last year or a thousand years ago. "At night, I once pass through here," recalled highland Hussein a half-dozen curves down the escarpment. "I see dead man in road. No problem. He's dead. I'm not. I keep going, but later that night I'm on my way back to Sana'a, I see crowd and can't help myself and stop and put my nose in. Dead man still there, and one in crowd he shouts, 'One *from Arhab* killed my friend!' As you know, I am Hussein al-Arhabi—from Arhab. I try lie. I say 'No, no, I . . . me . . . I from Hajeed.' They no buy this . . . so I take myself starting the car, flying with it. Wow! They run after me in their cars. Rocks in road they spin me. I keep going though. What a bad night! What a bad night!"

I wondered about today. In the passenger-side mirror I glimpsed the ack-ack several vehicles back, panning the countryside. The speaker of the Yemeni Parliament, Abdullah Ahmar, had recently noted, "It [kidnapping] is an adventure for the tourist, because the tourist will end up learning about the customs of the tribes as well as their good hospitality." A Sana'a newspaper had accordingly suggested that the Ministry of Tourism be renamed the Ministry of Kidnapping.

"They catch you and keep you in their house," desert Hussein explained. "But they let you call embassy, so everyone knows you're okay. They don't want to hurt you. They want to trade you for schools, a good road, a new well. A new Toyota or Explorer, maybe. Black is a good color."

He continued, "So it is not invisible you be in the desert."

"Invisible?" Ricardo queried.

"Invisible! Not invisible you visit desert!"

"Advisable?" David suggested.

"Yes, not advisable. For all the way on this trip, it dangerous!"

Which led to a spirited exchange between the Husseins.

"We go!"

"We go no matter!"

"We cra-zee bedouin. Crazee lot!"

"Cra-zee bedouin we!"

They laughed and slapped their thighs as a last curve catapulted us out across a raw gravel desert. Hazy blue mountains rose behind and beside us, except to the east. There the horizon shimmered with the beginning of the great sand sea of the Rub' al-Khali, the Empty Quarter. Cringing away from its vastness, the highway veered to the south. We slowed for a checkpoint flanked by dug-in artillery. There our escort vehicles pulled off to organize a return convoy to Sana'a. We were on our own.

Waves of sand streamed across the pavement. We drove on, through a landscape of brooding, long-dead volcanoes, to the old and new cities of Ma'rib. Old Ma'rib could well be Kitor, fabled as the queen of Sheba's capital. And the time would come for us to explore its remnants, but right now we had to attend to business in new Ma'rib, a gritty cluster of cement and cinder-block buildings interlaced with supply yards for oil field operations in the Rub' al-Khali. We checked in at the hotel of "The Garden of the Two Paradises" (honoring the Koran's description of Ma'rib), then crossed its dusty parking lot to seek Sheik Naser Zaied, king of the desert, quartered in a stuccoed mud-brick complex next door. A group of armed retainers gestured that we should slip off our shoes and enter Sheik Naser's mifraj, his council chamber.

The spare, whitewashed room was heaped with branches. Lounging on cushions ranged around the walls, some twenty glassy-eyed men were picking them clean of the shiny green qat leaves, which they chewed until their cheeks appeared stuffed with golf balls. A slight but steely man in his middle thirties—Sheik Naser—gestured for me to sit by his side and offered me a branch. I politely declined, passing the foliage on to desert Hussein, who pronounced, "Today is hot. Is qat good for hot. Qat circles the blood!"

Sheik Naser's words were few, characteristic of a leader who holds sway with long, unsettling pauses and dark looks. He nodded as I reviewed our route and took a passing interest in the two GPS receivers we would use to track our progress. He regretted that pressing but unspecified matters made it impossible for him to join us. He beckoned over a slender man wearing gold-rimmed spectacles, whose teeth when he grinned, as he often did, flashed gold as well. He was Ali al-Sharif, the king of the desert's cousin. As we were to find, he had a remarkably feline personality. Ever sinuous in his movements, he was a contrast to the also feline, but big-tom, desert Hussein. Certain cat species—the leopard, the rarely glimpsed sand cat—fare well in the desert, able in the blink of a yellow eye to spring from somnolence to high alert. Though only in his late twenties, Ali knew the sands; his father and grandfather had guided desert caravans, and perhaps an ancestor far back had shown the way for the queen of Sheba. In a pinch, Ali could invoke the specter of Sheik Naser's personal militia. "Five hundred he has," said Ali respectfully, "and he can call up more."

Concluded the sheik, "Enshallah, you will have a good journey." With a glint in his eyes he added, "Maybe we come at night and steal your satellite machine!"

We took our leave and prepared for the morrow. A shudder in the rear axle of desert Hussein's Land Cruiser needed attention. Everyone else, myself excepted, would stock up on groceries in the cool of the evening. I used the time for a last session with the Tactical Pilotage Charts (designed for aircraft) and our Landsat 5 satellite imagery. Sunk in a Naugahyde chair in the lobby of the Garden of the Two Paradises, I marked our key waypoints on both maps and space shots, then translated these waypoints into latitude and longitude coordinates that could be programmed into our GPS units.

Well after dark, I heard the crunch of tires on gravel. I stepped outside and helped swing five-gallon jerry cans of gas and water up onto the Land Cruiser's roof, to be lashed down by desert Hussein.

The shopping party hadn't returned with all that much: a stalk of bananas, a few tins of meat, a carton of eggs, and sacks of rice, sugar, and coffee.

"This is it?"

David and Ricardo sheepishly shrugged; it was the best they could find. "And we got some more Laughing Cow cheese—it doesn't go bad."

"Not worry, Nicholas, not worry," desert Hussein assured from up on the roof. "Enshallah!"

In predawn darkness we rumbled east on an asphalt oil-camp road. The sky lightened, a distant mauve silhouetting low dunes. Desert Hussein stretched and stroked the Kalashnikov by his side. He softly said, "It's simple. If you don't like life in the desert, you don't deserve to live." With that he wheeled off the road into the sands, where we stopped to let air out of the tires until they were down to sixteen pounds per square inch. David and Ricardo strolled about in their long robes and turbans. I was content with my usual khakis, rumpled denim shirt, and Aussie hat.

Headlights flashed from a vehicle turning off the oil road and heading our way. In a startlingly swift move, desert Hussein reached for his Kalashnikov, only to ease up as he recognized Ali al-Sharif's pickup. Pulling up to lower the air in his tires, Ali introduced his nephew, fourteen-year-old Muhammad, whom he had brought along to help out around camp and learn the sands.

Ali led the way out into the Rub' al-Khali and a region known as the Ramlat Sabateyn, translated by some as "the Desert of the Two Shebas." But according to the Husseins, it simply meant "the Desert of the Seven Ridges," a topography confirmed by our space images. For four hours we worked our way through and over larger and larger dunes. Ali sometimes followed the tracks of previous vehicles and sometimes struck out on his own, mindful of unmarked minefields laid in recent civil wars. A rare overcast sky kept temperatures in the mid-eighties.

Cresting a dune, we caught sight of a distant scattering of black dots and patches—goats and tents. It had rained in recent weeks, and the bedouin were taking advantage of quickly sprouting grasses and plants to graze their flocks. White and yellow flowers lined our route—and in the distance the face of a dune was not only vividly green but weirdly undulating. Ali raced ahead, then slammed to a stop, as we did. The Husseins tore off their turbans, leapt out, fell to their knees, and joined Ali and Muhammad in scooping up as many as they could capture of a wave of migrating, mating locusts.

"For later, for lunch!" shouted desert Hussein, adding with a wink, "Enshallah!" He popped a wriggling mating pair into his mouth. "Men locusts, women locusts! All good! Witamin B complex!"

Stocked up on the creatures, we drove on for another hour. The dunes gave way to a rolling sand plain, and Ali swung to the east, then back to the west in search of a bedouin encampment he had heard was in the area. We found it in a thicket of acacias. The man of the tent had gone off to fill up his water truck; his wife, veiled but not shy, invited us to rest and eat. Her two winsome little boys fetched a goat, we offered a good price for it, and soon strips of meat were spread to dry on thorny branches; they would be enough for three days' travel. Enshallah.

Luncheon, then, was grilled goat and locusts sautéed in desert herbs. With everyone joining a circle on the tent's carpeted floor, Ricardo was offered the first taste. Picking up a locust with his right hand (observing bedouin etiquette), he noted that it still looked very much like a locust, a big locust, three inches long, its wings, antennae, and backward little knees still intact, though brown and crusty rather than chartreuse and shiny. Ricardo closed his eyes and took a bite. The delicacy audibly crunched. His eyes remained closed, and he smiled, the smile of a mendicant afforded a glimpse of paradise.

"Delicia," he proclaimed, "que delicia!" I was next to nibble, and I couldn't argue, the locusts *were* tasty. When the bowl of bugs came around to Ali al-Sharif, he summed it up: "My goodness, is high class!"

The conversation turned to manners, as perceived by the irrepressible desert Hussein and the reserved highland Hussein. "Speaking is from silver," pronounced the latter, "and silence from gold. Allah gives you two ears to hear a lot and one tongue to speak a little."

"Me, I don't like silent," shot back desert Hussein. "And feet. Feet they don't matter!" He was referring to a traditional injunction against displaying the soles of one's feet. Virtually all Middle East guidebooks say you must not do this; for years, while eating in this part of the world, I had sat on my feet and on my left hand as well, lest they offend.

"And hands!" continued desert Hussein (who, like me, was left-handed). "Who cares? Who cares? Left or right is the same, both the path to the mouth."

Drawing himself up, highland Hussein responded, "When you eat with the left hand, Hussein al-Ajlan, you eat with the devil. And you watch out, the devil he put poison in your food."

Desert Hussein shrugged, left-handedly put away a locust, and echoed Ricardo's "Que delicia!"

As is the custom of the bedouin, everyone then reclined and dozed, enjoying the mild stupefaction that follows a good meal in the desert. A breeze rippled the tent and before long had it flapping. Ali looked out at a darkening sky and thought we had best move on.

Far away, the flat horizon was broken by a conical peak. We made for it: Jebel al-'Uqla, a beacon to desert travelers. At its base, I had read, a mass of boulders was incised with more than a hundred inscriptions in Epigraphic South Arabic, or ESA, the elegant script shared by the kingdoms of southern Arabia.

Al-'Uqla's inscriptions had been recorded in the late 1930s by Harry Philby; more recently, they had been meticulously translated by a learned Belgian Jesuit, Albert Jamme. I'd come to know and admire Father Jamme, and the past winter had visited him at Catholic University in Washington, D.C. Though troubled by ill health, he was enthusiastic and irascible, hoping that God would grant him the days to interpret as many as possible of the fourteen thousand inscriptions overflowing his office files. In parting, he had advised, "Go looking, but please don't do or say foolish things. Never deny the value of a clue, but never create it, either." As I walked away through the slush and snow, he cranked open his window and called after me, "Keep the fire burning!"

We pulled up at the foot of al-'Uqla.

What Jamme had determined from the al-'Uqla inscriptions was that this site had been used for the coronations of the kings of Hadramaut (the first of the three kingdoms we would traverse). Why at such an isolated and lonely place? Quite possibly the peak above figured in the Hadramis' cosmology. In addition, this would have been an ideal base for a ritual hunt that would assure king and court of the blessing and magic of animals symbolizing the sun, moon, and stars. In more temperate days, game was plentiful; an inscription translated by Jamme recorded that a party led by "Yad'il Bayim, King of Hadramaut . . . killed thirty-five oxen and eighty-two camels and twenty-five gazelles and eight leopards at the fortress 'Anwadum [which once existed at al-'Uqla]."[3]

A pair of inscriptions commemorated dignitaries from distant lands assembled for a single ceremony. So desirous was the ancient world of Arabia's incense, that they had come from Chaldea (Iraq), Hind (India), and Tadmor (Palmyra, in Syria). There were also fourteen ladies from Quraysh (in the Hijaz region of north-central Arabia). They may have been courtesans, though that is doubtful, given the sacrosanct nature of the site. More likely they were respected envoys; they, like a queen of Sheba, had traveled far on affairs of state.

Although here and there I could recognize a few words on the boulders, I couldn't fit them together; doing so required years of study, and even so, Father Jamme and his colleagues were often at odds as to the sense of a particular inscription. At al-'Uqla we could only admire the language's South Arabic letters, models of proportion and elegant form even though carved on irregular rock surfaces.

al-'Uqla inscription that begins, "Ill'add, King of Hadramaut . . ."

These letters were long believed to have been derived from the alphabet of the Greeks. If that theory was correct, it would seriously undermine the possibility of a Yemeni queen of Sheba at the time of Solomon. Written Greek dates back to approximately 800 B.C., so the earliest ESA inscriptions *derived* from Greek could logically date to no earlier than 650–700 B.C. Those dates would place an advanced civilization in the area two to three centuries *after* the queen of Sheba's appearance in the Bible in 950 B.C. When I began researching and looking for Sheba a few years before, prevailing wisdom held that she could not possibly have reigned in southern Arabia. But that certainty had been challenged, and in a few days we hoped to visit the site where a case had been made for a much earlier dating of the region's script and civilization.

Big drops, just a few at first, hissed as they stained the lost world of the al-'Uqla inscriptions. Around us their splatters raised tiny clouds of dust. The drops came harder and faster, and within minutes a sheet of rain was sweeping across the Ramlat Sabateyn, the front of a maverick storm that had turned inland from the Indian Ocean. Ali was worried; the stretch of desert ahead of us could quickly become a vast, impassable lake. We drove on. Lightning arced across the sky, and a rogue wind tore up scrub brush and hurled it against our windshield. Our Land Cruiser shaking and shuddering, we followed Ali's pickup as he made for a low ridge. Through the murk of the storm we dimly perceived walls and towers rising above us; we had made it to the ruins of Shabwa, once the capital of the Hadramaut. We pulled up beside Ali and, pinned for the time being in our vehicles, shouted back and forth as to where we might camp. The Husseins preferred the open desert, even at the risk of flooding, for the alternative was the ruins, which were rife with djinns. "Here before I see a strange light up there," gestured highland Hussein. "I shoot at it! It goes over there! I shoot some more, a lot! I never hit that spookey, or if I do it makes no difference!" We settled on a sheltered site at the outer edge of the ruins, above the floodplain.

The storm slacked off. It was dark by the time we organized a supper of leftover locust and partly dried goat, and afterward no one was quite ready to go to sleep. Would the djinns keep to the ruins? Would the rains return? By the light of a gas lantern, Ali and the Husseins regaled us, as they would for several Scheherezade-like nights, with stories of their desert and their world. I asked about the queen of Sheba, and we listened to an accurate retelling of her story as it appears in the Koran. The prime schooling for our Yemenis was the study of the Koran in the courtyard of a village mosque; if the Koran had anything to say about a character or event, that was the tale we heard, repeated nearly word for word. Beyond the Koran, however, their storytelling was amazing—bewildering—in its range of sources.

Ali recounted a fable of a scorpion and a snake, which he attributed to Luqman, an Arabian Aesop who in legend was the queen of Sheba's vizier.

A story or so later, highland Hussein casually mentioned the Sumerian goddess Ishtar (Sumeria's Astarte). "Ishtar!?" I blinked. "Most certainly Ishtar," he responded. "Everyone knows Ishtar." He went on to speak of Asa, the Arabic name for Jesus. The source for his story was not the Koran or even the Bible; it was, I later discovered, the "Infancy Gospel of St. Thomas," a document dating to the middle second century A.D. It was inconceivable that he had access to scholarly translations; the only explanation was hundreds of nights like this, endless tellings and retellings.

And there were stories attributed to Sheik Zubayr. They were stories from afar, the Husseins concurred, for Sheik Zubayr's characters didn't have Arabic names like Ali or Muhammad; their names were Hamlet and Romeo and Juliet. Who knows how Shakespeare's characters came to declaim and die in the sands of southern Arabia?[4]

A little after midnight, a full moon, no longer a hostage of the storm, shone on our camp and, beyond, the once crenellated ruins of Shabwa. "The djinns, they keep to themselves tonight," said a relieved highland Hussein.

Desert Hussein smoothed out his blanket and propped his Kalashnikov within easy reach.

Highland Hussein reflected, "What use, what good are things of the world to the bedouin?"

"My Toyota Land Cruiser is good," desert Hussein was quick to respond, "food is good, qat is good . . ."

Highland Hussein raised a finger to his lips and said, "Yes, but what are things when you stand before God? And what are things when you have stories and words? Think of it, when all is *khalas* [finished], it is a word, only one single word that matters . . . and that word is your name. That people no look down on your name, that they look up to it.

"That people they come to pray on your grave. And they whisper your name."

13
A Trail of Ruins

AT SHABWA we intercepted Arabia's Incense Road, which we would follow to the land, we hoped, of the queen of Sheba. The sky was clear, the temperature rising, and our bedouin savoring their coffee as David, Ricardo, and I set off to explore what was left of ancient Shabwa. Our expectations were not high, despite the words of the historian Pliny the Elder: "The harvested incense is transported by camel to Sabota [the Latin name for Shabwa] where only one gate-

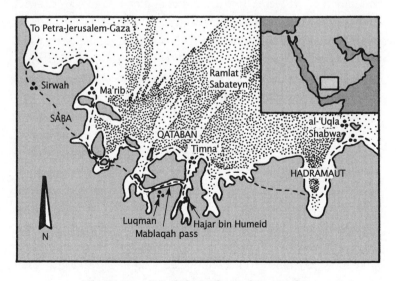

The Incense Road through southern Arabia

way is open to it. Taking another route is a crime that the kings punish by death. At Sabota a tithe estimated by measure and not by weight is taken for the priests for the god they call Sabis . . . Sabota is a walled town containing sixty temples."[1] In the 1930s, fired by this account—the great god Sabis, sixty temples!—Harry St. John Philby and the British solo adventuress Freya Stark vied to be the first to reach Shabwa, only to be laid low by fever and undone by feckless guides. They were beaten to the site by Hans Helfritz, an unassuming young German. During his brief and uncomfortable stay, hostile locals "deliberated not whether to kill him but how to kill him. His courage and resource, coupled with the bad marksmanship of the Shabwa folk enabled him to get away with at least a photographic record of some of the ruins."[2] Helfritz was disappointed by what he found, as was Philby, when he cajoled his way there the next year. Little was standing; at most there were six temples, not sixty.

Given Philby's appraisal of Shabwa as "disappointingly small and insignificant," we were surprised and enlightened by what we saw. A French team that recently spent several years at Shabwa had made sense of the site. Working their way through the rubble of a palace, they determined that it had risen seven stories and that its mud-brick construction had been earthquake-reinforced with an internal framework of flexible wooden joints.

This towering building bespoke a classic civilization in the desert of southern Arabia. The touchstone of that civilization was trade—and the beginnings of that trade, we now saw, were humble. After a breakfast of locust and eggs at our camp, highland Hussein guided us to a cluster of murky pools. These were flooded salt mines, their white walls furrowed with the slashes of ancient adzes. In Neolithic times the demand for salt (and for such homely commodities as sea shells and flakes of obsidian) gave rise to trails that were eventually linked and expanded to accommodate long-range caravans laden with incense, spices, and a host of luxuries.

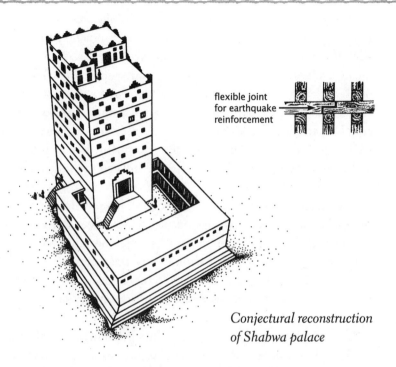

flexible joint
for earthquake
reinforcement

*Conjectural reconstruction
of Shabwa palace*

By midmorning we were on our way again, a one-pickup, one–
Land Cruiser caravan on the Incense Road. We jolted along a dirt
track, then cruised a two-lane paved highway. New roads in Arabia,
unless they're venturing into virgin territory, generally follow old
tracks. It's difficult to improve on their sense of the terrain, their
logic.

Only upon following it through Arabia did we grasp the Incense
Road's guiding logic: it followed the very easiest possible route, even
at the expense of adding miles and days of travel. The road also took
into account the terrain-specific evolution of camels' feet. Camels
that roamed the sands of the Rub' al-Khali developed large, floppy,
saucerlike feet; flinty plains produced camels with small, hard

hooves. Over time, the bedouin recognized and bred more than forty "houses," or variants, of the animals, each uniquely suited to what was underfoot and what was expected of them. As a consequence, once formed, a caravan had to go out of its way, often far out of its way, to hew to consistent terrain that was comfortable for its camels. By contrast, Hussein's "son of the camel" Land Cruiser could readily handle the sands if its tire pressure was lowered to sixteen pounds per square inch—the equivalent of floppy feet— and hard-packed stretches if its tires were inflated to thirty or more pounds.

The Incense Road consistently sought firm but not flinty or overly rocky terrain. Wherever possible, its path was between the sands of the open desert and the mountains that rose abruptly from those sands. We could see on our space imagery a gap ranging in width from miles to just a few hundred feet. If there was no gap at all, the route took to the mountains rather than risk miring hard-hooved camels out in the dunes.

After what would have been eight days by camel from Shabwa (and two days with several side trips for us), we crossed into what was once the kingdom of Qataban and made our way to Timna', its unexcavated capital. Other than the massive foundations of a palace and a still-standing gate, there was little to see. As at Shabwa, a gate was an instrument of taxation. Pliny recounts that a hefty share of frankincense was "paid to the king of that people . . . Fixed rations of the frankincense are also given to the priests and the king's secretaries, but besides these the guards and their attendants and the gatekeepers and their servants also have their pickings: indeed all along the route they kept on paying, at one place for water, at another for foods, or the charges for lodging at the halts."[3] And so it went, with caravans fleeced at every stop along what Pliny calculated as 2,437,500 arduous paces from Timna' to the shores of the Mediterranean.

Timna' was forlorn, its glory and greed smothered by the encroaching sands of the Ramlat Sabateyn. The valley to the south—into the mountains and away from the desert—was still farmed, irrigated by a network of canals dating to Qatabanian times. From the tell at Timna' we could see the contemporary village of Aseilan, where an uncle of desert Hussein presided as the Arabian equivalent of a mayor. And was it not time to experience the hospitality of the desert? As Ricardo had admiringly noted, desert Hussein was a creature of earthly pleasures. Between meals he got along with a mouthful of qat, a cigarette in one hand, a Coke or Mountain Dew in the other. On occasion, as when reaching for a weapon, he'd hold his cigarette, pop can, and twigs in a single hand. Now the prospect of lunch had him barreling cross-country "to eat until I full up like a gas tank—and then you will see that I have extra 'full.'"

Hussein's uncle welcomed us, called for fresh tea, and ushered us into his high-ceilinged, invitingly cool mifraj, there to relax among a plethora of blue cushions. In short order we were served *bint al-Shahan*—"the daughter of the dish," a Jell-O–like mold of wheat flour, ghee, and local honey. We were joined by more guests, arriving in Toyotas, Nissans, and old Land Rovers. Each man stacked his automatic weapon by the door; each solemnly shook our hands. More trays and platters were brought forth, one bearing the better part of a sheep. And the more there was to eat, the more company arrived, until the mifraj was abuzz with several dozen robed and bedaggered men. They ate rapidly, as is the custom of the bedouin.

Then, as if by invisible command, all fell silent. A man with a large turban and a sheaf of papers rose and solemnly addressed the assembly. "Is making accusations," whispered highland Hussein. He nodded in the direction of two downcast teenagers, who, it developed, had been caught red-handed in an act of vandalism. A trial was under way. It was handled as a tribal matter, beyond the jurisdiction of the Yemeni government.

A bent-over older man had his say, his voice trembling with anger and passion. He shouted. Another man was suddenly on his feet, reaching for his dagger. The room tensed. In one swift motion he unsheathed it, defiantly sliced it through the air, and cast it upon the carpet at his feet. He then sank to the floor. A gesture that I thought would have everyone scrambling for their weapons was in fact an age-old signal of resignation. This was the father of the accused, and he was indicating his willingness to accept the judgment of the offended family, who now rose and retired to the courtyard outside the mifraj to discuss and agree on an appropriate punishment.

We took our leave. Desert Hussein was concerned that he had inadvertently thrust us into an unseemly airing of grievances, but no, we assured him, we had been impressed by the trial's somber formality. That afternoon, as we explored archaeological byways of the kingdom of Qataban, we asked more about the ins and outs of Yemeni society. We knew that the central government held sway in the major cities, particularly in the highlands, but beyond that the country appeared to be functionally feudal, in the hands of sometimes rival, sometimes conciliatory sheiks and their heavily armed tribesmen. Yet this feudalism was tempered by a tradition of common assent, a trust in the wisdom of the Koran, and a variety of checks and balances. With everyone toting guns, for instance, a certain, if touchy, equilibrium was achieved.

Feudal democracy? Lord knows Yemen had its problems—an economy undermined by qat, a society facing severe overpopulation—but the Husseins took pride in the fact that theirs was a country of free assembly and free speech, the only democracy in Arabia. Passing a poster of Yemen's president plastered on a mud-brick wall, desert Hussein asserted, "If I feel like it, *I* can put up posters. As many posters of myself as I want, and *still* not be thrown in jail."

There were, in fact, parallels to the social structure of ancient Yemen, which also was rooted in local independence and given to bouts of chaos. The building block of that society was an economic entity called a *sha'b*. A sha'b could be as small as a few dozen square kilometers in area and was politically autonomous. Imagine an American county, but with little or no legal connection to a larger state. A sha'b customarily had a distinct religious and administrative center known as a *hajar*. A feature of the hajar was a sanctuary enshrining a *betyl*, a slab of unfinished stone symbolizing the sha'b's tutelary deity.[4] A sha'b's temporal leader was sometimes modestly called a *bikr*, or "first born," and sometimes a *malik*, or king, though a king of not very much. King or not, the governance of a sha'b had a strong collective and consensual component, as demonstrated by the trial back in Aseilan. The guiding force there had been the will of the people, not that of Hussein's uncle or any one individual.

Creating a next tier, clusters of two or three sha'bs often joined forces to become a super-sha'b, whose combined territory might be as much as several thousand square kilometers. These ethno-cultural entities were held together by a tribal name and deity and by a sense of territorial integrity, often defined by a cooperative system for diverting the seasonal runoff of a major wadi into canals and a complex irrigation system. A super-sha'b was headed by a *qayl*, a tribal chief.

Finally there were confederations of sha'bs super and small. Such were both Qataban and Saba, states that to a degree arose in response to the organizational demands of long-distance trade. Yet by no means was local autonomy forsaken. Yemen's ancient political superstructure lacked "a formalized and legal means of coercion" of wayward sha'bs and their maliks.[5] A parallel would be a U.S. government with little control over its fifty states—no FBI or Supreme Court—but able to present a unified face to the world outside. This ability was essential for organizing the incense trade and dividing its spoils. At the head of such a confederation was a *mukarrib*, a title first thought to mean "priest-king," then "chief of chiefs," and more recently interpreted as "unifier."

The queen of Sheba—or her husband—could have been an early-day mukarrib, precariously poised at the top of a pyramid of go-their-own-way sha'bs and super-sha'bs. To rule as a mukarrib was to face and deal with a contentious lot of bikrs, maliks, and qayls.

From what the Husseins said and from what we saw, the essentials of this social order were preserved in contemporary Yemeni society. It was no joke that our patron Sheik Naser was called "king of the desert"; he was malik of his sha'b, as was Hussein's uncle in and around his village of Aseilan. Yemen still had its sometimes fractious tribal confederations, and in dealing with them the country's president functioned as a mukarrib—including the handicap of diminished "formalized and legal means of coercion."

By the last light of day we investigated a hillside of jumbled and long-ago-looted Qatabanian tombs, then drove on in search of a campsite. I saw several places that looked fine to me, but ahead of us Ali's pickup passed them by, until his headlights fell upon a dune that had the look of an *Arabian Nights* sandcastle city, its sinuous battlements and domes silhouetted against a blue-black sky. Ali shifted into his lowest gear and after a running start spiraled up to a hollow just below the summit. We followed, though not without wheel-spinning, backsliding, and a lesson personally learned: don't make jokes when a bedouin gets stuck in the sand. Additional bedouin don'ts: no tapping on the shoulder from behind; the resulting reflex action will be startling at best, life-threatening at worst. And no initiating good-will discussions of comparative religion. There's only one, and it's not yours.

Said Ali, alighting from his pickup, "So look. Is wonderful. You like?" The goal of his search had been nothing more or less than a sublime view: farmland and patches of twinkling lights in the valley of the Wadi Beihan to the south, and, to the north, dune after moonlit dune of the Ramlat Sabateyn and the eternity of the Rub' al-Khali. What better backdrop for an omelette supper, embellished by

Ricardo with herbs and cheese. We were in good spirits, even sulky teenaged Muhammad—everyone but desert Hussein, who grumpily clambered up onto the roof of his Toyota to spend the night.

"Is bad qat for him he chew today. No good qat in this part of Yemen," Ali commented. "I think pesticide in it."

Hussein indeed had a bad night, but over breakfast (eggs again, for they were beginning to go bad) he brightened as Muhammad described a dream he'd had. It foretold that he would very soon find $100,000 in U.S. dollars.

"Is good, is good, but where?" asked desert Hussein.

"Maybe here, maybe where we go next," Muhammad replied.

"A new truck for us!" exclaimed Ali. "That would be excellent."

"Yes," agreed Muhammad, "and maybe new tires for Hussein." Hussein grinned, though not a big grin, for it appeared that the windfall was not to be equally shared.

"Gee, how about us?" asked David.

"What's for us?" Ricardo echoed.

"You? Nothing . . . though we maybe not leave you behind when we go off to spend the dollars."

"Oh?"

"You'd abandon us?" asked Ricardo.

Assured Ali, "Oh, we take you along. I think."

Barring young Muhammad's windfall, our next destination was Hajar bin Humeid, a site that merited no mention by Pliny or other classical or Arab writers. Yet discoveries there in 1951 were to profoundly influence the archaeology of all southern Arabia. In February of that year Gus Van Beek, a young archaeologist with a recently earned Ph.D. from Johns Hopkins and a hundred dollars in his pocket, stepped off the gangway of an oil-company supply ship docked at what was then the British Crown Colony of Aden. He headed off into the interior to rendezvous with fellow archaeologist

Don Dragoo. At Hajar bin Humeid, Don supervised the digging and Gus analyzed what was uncovered, hoping to establish an occupational chronology. Previous estimates as to when southern Arabian civilization had arisen and fallen had diverged by as much as a thousand years.[6]

Ricardo programmed his GPS unit to lead us to Hajar bin Humeid, which it efficiently did, beeping with joy as we came within a tenth of a kilometer of a tell rising to the east of the Wadi Beihan. We saw that in the last few hundred years, seasonal rains coursing down the wadi had seriously eroded the site—which was fortunate, for the erosion had exposed a vertical cross-section of layer upon layer of occupation. Fragments of floors and walls protruded from the cut.

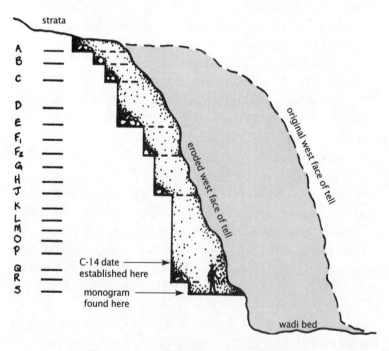

Cross-section of tell of Hajar bin Humeid

A tell is a sizable mound created by successive settlements that, over time, rise higher and higher on their accumulated refuse and collapsed structures. The use of mud brick accelerates the buildup, for when even a single story falls to ruin, it creates three or more vertical feet of debris. In addition there is whatever gets swept out the door or thrown out the window. On top of this the next family builds its house, and so on and on, up here to a height of seventy feet—in essence a man-made hill.

To probe the secrets of a tell, archaeologists frequently sink a vertical test shaft called a *sondage*. But at Hajar bin Humeid, Don Dragoo and Gus Van Beek could bypass that. The chronology of the tell could be probed by relatively modest stair-step excavations on the face of the flood-created cut.

Dragoo retrieved varying types of pottery from nineteen levels of occupation, from the most recent (but still old) Stratum A to the oldest, S, which rested on sterile dirt. With an innovative coding system, Van Beek classified hundreds of pottery shards by their shape, temper, surface coating, finish, and decoration—and laid out the first-ever pottery sequence for southern Arabia. It was a remarkable achievement, enhanced by the fact that in Stratum Q he found a charred roof beam, which became a candidate for the then newly developed technique of carbon-14 dating. Noted the report from the U.S. Geological Survey Radiocarbon Laboratory:

```
W-437 Charcoal from Stratum 2, Phase 2, Area 4      2,807 + or
     [same as Stratum Q] of Hajar Bin Humeid        -160 yrs.
     excavation, Western Aden Protectorate,
     South Arabia. Collected by D. W. Dragoo
     and G. W. Van Beek, 1951.
```

Now back in America (and on the staff of the Smithsonian), Gus Van Beek was elated by this news, for here was an anchor for his pottery sequence, fixing it in time. And the C-14 dating gave special meaning to a single homely artifact: a fragment of a jar found in Stratum S, five feet below the carbon-dated roof beam in Stratum Q. It featured a raised monogram, which Albert Jamme identified as an imaginative combination of the Epigraphic South Arabic letters K, H, L, and M. Add vowels between these consonants and you have the name Kahalum, probably the owner of the jar and its contents.

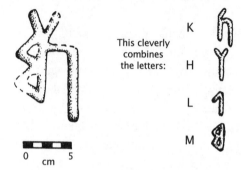

This cleverly combines the letters:

K

H

L

M

0 cm 5

Hajar bin Humeid monogram, Stratum S

Take a moment to consider what arithmetic and logic make of this:

Start with the fact that a carbon date for Stratum Q—2,807 years before 1956, when the test was run—translates as 852 B.C. (with a possible error range of 692–1010 B.C.).

Next, conservatively add 150 years to get back in time to Stratum S. That dates the monogram to something like 1000 B.C. (and it could be as old as 1160 B.C. if we factor in the plus-or-minus range of the C-14 test).

Finally, note that the monogram is a sophisticated composite of four letters, not what one would expect to find in the early days of an alphabet. Estimate the *origin* of that alphabet to be at least two centuries earlier—in the neighborhood of 1200 B.C.

What Gus Van Beek had found at Hajar bin Humeid was that the southern Arabian alphabet—and by definition southern Arabian civilization, for civilization is traditionally defined as a culture with a system of writing—dated to the twelfth century B.C. or earlier.[7] This discovery had many implications, and one that immediately struck Gus was that it comfortably cleared the way for a tenth-century, flesh-and-blood queen of Sheba. He was delighted and relieved. If his Stratum Q sample had carbon-dated to a few centuries later, her existence would be in serious doubt, for there would have been no writing, no civilization, in her time.

Van Beek's final report and findings were well received by his American colleagues but were criticized, derided, and dismissed abroad. In a review in a French journal, epigrapher Jacqueline Pirenne could only conclude that he had seriously confused his strata. In her opinion the script on his monogram could not possibly date to before 700 B.C., since its letters were clearly derived from the Greek alphabet, which dated to approximately 800 B.C. The august Académie Française backed her view, as did academics in Britain, Italy, and Germany. In their opinion, civilization in southern Arabia dated to no earlier than 800 B.C., so *there could have been no significant Sabean state, no queen of Sheba.*

Van Beek and Jamme temperately responded by suggesting a non-Greek provenance for the lettering on the Hajar bin Humeid monogram:

> The origin of its script is still somewhat obscure, but it perhaps derives from one of the earliest Semitic scripts, the Proto-Sinaitic script of about the seventeenth century B.C., with some Canaanite influence. It seems to have split off from its northern progenitors no later than the thirteenth century B.C., by which time consonants in such dialects as Canaanite and Hebrew had begun to coalesce.[8]

European experts sniffed, reiterating that the southern Arabian script resembled Greek—which, admittedly, it does—and therefore was derived from Greek. And there, for decades, the matter rested.

When I first visited Yemen in 1993, I photographed and studied inscriptions with a mixture of awe and melancholy, for the prevailing wisdom was that they were old, but nowhere near old enough to accommodate Sheba.

But now, several recent C-14 dates had been linked to further inscriptions, and evidence was piling up in favor of Van Beek and Jamme's groundbreaking interpretation. A team from the American Foundation for the Study of Man reported corroborative dates from the Wadi al-Jubah. Their findings were backed up by a French team's excavations at Shabwa, which confirmed the accuracy of Van Beek's Hajar bin Humeid pottery sequence and its proof of an early threshold for southern Arabian civilization. Young Gus, it appears, had been right all along. Though some scholars may still have a hard time accepting this conclusion, it's clear that for close to fifty years all the experts of Europe and all their surmises had been dead wrong.

This meant that what we had seen in Yemen—and whatever lay along the Incense Road ahead—might date to the days of Solomon and Sheba.

Just to the west of Hajar bin Humeid we came upon an intact, rock-paved stretch of the Incense Road. As it climbed up a long valley, a landslide blocked our way with refrigerator-sized boulders. David, Ricardo, and I continued on foot, up six miles of well-engineered switchbacks and an altitude gain of 2,600 feet at Mablaqah Pass, where a seventy-five-foot rock cut had spared camels further ascent. The hand-hewn, narrow cut forced caravans to fall into single file so that loads could be counted and, no surprise, a toll extracted.

We backtracked and rejoined the Husseins, Ali, and Muhammad. A long detour took us to the other side of Mablaqah Pass—and into trouble.

Our Incense Road passage had been loosely planned so that we could act on suggestions by Yemenis we met along the way. Desert Hussein alone had an inexhaustible supply of helpful uncles and cousins. On their advice, we had detoured to inspect inscriptions, ponder tombs, and peer down wells of finely laid masonry, so deep you could count to five before a stone splashed. That Thursday afternoon we drove up a remote canyon looking for "Luqman," a site known to locals—desert Hussein hazily recalled being taken there as a child—but not to archaeologists.[9] The canyon is marked on a 1951 archaeological map but with no indication of ruins. Perhaps the survey party didn't reach the canyon's end, and perhaps there was a reason they didn't.

We drove along the canyon's sandy wadi until it became choked with boulders. Finding a footpath, we left Ali and Muhammad behind with the vehicles and hiked through a narrow defile into an Arabian rarity, a forest. Gnarled trees, the kind that grow in fairy tales, were backlit by golden late-afternoon sunlight. The effect was enchanting, a magical copse concealed in sere desert mountains.

We were surprised to see, off the path to our left, stone-walled buildings, long abandoned and roofless. The only similar structures I was aware of were at the ritual hunt site of Yala, forty miles to the west; there a party of Italian archaeologists had reported C-14 dates ranging from 980 B.C. back to 1395 B.C.

Through an overhead tangle of branches, we could see that the canyon ended abruptly at a spectacular thousand-foot-high headwall of banded gneiss.

We came upon steps, hewn stone steps, the beginning of what archaeologists call a monumental staircase. It curved to the left, up the canyon wall and out of the forest. "Hold it," said Ricardo, switching on his GPS unit. "Let's get this." He recorded a bearing.

As we ascended the stairs, a slender, graceful waterfall came into view, cascading down the headwall to a beautiful oval lake, a lake worthy of *The Arabian Nights*, in which great palaces are frequently mirrored in magical ponds. And indeed we saw ruins ahead, tucked on a precipitous canyon shelf. Nearing them, Ricardo reported, "Latitude now 45 degrees 35 minutes 10.1 seconds, longitude 14 degrees 51 minutes 42 seconds even." The staircase to this point, he calculated, was close to 250 feet long with some 600 steps.

What those steps led to we could not even guess, for whatever had been here had been dynamited and looted, and not long ago. The stones were dusted with fine white powder, created as they were fractured and hurled skyward. Judging by the mass of jumbled rock, there had been one or more impressive structures here, but only a few fragments of walls remained. What a loss. Even with rescue archaeology it would be difficult to determine whether this had been the site of a temple or, conceivably, in this splendid setting, a summer palace of the Qatabanians.[10]

We photographed the site in the day's fading light, then retreated down its grand staircase and back through the shadowy forest. Desert Hussein now had a clearer memory of coming here as a boy, and he recalled another site in a cave high above us to the east. "It's where they made their stamps and tussauds."

"Their stamp seals? And their what?"

"Tussauds. Peoples."

"Tussauds?"

"You know, you should know, it's English word," he said with an air of exasperation. "It means copy of peoples."

As in Madame Tussaud's London waxworks! Statues. And if there was a special place of manufacture for sculptures and stamp seals, they probably were not hewn of stone, but rather cast—as in a foundry. The Qatabanians had issued coins; could this possibly have been their mint? We could return the next day to look for slag, smoke stains, and traces of bronze, even gold.

Then I saw, ahead, three vehicles blocking the wadi and eight furious and heavily armed tribesmen confronting Ali and Muhammad. The tribesmen saw us and shouted. "Bad peoples," muttered desert Hussein; highland Hussein advised us to hang back. The two would join Ali and see what the problem was.

It became apparent that the bad people felt they had some claim to the canyon, with the drift that they may have been the ones who had blown up its major archaeological site and didn't want anyone to know. On our behalf, Ali did most of the talking, and he appeared to be forcefully rising to the occasion, a shift from his customary fey, catlike self.

In Arabia, if you're not talking your way into something, you're talking your way out, and, after being on the sidelines of many a negotiation, I had learned to listen for two key words: *imkin* and *mumkin*.

Imkin means "maybe," and *mumkin* means "probably." If *imkin* peppers the discussion, it's highly unlikely you'll get what you want. *Imkin* is a polite "no." But if a *mumkin* surfaces now and again, your prospects may be improving. It was a relief when we caught a first *mumkin*. Then, a few minutes later, another. And not long after that we were on our way, though not without the casting of evil looks.

When we stopped for the night well beyond Mablaqah Pass, Ali was pleased with himself. He recounted, "I first tell them that if they come to where I live, they be my guest, so then if we come here we should be their guest. This no work. Not one bit. So then I get them thinking, thinking what will happen . . . what will happen if they put a hand on you and do bad things to you and my boss Sheik Naser finds out. I let them be thinking about this, how they don't want to look down their canyon and see a lot of guns. Little guns. Big guns. I finally ask, 'What you want? What you want?' They think about this and they say, 'Don't you ever come again. Don't you ever bring anyone here again.' And I say okay."

Quitting a field of near-battle with honor, Ali asked, "Am I not some wonderful, some silver talker?" We all smiled and nodded, but I could see that the Husseins were edgy. Word travels. And the road ahead, though fast and well paved, was singularly known for its perils.

A half hour along our way the next morning, we were ordered to stop at a roadblock, manned, to our relief, by bona fide government soldiers.

"Who them?" asked one, looking in at us.

"Americans," answered desert Hussein.

"Ow, ow!" the soldier exclaimed, the "ow" the cry of a baleful pooch. "Be careful, ow, ow!"

"Yellah!" exclaimed Hussein through clenched teeth. Depending on the tone of voice, *yellah* can be a good-natured "let's go" suggestion, or it can be a decision to do what we now did: fly hell-bent down the road, slowing only—and only a little—when our bald-tired Toyota careened through mountain curves. We had hoped to stop at three archaeological sites not far off the highway. Not today.

Sometime that morning we crossed the lost border of the ancient kingdom of Qataban—and were in the land of Saba.

Desert Hussein squinted. Ahead we could see figures milling. A roadblock, but with no government-type vehicles in evidence. Hussein slowed. The figures signaled him to stop. He jammed the accelerator and tore on through, leaving whoever it was frantically waving in the rear-view mirror.

We passed a volcanic outcropping with antigovernment invective scrawled in white paint. It marked, said highland Hussein, the spot where a busload of French travel-adventurers had been kidnapped and spirited to a mountain hideaway and there held for ransom. Desert Hussein tightened his grip on the wheel, for once two-handed, forsaking his customary soda, cigarette, or twig of qat. Even so, it was hard to imagine the danger of kidnapping on this calm and sunny day, with the road in excellent repair. Off toward the serrated mountains to the west, life was quietly going on in scattered mud-brick villages as it had for ages. To the east lay the still, sun-baked dunes of the Ramlat Sabateyn.

The road curved around a low hill, and we came skidding to a stop, face to face with an antiaircraft gun mounted on a truck and leveled at our windshield. Several dozen heavily armed tribesmen swarmed up from flanking gullies to surround us—and were disappointed. "This day," interpreted highland Hussein, "they look to snatch some people from another tribe. To settle old score, as they say in the movies. Hamdullalah, we okay, we can go on." Normally, he explained, we would be fair game, but not today.

A few minutes and miles later we passed between twin volcanic peaks via a low pass known as the Bab al-Balaq, which may be a corruption of Bab al-Balqis . . . "the Gate of Sheba." We looked out across a beige desert plain, crossed by the dry Wadi Adana and dotted with patches of green, though not many. The temperature nudged 115 degrees on Ricardo's thermometer. Crooked-columned dust devils rose up, whirled like dervishes, and collapsed as if exhausted from the heat. There was little sign of the splendor that once rose from this plain, striking caravaneers with wonder as they looked down upon the city that might be fabled Kitor, known as Ma'rib in Arabic and Maryab in Latin.

A quote attributed to Pliny the Elder praised Maryab as "the mistress of cities and a diadem on the brow of the universe." In the words of Agatharchides of Cnidus, here was once the capital of a land of "divine and mysterious pleasure."[11]

14

City of Divine and Mysterious Pleasure

TIME, THE SANDS, and looters had taken their toll on Ma'rib. After its civilization fell in the late sixth century A.D., fingers of the Ramlat Sabateyn crept across no longer fertile fields, stole into dwellings, smothered monuments. In the Temple of the Moon once proud Sabeans lit dung fires and melted down votive statues and plaques cast in brass, bronze, and possibly gold. They pillaged Ma'rib's masonry, reusing it in a succession of rude towns built each on top of the last. Some blocks were dragged off to settlements twenty to thirty miles distant. Looting continued for centuries and has yet to cease. A 1930s Royal Air Force aerial photo shows much of the city wall still intact; now hardly a trace remains, its stones reused in the boomtown of new Ma'rib, which we could see as a smudge of gray and rust on the horizon.

Still, not everything had crumbled or been swept away. Ma'rib was too much a wonder for that. Ruins survive, and archaeologists can only guess at and dream of what lies buried. Only a fraction of a percent of Ma'rib, the most promising—and most daunting—site in Arabia, has been investigated.

It took us some time to grasp the size and scope of the site and the significance of its monuments. In the next several days, we sought what remained and imagined what had been destroyed or still lay buried. Here now is a Baedeker of our wanderings as we visited and revisited the remains of a mighty dam (A) spanning the Wadi Adana;

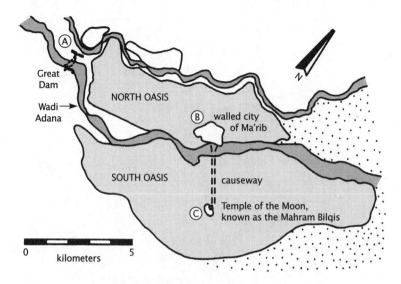

Map of Ma'rib plain

a tell (B) that may conceal the royal palace of the house of Salhan; and the Temple of the Moon (C), long known as the Mahram Bilqis.

A GREAT DAM AND
THE GARDEN OF THE TWO PARADISES

Its bed a mosaic of dried and cracked mud, the Wadi Adana is the key to how and why the Sabean civilization flourished on the edge of the desert. Two to three times a year, in the past as now, rains drenched the Yemeni highlands to the west. Runoff trickled, flowed, then raged down the wadi as it snaked through rugged mountains, crossed the Ma'rib plain, and vanished in the thirsty sands of the Ramlat Sabateyn. All that came of this torrent was an ephemeral bloom of bindweed and catchfly and sustenance for skittish jerboas, and fennecs. But beginning in late Neolithic times, the Wadi

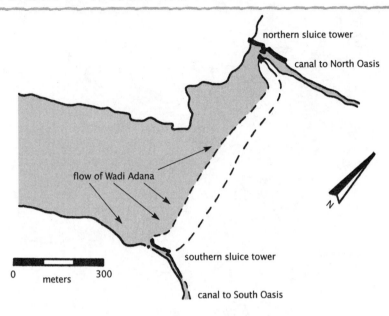

The Great Dam of Ma'rib

Adana's waters were slowed and tamed by a succession of dams. The mightiest of these, built in the fifth century B.C., was 2,033 feet (680 meters) across, half again as wide as Boulder Dam.

Long since washed away, the Great Dam of Ma'rib was a massive earthen barrier faced with stone slabs set with lime mortar. It was built to withstand the assault of seasonal flash floods surging down the wadi at a rate of 1,700 cubic meters a second—that is, *bearing 2,000 or more tons of water and silt per second*. The dam's purpose was not to create a reservoir but to divert this turbulent mass into two sluices, north and south, and then into stilling basins. From there two broad canals further calmed the water before distributing it through a vast network of smaller and smaller canals and an irrigation system that reached twenty miles or more into the Ramlat Sabateyn. All told, 24,000 acres (9,600 hectares) were brought under cultivation, enough to sustain a city of 30,000 to 50,000 people.

This man-made oasis—the "Garden of the Two Paradises"—was actually two oases, one to the north of the Wadi Adana and the other to the south. And it was said that "if a woman or servant walked under the trees of the two gardens with a basket on the head, it used to fill of itself with fruits in a short time, without it being necessary to pluck them by hand or pick them up from the ground."[1] Though extravagant, the image is an apt metaphor for one of history's greatest agricultural schemes. When in the 1980s Jürgen Schmidt of the Deutsches Archäologisches Institut surveyed the Ma'rib plain, he wrote admiringly, "It was here that the most perfect specimen of an ancient irrigation system was created, a complex and technically highly elaborate piece of construction engineering."[2] He was impressed that the system could handle sudden, violent floods at any time, day or night, without warning; he concluded that only in the twentieth century had the Sabeans' hydraulic ingenuity been equaled, though not surpassed.

Highland Hussein, David, Ricardo, and I scrambled up the Great Dam's still-intact fifty-foot-high southern sluice tower. The locals call the tower Marbat al-Dimm, "the place where the cat was tied," an allusion to an incident in the legend of the queen of Sheba, when all the cats of Saba were no match for red rats tearing apart the dam and its supports. We marveled at the sturdiness of the structure and, gazing off to the east, imagined the green and fragrant Garden of the Two Paradises stretching as far as the eye could see. Ricardo was

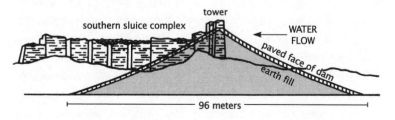

The Great Dam (cross-section reconstruction)

moved to remark, "What a woman!" but then thought to add a qualifying "maybe." He was mindful that everywhere we looked we saw only Ma'rib's *final* ruins, of which the Great Dam was a good example. Inscriptions on the sluice towers dated their construction to the mid 600s B.C., some three hundred years later than the queen of Sheba's tenth century.

We had hoped to investigate earlier times—her times—by hiking down the Wadi Adana to look for remnants of waterworks predating the Great Dam. But at the foot of the southern sluice tower, desert Hussein was nervously pacing, his Kalashnikov at the ready. If this part of Yemen was a latterday Wild West, he had given us to understand that here we were in Dodge City and on the wrong side of town. Desert Hussein warned, "We be careful, we must. Looks like nobody around, but they around. I was here once with a Dutchmen, foolish Dutchmen. Shooting it starts and he not keep his head down and took bullet in shoulder. Took us an hour, a whole hour, to shoot our way through! What a mess! I in no mood for mess today."

In more settled times, Jürgen Schmidt had stood where we stood (I'd brought along his reports and maps) and considered how a wadi in flood sweeps up and then deposits silt. When nature had its way, the Wadi Adana's silt was dumped out in the Ramlat Sabateyn. When man had his way, that silt was instead deposited on Ma'rib's irrigated plots. When did this first occur? When, by inference, was the Wadi Adana first diverted? In search of the dawn of agriculture at Ma'rib, Schmidt profiled the silt in the Garden of the Two Paradises and found it to be an astonishing 30 meters deep—more than 90 feet! Based on a rate of deposit of .7 centimeters a year, he estimated a 2,700-year span of artificial irrigation dating back to 3200 B.C. and predating our queen of Sheba by more than a millennium.

To back up this extraordinarily early date, Schmidt reconnoitered the dry bed of Wadi Adana, and downstream from the Great Dam he found fragments of early but sturdy flood-diverting structures, in use from 2400 to 1500 B.C.

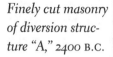

Finely cut masonry of diversion structure "A," 2400 B.C.

The next step for the Sabeans was a bold one: in approximately 1500 B.C. they *completely blocked* the Wadi Adana with a dam that continued in use through 940 B.C., that is, through the time of Solomon and Sheba. It's difficult to estimate the yield of the cropland irrigated, but a conservative guess would be that it was enough to feed a population of 20,000 (against Ma'rib's peak population of 30,000–50,000).

The upshot is that well before the days of the queen of Sheba, Ma'rib was a major city with an agricultural base that was both dependable and bountiful. The Sabeans were extraordinarily well off *even without* a trade in incense and spices. Grant them that trade and they would be, as in the myth of "Kitor to the East," the envy of nations.

In new Ma'rib we stayed at the cheerily decrepit Garden of the Two Paradises, a hotel of wide hallways and cavernous public rooms, its aspirations to grandeur reflected in the bathroom mirrors, which were placed so high on the wall that even on tiptoe you could see only the top of your head. In the days we were there a handful of Dutch and French tourists and a few oil-field roughnecks stopped in for a night's sleep. We dined at a lone table in a hall that could seat hundreds. The lamb kebab was quite tasty, and the accompanying french fries extraordinary, which was good, for the menu began and ended with lamb and fries. Maybe the crowds, the buses would someday come, but not yet. What could you expect when the only way here from Sana'a was in an armed-to-the-teeth convoy? Moreover, there were rumors that if you wandered out of bounds on Ma'rib plain you might be stoned, shot, or abducted.

Every midday we retreated to the Two Paradises to wait out the worst of the heat, catch up on homework, and give the Husseins quality qat time next door in Sheik Naser's mifraj. Around noon the sky would often dim as sandstorms swept in from the open desert, filling the hotel's cracked and empty swimming pool with uprooted nettle shrubs and skeletal zizyphus trees. To an accompaniment of rattling hotel windows, we studied and marked up our Ma'rib space imagery, on which ancient canals and channels were visible as a crosshatching of blue lines (see plate 11).

At latitude 45° 20' 09.2", longitude 15° 25' 23.8" there was a substantial tell, the likely location of the royal "house of Salhan in war and peace," a palace that may have been that of the queen of Sheba.[3]

THE PALACE OF SALHAN IN WALLED OLD MA'RIB

For the trip to the tell of the Old City of Ma'rib, the Husseins thought it best to take on additional security, so an Askari mercenary and his Czech semi-automatic were now squeezed into our Toyota's back seat. This day, as on all our days out on the Ma'rib plain, we crossed boundaries beyond our perception. Cruising a landscape that to us was relatively featureless, we would enter an invisible danger zone and the Husseins would tense up. A few miles down the road they would relax again, without a care in the world.

A heavy mist shrouded the plain, a pall of humidity and suspended debris hanging in the wake of a midday sandstorm. Desert Hussein slowed and squinted to determine where we should go. The mist had an eerie greenish tinge, and driving through it was like driving in a dream in which you're searching for something but can't quite grasp what it is or if it even exists. The track ended, and the tell of Salhan loomed before us. The mist muffled car door slams and footfalls as we swung out and trudged up a crumbling mound of dirt, sand, and civilization. Here, in the twelfth century A.D., traveler Nashwan ibn Said described immense columns, more than twelve feet in circumference, protruding from the earth, though by then only to the height of a spear. The columns have long since been obscured by a succession of villages, dating from the early days of Islam to the relatively recent occupation of Yemen by the Ottoman Turks. Whatever remained of Salhan palace (if this was indeed its site) was now under fifty or more feet of later occupation and collapsed overburden. Even so, there were traces here of something once grand. Fallen columns, though only half the circumference of those reported by ibn Said, lay at the foot of the tell; a number had been reused—upside down—in a mosque, itself now abandoned. The column's capitals were geometrical and austere, quite different from the conventions of the classical world. Sabean architecture, judging from its few remaining fragments, had been well proportioned and imposing.

All around the tell—as far as we could see into the mist—a great

Capitals from Ma'rib

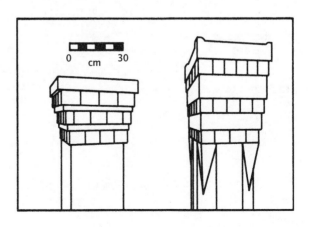

city had once risen. "Maryaba, meaning 'lord of all men,'" wrote Pliny the Elder, "measures six miles round." Though this was an exaggeration—two and a half miles is more like it—the six-gated walls of Ma'rib encompassed 275 acres (110 hectares).

We walked back and forth across the site, though there was little to see on its surface. Southwest of the tell we crossed a large circular depression that may have been an open-air market. Scattered limestone blocks were all that remained of the foundations of hundreds of rectangular mud-brick dwellings that once soared eighty feet or more, some of the world's first skyscrapers. They're long gone, the mud brick dissolved by infrequent but torrential desert rains.

Even so, archaeologists have ascertained the probable layout of a typical Sabean tower house. From street level a stone stair led to a

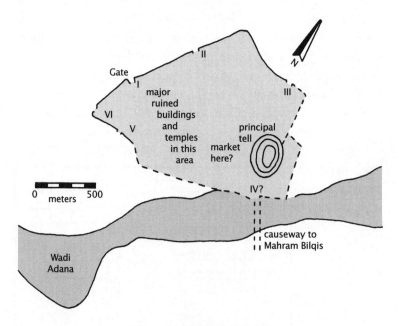

Plan of walled Old Ma'rib

stout wooden door fitted with brass bolts. Within, the ground floor was a warren of rooms with high thresholds, storerooms for grain, firewood, and fodder. Water was stored in large jars and plastered cisterns. Animals were stabled on this level and the next. (In present-day Yemeni tower houses, goats clatter up to their second-floor quarters.) The dwellings rose two, three, or even six more stories to accommodate an extended family's bedrooms, kitchens, and one or more ceremonial rooms: a reception room or *diwan*; a *maswad*, or room of honor; a *manzar*, a chamber sited for the best view of the surrounding oasis and distant desert; and finally a top-floor *mifraj*, the spacious, exclusive domain of the household's men and their guests.[4] Larger households may have had one or more chapels furnished with incense altars and votive objects. And, life having its necessities, there were upper-story toilets with the waste plunging either inside or outside the building's walls to street level, where once or twice a day a Sabean sanitation worker sprinkled lime on a growing mound. Every week or so the waste was shoveled into a cart and taken to the sealed-off furnace of the neighborhood bathhouse; the resulting ashes would be efficiently recycled as fertilizer for the Garden of the Two Paradises.

The essence of this architecture was the height of the houses, distancing the better-off Sabeans from the clamor and odors of the workaday world, allowing them to watch over their lands, and bearing witness to their prestige and wealth.

As the grandest of the city's tower houses, the palace of Salhan would have had, along with the salient features of lesser dwellings, one or more impressive and airy pillar-lined courtyards. If its decor was typically Sabean, it would have been austere, yet there may have been bursts of oriental opulence, with golden light filtering through alabaster skylights to illuminate walls studded with multicolored stones and floors laid with richly textured carpets.[5] The house of Salhan's epicenter would have been its assembly hall and throne . . . a throne that in legend Solomon's djinns magically whisked to Jerusalem so that all could see how it paled beside their king's. Or did it? Solomon's anxiety (and envy?) suggests that perhaps Sheba's was the more magnificent.[6]

Was there a Sabean throne beneath our feet as we walked Old Ma'rib on this mist-shrouded day?

The fact is that until it is at least partially excavated, this once-great city is destined to be a phantom conjured in the mind's eye. And this, in truth, has ever been the case, even in antiquity. For all of Ma'rib's fame, there is not a single eyewitness account of the build-ings within its walls, the activities of its marketplace, the splendor and secrets of its palace. The closest any known outsider came was in 24 B.C., when the Emperor Augustus dispatched a detachment of le-gionnaires under the command of Aelius Gallus, first prefect of Egypt, to discover the source of Arabia's frankincense and gold. Ex-perts are at odds as to whether Aelius's friend the historian Strabo ac-companied him, or whether Strabo's account was secondhand. In any case, Aelius Gallus may have come within sight of Ma'rib's walls and even attempted a siege before he and his troops, desert-worn and decimated, retreated back to Egypt.

Though it is the best that survives, Strabo's narrative is sketchy. He tells us that "the country is in general fertile, and abounds in particu-lar with places for making honey; and, with the exception of horses and mules and hogs, it has an abundance of domesticated animals; and, with the exception of geese and chickens, has all kinds of birds."[7] He describes the towns and cities of this bucolic landscape as "ruled by monarchs and prosperous, beautifully adorned with both temples and royal palaces." At Ma'rib, "he himself [a king] and those about him live in effeminate luxury; but the masses engage partly in farming and partly in the traffic in aromatics."

Living was easy: "the people are lazy and easy-going in their modes of life," so much so that they had to strive to stay alert as they

A merchant and
a matron of Ma'rib

conducted their trade in frankincense, myrrh, and cinnamon: "when they are made drowsy by the sweet odors they overcome this drowsiness by inhaling the incense of asphalt and goats' beard."

And over this populace, Strabo informs us, Ma'rib's king "has authority in lawsuits . . . but it is not lawful for him to leave the palace, or, if he does, the rabble, in accordance with some oracle, stone him to death on the spot."

This last observation is curious but not unprecedented. Strabo is describing a sort of Wizard of Oz arrangement—documented in later African cultures—in which a monarch is never seen by his subjects, who therefore believe he is awesome, almighty.[8] Invisibility enhances power. Conversely, if a king is revealed as all too human, that power is forfeited, and the rabble has its way. If this really was the

Sabean scenes:
a banquet and a caravan

Sabeans' practice—and if it dated to the days when they first realized the market potential of their frankincense and other aromatics—who then could travel afar and be trusted to negotiate arrangements for long-range trade?

Why not an enterprising and spirited queen?

This, of course, is speculation; the sequestering of the king may have been a Sabean custom closer to Strabo's day. But because Ma'rib is a slate with little upon it, the site invites speculation. Who knows who and what was here? Strabo wrote that he had heard that within the city's walls the Sabeans enjoyed "a vast equipment of both gold and silver articles, such as couches and tripods and bowls, together with drinking-vessels and very costly houses; for doors and walls and ceilings are variegated with ivory and gold set with precious stones."

If only a fraction of this was true, and only a fraction of a fraction of such splendor remains, what discoveries await archaeology!

A consensus arose among classical authors. "Taken as a whole, they are the richest races in the world," wrote Pliny of the tribes of Arabia. And of these, "the Sabaei are the most wealthy."

MAHRAM BILQIS, SACRED PRECINCT OF THE QUEEN OF SHEBA

A ceremonial way once led south from walled Ma'rib, across the bed of the Wadi Adana to a lofty columned portico and entrance hall, which in turn opened onto an enormous open-to-the-sky masonry-walled oval. The oval so amazed—and confounded—early explorers that not one accurately reported its dimensions. Only in 1998 did a survey by the American Foundation for the Study of Man, supervised by Canadian archaeologist Bill Glanzman, determine with a laser-driven theodolite that at its widest the temple's "irregular ovoid" was 314.3 feet (95.8 meters) across, that its walls had once been 53 feet (16 meters) high, and that its total enclosed area was 54,959.9 square feet (5107.8 square meters), in area two and a half times the size of the Parthenon.

Several inscriptions identify this as the Temple Awwam, meaning "place of refuge," and attest that it was dedicated to the god 'Ilumqah, probably (but not certainly) the god of the moon. The sex, astral identities, and other characteristics of the gods of the Sabeans have long been debated, and every time someone comes up with a coherent explanation, someone else throws an equally believable brick at it. 'Ilumqah, for instance, has traditionally been considered a male moon god, frequently represented by crescent horns cradling a

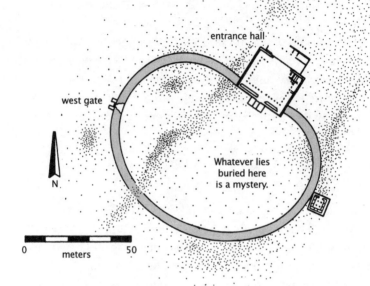

Plan of the Mahram Bilqis, the Moon Temple of the Queen of Sheba

disk. Recently, though, it has been argued that the disk is not the moon but the sun and that 'Ilumqah is not so much an astral god as a warrior deity, like Herakles, or maybe a vegetation god, like Dionysus. Whatever his identity, a temple inscription tells us that the Sabeans were "children of 'Ilumqah."

While the temple's formal inscriptional name is Awwam, its long-held common name—the name used by today's Yemenis—is Mahram Bilqis, "the sacred precinct of Bilqis"—the queen of Sheba.

The Mahram Bilqis entryway portico is marked by the shafts of eight square columns rising from the sand. As we pulled up in desert Hussein's Toyota, Ma'rib urchins had shimmied up them and were daring each other to leap from one to another (see plate 24). We waved hello and walked up a curved dune to where we could step onto the crown of the temple's encircling wall and examine its finely dressed masonry and ten-foot-thick casemate construction (boxed sections packed with rubble fill). We had many questions. Was the oval below us built to accommodate thousands of pilgrims? Did the encroaching sands conceal one or more royal tombs, possibly even that of the queen of Sheba? Could the oval's focus have been a sacred pool? Or might a sacred rock cube, a forerunner of Islam's Ka'aba, venerated in Mecca, lie buried here? We had no idea, and neither did anyone else, amateur or expert.

As we walked the wall, the urchins from the pillars tagged along, shoving each other out of the way as they tried to sell us fake bits of statuary—or maybe they weren't fakes.

One kid pestered David to take a picture of him cradling his Kalashnikov. David obliged. The youngster then demanded money, leveling the weapon and chambering a round. "Hey," said David, "you cut that out. Put that thing down!" A sidekick, mean-eyed and feral, drew a knife. From the interior of the temple's oval, highland Hussein rushed to join us at the top of the wall, exclaiming in Arabic, "No, no, he is your guest!"

The gun-toting kid, no more than ten or twelve years old, stood his ground. David, mercifully, didn't understand Hussein's heated Arabic: "So shoot him! You go ahead, try it! Shoot! Then see what I do to you, see what my people do to you and your people. I am Hussein al-Arhabi from Arhab!"

Arhab must be a tough place, because that threat did it. The kid lowered his gun, explaining, "I was only going to shoot by his head." He and his friends scampered away.

Exploring the mystery of the Mahram Bilqis has long been a touchy proposition. The first Westerner to come this way was Joseph-Thomas Arnaud, a French apothecary curious about the exotic spices traded by the queen of Sheba. That was in 1843. In 1869 the mystique of the queen beckoned a cleverly disguised Joseph Halevy to Ma'rib, followed in 1892 by the German epigrapher Eduard Glaser, who cited Sheba's appearance in the Bible and asked, "How then could I remain indifferent to its inspiration? From the very day I set foot on Arabian soil all my scheming and strivings were concentrated on reaching Ma'rib . . . to admire the remains of its glory and lift the veil which shrouds its legendary past with dementing obstinacy."[9] All three explorers found Ma'rib's tribesmen mercurial and hostile and considered themselves lucky to make off with crude diagrams of the Mahram Bilqis and hand-drawn copies of its inscriptions.

It wasn't until 1951 that the temple saw the archaeologist's spade. In April of that year, a flotilla of Dodge trucks and Power Wagons rolled over the horizon of the Ramlat Sabateyn; they had been shipped from America and rafted ashore at the British crown colony of Aden. Wendell Phillips, a brash and brilliant young American still in his twenties, directed the lead wagon. Appealing to armchair adventurers in major U.S. corporations, he had raised sufficient funds to found the American Foundation for the Study of Man, recruit a first-rate team, and mount an all-out assault on the antiquities of southern Arabia. Phillips embodied "the cocksureness of a swashbuckling adventurer, the coolness of a gambler and the cunning of an American backwoodsman," wrote the noted archaeologist Nelson Glueck; added Lowell Thomas, "in little-known Araby, young Wendell is a combination of Aladdin, Sindbad the Sailor, and Ali Baba."[10]

Phillips impressed Ma'rib's sheiks and tribesmen. He was versed in traditional Arab ways, and he was quite the quick-draw artist, a skill he demonstrated by setting out tin cans in the dunes and riddling them with bullets. His signature attire was cowboy boots, a low-slung tooled leather belt holstering a pair of pearl-handled Colts, a keffiyah headcloth, and Aviator sunglasses. Proud to lead "the first American exploratory party ever" to Ma'rib, he "hoped to reconstruct an entire civilization and perhaps bring to light the story of a queen whose visit to Solomon had made her famous."

With sixty oxen and a brigade of one hundred eighty Yemeni diggers, Phillips attacked the formidable sands clogging the entrance court of the Mahram Bilqis. At first only the tops of pillars were visible, but soon their full 17-foot (5.3-meter) height was revealed, as well as walls decorated with false windows that were more Frank Lloyd Wright than ancient world.

The team discovered artifacts, among them the arms, right foot, then all of a bronze statue (possibly once gilded) of a stiff-kneed man with a lion-skin cloak. The cloak was inscribed with his name: Ma'adkarib. His right hand may have held a staff or scepter and his left still held an official seal, as if preparing to stamp a document. His role as a high government official is confirmed by what may be either an elaborate cap or a three-layered hairdo, held in place by a double band of ribbons.

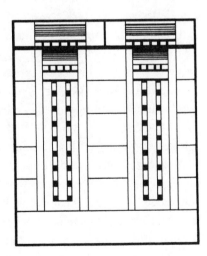

*Mahram Bilqis wall set
with false windows*

Bronze statue of
Ma'adkarib

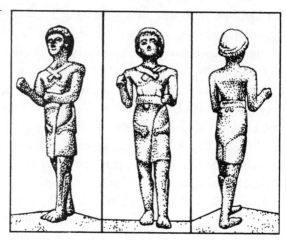

Everywhere they found inscriptions—painted in red, chiseled in stone, cast in bronze. The expedition's epigrapher—Father Albert Jamme—was beside himself. He rushed from one inscription to the next, coating each with liquid latex, letting it dry, then peeling back a "squeeze" that was better than a photograph for deciphering ancient lettering.

It is difficult for us to understand, but this activity spelled trouble for the expedition. A local judge, Qadi Zeid Inan, knew there was only one reason for anyone but a madman to waste time scouring ruins: hidden treasure. Gold and pearls. How then, could he understand Jamme's elation, when all that appeared to be at stake was rock and rubber?

Puzzled, Qadi Zeid Inan demanded and received his own set of latex squeezes, only to find the indecipherable rubber letters unrewarding. They brought him no wealth, no happiness. So the judge demanded the pure raw latex itself, fifty-five-gallon drums of it. Phillips and Jamme at first refused; they had barely enough for the work at hand. But facing a contingent of soldiers beholden to the qadi, they handed over the latex with a sinking feeling that their troubles were just beginning.

Though a few Yemeni officials had an idea of what archaeology was all about, they were outnumbered by the qadi and others who regarded the American Foundation's team as fortune-hunting infidels and did their best to sabotage the expedition. They held up urgently needed supplies. They cut off outside communication. As Phillips scrambled to salvage the expedition, they held Jamme virtual prisoner. Qadi Zeid Inan, Phillips fumed, was "constitutionally malevolent," and it didn't help that his strings were pulled by Yemen's King Ahmed, a scheming, paranoid, drug-addled despot. To keep his servants in the dark as he went about his Byzantine ways in his highland palace, King Ahmed insisted they wear opaque lead-lensed glasses. Even so, over the squeak and clank of his electric rocking bed, they heard him talking to djinns in his chambers. And if it wasn't djinns, it was poisonous snakes, updating the king on Yemen's malcontents and their plots to assassinate him.

King Ahmed would impress and cow his subjects by periodically wrestling with a tiger. A crowd would assemble outside the palace gates and glimpse in a lofty tower window a flash of orange, then a flash of Ahmed—and invariably he was the victor in a fight to the death with a three-foot-long stuffed toy tiger from Harrod's, a gift from a foreign envoy.

King Ahmed's dictates and whims were undermining the situation in Ma'rib. Phillips fired off a cable to the newly inaugurated U.S. president, Dwight D. Eisenhower:

DEAR MR PRESIDENT: EXPEDITION TO QUEEN OF SHEBAS CAPITAL MARIB YEMEN IS IN DESPERATE SITUATION STOP MY RELIEF CONVOY WITH NAVY MEDICAL SUPPLIES FOOD GASOLINE FORBIDDEN TO REACH US BY KING AHMED STOP PLEASE PERSONALLY INTERVENE URGENTLY WITH KING

TO HOLD OFF HIS SOLDIERS AND ALLOW ME TO EVACUATE
MY AMERICAN SCIENTISTS AND TECHNICIANS STOP UN-
LESS YOUR IMMEDIATE ACTION IS TAKEN AMERICAN LIVES
WILL BE GRAVELY ENDANGERED MY GRATEFUL THANKS
WENDELL PHILLIPS

The American Foundation continued, however nervously, to excavate the Mahram Bilqis. The temple's entrance court was cleared,
and the team was set to move into the great oval, where they felt
they could reach a stratum contemporaneous with the queen of
Sheba. Phillips later recalled, "In five more days I would have got to
the queen. What would we have found? The queen's name is not
known. But at least we would have found evidence of her reign." It
was then that he had a chilling conversation with Jama al-Gufty, his
Egyptian foreman. As soldiers watched the two from the wall of the
Mahram Bilqis, Phillips asked,

"Jama, which one do they want to kill the most?"

"Number one is probably Dr. Jamme. They hate him because he
works so hard and is not afraid."

"Jama, tell me, what do you think is likely to happen?"

"Sahib, it will probably start with Dr. Jamme. One of the soldiers
will give him some ridiculous order and he will not obey at once. A
soldier will pull out his jambiya, and the rest will join in. They will
cut Jamme apart, and when you or one of us comes to his rescue,
they will have the excuse they are looking for to kill some of us. They
will cut you down with rifles from the wall or watchtower."

To dig even a foot more, Phillips concluded, would be suicidal.
The only option was to use the cover of darkness to pack up the expe-
dition's two remaining drivable vehicles, one with a bad battery, the
other with "a rear differential scheduled to go out at any second."
With luck, they would have enough fuel to take them to Aden on the
Indian Ocean.

At daybreak on February 12, 1952, the American Foundation team distracted Qadi Zeid Inan and got him out of sight of their vehicles. If anything went wrong now, Phillips later wrote, "I had never doubted for an instant my ability to outgun the handful of Yemeni soldiers near our trucks, should the lives of my party depend on it, for I had on my side the element of surprise plus a Colt for each hand."

The expedition fled across the desert.

The duped and furious qadi dispatched shouting, gun-waving tribesmen on camel- and horseback in hot pursuit. One of Phillips's vehicles stalled, the one with the bad battery, but it had just enough juice for one last start. The tribesmen faded. The second vehicle's rear differential held, all the way to Aden.

It would be a very long time before archaeologists were allowed back in Yemen, and even then they would never know if their current season would be their last. Rid of Phillips, an unctuous courtier had declared on behalf of King Ahmed, "These antiquities [of Ma'rib] were a window through which the eye of the world might have scrutinized us. We have now closed that window."

Soon, all that Phillips and his team had laboriously cleared was reclaimed by the sands. What is within the great oval of the Mahram Bilqis remained a mystery.

15
Chiseled in Stone

THE WINDOW to Yemen's past may have been slammed shut after Phillips's hasty retreat, but not before some key evidence was spirited back to America, at first concealed in Post Toasties cereal boxes, in the end packed aboard the group's fleeing vehicles. Though Father Jamme had forfeited his latex squeezes, he still had hand copies and photographs of close to two hundred inscriptions from the Mahram Bilqis. He was to spend a decade translating and making sense of them. It was solitary, painstaking work, for he had no one to debate with but himself, so few were the scholars who comprehended the syntax and nuances of Epigraphic South Arabic.

What Jamme diligently rendered into English was at once disappointing and enlightening. There was no transcendent poetry or philosophy on the walls of the Mahram Bilqis, nothing approaching biblical writ. The phraseology was formulaic and most often recorded deals between the donor of an inscription and the deity 'Ilumquh. After identifying himself, the donor stated what he was offering the moon god: typically, the inscription itself (carved at some expense) plus a votive statue or temple enhancement. It all had the air of a business transaction. A donor "paid off to the lord 'Ilumquh, master of Awwam, what he had promised to Him." The donor then went on to credit the moon god for granting a favor, anything from a mended bone to success in a military campaign. The inscription usually closed with a simple "By 'Ilumquh," though sometimes the

donor would ramble on, demanding that the moon god deliver future favors. Cursing and smiting were popular requests, with a recurrent phrase being the "crushing and breaking down and withering of
every foe and enemy."

Jamme was especially interested in inscriptions that began with an
S-shaped symbol, probably an abstraction of a cudgel (or what a German archaeologist called a *Tod-schläger*, or "death beater"). The
symbol was exclusive to royal inscriptions. One example opens:

'Ilsarah, son of Sumhu'aly Darih, king of Saba, has dedicated
to 'Ilumquh the whole mass of the enclosing wall from the line of
the inscription to the top and all the recesses and towers on this
wide wall, as 'Ilumquh had ordered to 'Ilsarah through an oracle,
because 'Ilumquh had granted him and shall grant what he had
promised to him . . . by 'Ilumquh . . .

This particular text is intriguing because it records a major phase
in the construction of the Mahram Bilqis. We also learn that the
temple had a resident oracle. But best of all, it gives us the name of
both a king and his father, who (another inscription tells us) also sat
on the Sabean throne. Jamme found many such inscriptions, some
chock full of royal names, not unlike the dedicatory plaques on our
own public buildings. Sorting through and linking this information,
Jamme was able to reconstruct in detail dynasties dating back to 185
B.C. Some additional fragments of genealogy harked back to several
centuries earlier.

Following the publication of his landmark *Sabaean Inscriptions
from Mahram Bilqis*, Father Jamme's pioneering genealogical work
was taken up by epigraphers who had collected inscriptions from
other sites. Among them was Kenneth Kitchen of the University of
Liverpool. An Egyptologist for most of his career, he realized he

could apply what he had learned of the whys and wherefores of dynastic succession to the little-known kingdoms down the Red Sea in southern Arabia. By the middle 1990s he felt he had sufficient information to compile a working chronology of some 115 known Sabean kings and mukarribs (a mukarrib being an early ruler, a "unifier").

The question arose: where might a queen of Sheba fall on such a dynastic list? Until recently, the queen's assumed dates in the middle 900s B.C. would have put her out of the running, for it was held that the earliest names on the list couldn't date to much before 500 B.C. Kitchen was uncomfortable with that as a cutoff date, for it meant that a lot of rulers had to be squeezed into a short time; the average reign would be less than ten years. But now this radical compression was no longer necessary or appropriate, for Gus Van Beek's chronology at Hajar bin Humeid had shown that the southern Arabian script dated back to at least 1200 B.C. Using this expanded time frame, Kitchen began to rough in who might have ruled when. This was daunting work and somewhat speculative, for if the Sabeans had a dating system, they neglected to employ it in their inscriptions, leaving their royalty afloat in time.

And so they might have remained, but for the mukarrib Karibil Watar I. A huge slab at Sirwah, a site in the mountains to the west of Ma'rib, boasts that in his military campaigns he killed in excess of 30,000 people and took captive no less than 73,000. A rapacious mukarrib, this Karibil. And a man with a reputation, for Kitchen believes that he was the "Karibilu" who is mentioned in Assyrian texts that can be firmly dated to 685 B.C.[1] This correlation, or *synchronism*, as archaeologists call it, allowed Kitchen to "anchor" his royal chronology. He established that Karibil Watar I ruled from roughly 695 to 660 B.C. and then, working backward, estimated the lengths of earlier reigns as far back as there were known mukarribs.

Gus Van Beek, Father Albert Jamme, Kenneth Kitchen . . . these time detectives worked their case for more than forty years and pushed back the dates of Arabian writing, rulers, and civilization to the era of Solomon and Sheba. Here, then, are the opening lines of what Kitchen calls "An Exercise in Maximal Chronology," which he fully acknowledges is hypothetical. Says he, "No cast iron certainties here!"

DATE B.C.	NO.	RULERS — SABA	LENGTH OF REIGN
		Mukarribs	
c. 1200–1000	x1–15	(Perhaps 15 early rulers, beginning of mercantile state)	240
c. 1000–990	1	Karibil A	40
c. 990–970*	2	Yada'il Yanuf, son of Karibil	20
c. 970–955	3	**Dhamar'alay A**	15
c. 955–940	4	**Yakrubmalik A, son of Dhamar'alay**	15
c. 940–925	5	**Yada'il Bayyin I, son of Dhamar'alay**	15
c. 925–905	6	Sumhu'alay Dharih I, son of Yada'il	20

And so on, all the way to A.D. 577

*The era of King Solomon—and, by association, the queen of Sheba—is in boldface.

But . . . no queen? Instead, we have a Dhamar'alay or a Yakrub-malik? No queen—*unless* she shared the throne of Saba with either her husband or, as regent, her son or another close relative. Either scenario is possible; Kitchen leans toward the idea that she was an "executive queen," an emissary empowered to carry out a critical long-distance trade mission. This certainly makes sense if you think about it. What ruler in those days could leave his palace for three months or more and expect to find his throne still empty on his return? Better to dispatch his queen, better yet if she had the met-tle and resourcefulness of subsequent Arab queens (from Zabibi to Zenobia).

"There was this certain woman who is known as the queen of Sheba—she has ruled over the Shebans since the death of her husband." This line from a traditional Yemeni tale suggests a second, and for me more likely, option: that the queen of Sheba was a regent. In the Solomonic era (shown in boldface in the table) of Kitchen's chronology, three of the four successions are father-to-son. If just one of these sons was not of age when his father died, a regent would be in order, and that regent could have been his mother. In myth, Sheba reigns for seventeen years—and there is no mention that her reign was terminated by her death. This would make sense if she had guided a young son to manhood and then stepped aside: the widow of Dhamar'alay, say, ruling until her eldest son, Yakrubmalik, was of age.

The low sun cast the chiseled letters of the Mahram Bilqis in dramatic relief. The temple was free of urchin-assassins, and we took our time seeking out and photographing inscriptions not covered by sand. Away from the temple I found a slab incised with inch-high lightning-bolt lettering:

On the temple's outer wall we admired an inscription with spare and elegant lettering more than a foot high.

This was one of a series of inscriptions (including the one that begins "'Ilsarah, son of Sumhu'aly Darih,") that documented the construction of the oval wall over a span of six hundred years. Why so long? one might ask. It's difficult to grasp, but what is now visible of the Mahram Bilqis is nothing compared to the grandeur that once was. Before the wall's top courses were toppled and its bottom courses buried, it rose to a height of 53 feet (16 meters). More than five stories.

Ricardo thought the wall might be defensive, as befits the name Awwam, "place of refuge." I wondered if it might have served to block out the view of the surrounding mountains, so that priests and pilgrims would gaze toward the heavens and the passage of gods of the sun, moon, and stars. If that were the case, the temple could have functioned as a Sabean astronomical-astrological observatory.

A day will come—maybe soon, maybe years from now—when the temple is fully excavated, more inscriptions are uncovered, and its mysteries solved. For now, epigraphers like Albert Jamme and Kenneth Kitchen, wringing every possible detail from what has been

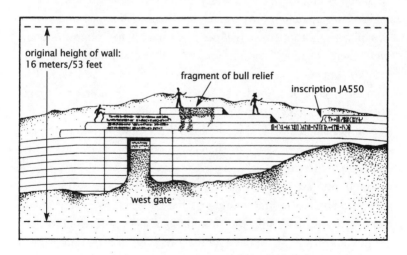

original height of wall:
16 meters/53 feet

fragment of bull relief

inscription JA550

west gate

Height of outer wall of Mahram Bilqis

found, have learned not only of dynastic successions but of everyday life, agriculture, temple practices, and—quite significantly—the geography and additional cities and towns of the Sabean state.

While camped in Ma'rib, Father Jamme roamed the forbidding mountains to the west, where he found and copied additional inscriptions. At the site of Sirwah, a text recorded that a

> king of Saba . . .
> has dedicated to
> 'Ilumquh, master of the ibexes of Sirwah, six
> statues which [are] of bronze for his own safety
> and the safety of the house of Salhan.[2]

This was intriguing, for here was a Sabean king and the royal house of Salhan linked to a site other than Ma'rib: Sirwah. This, I found, related to a persistent if vague tradition that Sirwah had been the capital of the Sabean state *before* Ma'rib.[3] If that were true, Ma'rib, though thriving and commercially significant in the queen of Sheba's time, may not have been the city of her court and throne.

As a last stop on our travels along the Incense Road, we had hoped to visit Sirwah, though we had been advised not to.[4] Almost nobody went there, for good reason. The tribe that controlled the region had kidnapped dozens of tourists and oil workers as well as a BBC film crew. We understood that they were currently holding hostage the sons of four government ministers, hoping to swap them for Sirwahites jailed for prior kidnappings. With some hesitation our patron, Sheik Naser, had said that *imkin* (maybe, only maybe) we could go to Sirwah.

But in our last days in Ma'rib, *imkin* jumped to *aiwa*—sure!—and a sunny, windless morning found us, the Husseins, and Ali al-Sharif packing up to drive into the mountains and explore whatever remained of Sirwah. The only pictures I had found of the site were a few grainy black-and-whites dating to 1947. It looked impressive: tow-

ering battlements and, as at Ma'rib, a major temple dedicated to
'Ilumquh. But in the early 1950s the ruins had been plundered for
defensive emplacements in a Yemeni civil war battle, and periodically to the present, disputes between the government and renegade
Sirwahites had been argued with artillery and mortars.

Was it foolhardy to venture to Sirwah? Certainly, but in the words
of the Husseins weeks earlier as we had descended from the Yemeni
highlands into the desert, "For all the way on this trip, it dangerous
. . . We go no matter!" We had come this far, and there is nothing you
desire more than what you can't have, especially if it is to walk a city
that might have been walked by the queen of Sheba.

In the late morning of June 23, 1997, we were about to leave the
hotel parking lot at the Garden of the Two Paradises when a military
jet, a vintage F-4, Ricardo thought, roared out of the desert's cloudless, deep blue sky. The fighter banked overhead and vanished over a
ridge to the west.

A few seconds later we heard an explosion. I looked at my watch:
11:05 A.M. A few minutes later, smoke lazily drifted up from somewhere in the mountains beyond the ridge. Ali al-Sharif rushed off to
Sheik Naser's mifraj to find out if anyone had any idea what was happening. There were varied opinions. The sheik suspected that the
central Yemeni government, obstinately insisting on the return of
the snatched sons of four government ministers, had run out of pa-
tience with the Sirwahites.

This proved to be the case. On this day the government had had
enough and had bombed Sirwah.

"I can't believe it, I just can't believe it," said David.

Questioned Ricardo, "So there go the ruins? Three thousand
years and . . . pffft?"

"But maybe okay!" volunteered desert Hussein. "Is archaeology!
Is archaeology! Put dynamites into mountain and see what comes
out!"

16

A Secret of the Sands

WITHIN AN HOUR, elite emergency forces in blue camouflage uniforms were wheeling around new Ma'rib, assembling for a ground assault on Sirwah. Rattletrap Russian helicopters, camouflaged blue as well, came and went. As with almost everything that transpires in Yemen, what was happening was unclear. We were puzzled by the variegated bright blue camouflage. To blend in with what—a mirage?

We let a few hours go by and then with the Husseins paid a visit to Sheik Naser's mifraj. The frantic events of the day were insufficient to interrupt the sheik's afternoon qat chew.

"So they bombed Sirwah?"

The sheik nodded.

"Anybody hurt?"

The sheik shrugged. Not that he'd heard.

"In any case, there is no way we're going to Sirwah."

He nodded. No, we could not go to Sirwah. "But you go somewhere else maybe."

"We could?"

The sheik stripped fresh leaves from a twig of qat and added them to the sizable wad in his cheek. He picked at a second twig, then took a drag on a communal hubble-bubble. "How about you go to Wadi Raghwan?"

He had in mind a pair of minor sites north of Ma'rib with little to see, and nothing relevant to a queen of Sheba. "How about some-where else?" I asked. "Something better?"

For the longest time he said nothing, and the only sound was the hubble-bubble of the hubble-bubble. The sheik's gaze wandered off into space, then returned and focused on Ali al-Sharif, curled catlike opposite us. "Ali will take you to al-Alam. It is where little people lived. You will like it. There are buildings there."

"Where is this?" asked Ricardo.

"Out in the sands," said the sheik.

"Short-Man City," confirmed Ali. "We must leave early. Tomorrow at five."

In the half-light before dawn we followed Ali's pickup as he angled north well away from Ma'rib. Weaving through the dunes, we clicked off thirty, forty, fifty kilometers. Ricardo switched on his GPS receiver and held it at arm's length out the window: "Heading due north."

Ten minutes later: "Veering now to the west."

Another twenty minutes: "Doubling back."

Rather than following a direct route, Ali was evidently navigating from landmark to landmark. It was as if he had been this way, but not often. As he slowed, scanned the terrain ahead, then shifted direction and sped up, we second-guessed what he might be looking for: subtle features like an elephant-shaped dune or a depression with a patch of vegetation.

After a long featureless stretch, Ali honked and gestured out the window. He had spied a low limestone hill, easily missed if we had been half a kilometer to the north or south. Before us was al-Alam, Short-Man City. As we pulled up beside his pickup, Ali grinned. We weren't all that elated, for all we saw was a low limestone hill. There was not a sign of habitation, let alone a city.

There is a long tradition, we were aware, of bedouin mistaking natural features for ancient splendors. In the 1920s, guides led Harry Philby far out into the Rub' al-Khali to show him the scorched walls of Wabar (also known as Ubar), a city destroyed by the wrath of God. Black pearls, they promised, lay scattered in the sands, evidence of Wabar's wealth. The site proved to be the impact crater of a meteorite that fell to earth in the nineteenth century; the black pearls were globules of heat-crystallized glass.

Ricardo dutifully recorded our bearing: 45° 37' 14.1" latitude, 15° 57' 29.6" longitude. We had driven 92 kilometers from Ma'rib, 70 kilometers as the crow flies.

We trudged up the hill. Desert Hussein and Ali thought it would be best if they remained with the vehicles in case the tribesmen who roamed this part of the Rub' al-Khali showed up. Ali explained, "They Jahan and Dahn. They son-of-a-bitch people. They kill for nothing."

Out of breath after considerable slipping and sliding in the loose sand, we gained the crest of the hill—and blinked and gasped at what had been hidden from sight where we parked our vehicles: a panorama of hundreds upon hundreds of stone domes sprawled over a tableland and spilling down to the red sands beyond the hill.

Al-Alam wasn't a lost colony of little people. It was a vast necropolis.

The domes were waist high, with west-facing doors and no windows. Though most of their roofs had collapsed, there was no evidence of the wanton destruction that facilitates looting. We looked for surface artifacts and found just one, a stone scraper. No shards. The necropolis of al-Alam, we guessed, was Neolithic, dating to somewhere in the range of 3000–5000 B.C.[1]

There were rows of a dozen and more tombs. There were circles of tombs. There were random scatterings of tombs. We shot rolls of film. Just below the highest point of al-Alam several tombs were clustered together as if to form a single structure whose interior was once lit by a window (the only window we saw). This, we thought, might have been a mortuary temple.

"And look!" Ricardo exclaimed. "What are those?" We looked south to see long lines of dark rocks that stretched hundreds of meters out across the desert. No two shared the same alignment, except for a pair that resembled ruts in an unpaved road.

A way away and out of sight, desert Hussein honked. It was ten A.M., and the temperature was already 115 degrees. We shouldn't linger.

"Bearings," I thought out loud. "For the lines. We should take bearings."

We did, I with a magnetic compass and Ricardo with his GPS unit.

"The two parallel lines off to the right, 168 degrees."

Was this a meaningful alignment? We could check later, I thought. But Ricardo, intently punching the GPS's keypad, then and there determined that the lines pointed to Timna', once the capital of the kingdom of Qataban. When we were there ten days before, Ricardo had recorded the location of the ruins in the device's memory.

"Do the lines point straight to Timna', or sort of to Timna'?"

"Directly. No error. No measurable error."

Quickly, Ricardo took the bearings of two more lines: 186 degrees and, angling off to the west, 283 degrees.

Desert Hussein once again leaned on his horn.

We hastened back the way we had come. To everyone's relief, no fearsome Jahan or Dahn in sight. But our vehicles could overheat if it got much hotter. We were quickly on our way—but not south to Ma'rib; Ali was driving due east. "He sees you likes what he shows you," explained desert Hussein, "so he want to show you a little more. You have been to White al-Alam. Now we go to Black al-Alam. But we stay only a few minutes."

Neolithic tombs and rock lines at "White al-Alam"

Twenty minutes later, a somber black ridge rose ahead of us. Black al-Alam. At its base more lines of stones radiated out into the desert. Desert Hussein was still braking as Ricardo sprang from the vehicle and ran the length of a line, his GPS held high. He was recording a track to get a more precise bearing.

"It's 298 degrees! Or maybe the reverse of that," he shouted, rushing off to measure a second line.

"Up there," said Ali, gesturing to the ridge above us. "You see how long ago the little people here put up guards to frighten bigger people away!"

Evenly spaced along the crest of Black al-Alam were dozens of cylindrical stone monuments. From afar they looked to be about two feet in diameter and four to five feet high. Were they markers to take the measure of the heavens? Was there a link to the long stone lines?

We would have loved to climb up for a close look, but . . . "This is all good and very wonderful," said Ali. "But now we go."

In the Land Cruiser's rear-view mirror Black al-Alam vanished beyond the curvature of the earth, and desert Hussein sighed. "Jahan and Dahn. Those people so tough. Lucky today they busy with something else, not busy with us."

The return trip was far speedier than when we were finding our way out. Ali had absorbed the lay of the land and struck out directly for Ma'rib. By early afternoon, I was back at my room in the Garden of the Two Paradises. Under a ceiling fan that could barely summon energy for the next time around, I spread out our space images and Tactical Pilotage Chart K6-A. One by one, utilizing the straight-edge of my battered but trusty Silva compass, I plotted Ricardo's bearings from White and Black al-Alam. I took care *not* to peek at where the lines might lead; I didn't want—even unconsciously—to force an incorrect alignment. The results:

FROM	BEARING	POINTS TO	ERROR
Black	67°	Al-'Uqla, ceremonial site near Shabwa, capital of Hadramaut	1°
White	168°	Timna', capital of Qataban	None perceivable
White	186°	Uncertain	?
White	187°	Harabat, a major city of Qataban	None perceivable
White	283°	Qarnaw, capital of Ma'in, a kingdom north of Saba	None perceivable

Of the five bearings we had recorded, four were direct hits on major sites along the Incense Road. (And the other couldn't be written off; it might point to an unknown site.) I rounded up David and Ricardo and had them double-check my marked-up map. Puzzling over the lines, we thought of early-day caravans crossing the Ramlat Sabateyn, never sure of landmarks in the shifting sands. Perhaps, we theorized, the lines were guides. Once headed in the right direction, the caravans could maintain their course by orientation to the stars. But how the lines were laid with such precision we had no idea. Here was a navigational challenge that confronted both caravaneers and early-day mariners. Both set out from a port to cross an open sea to a far port. Only in the Ramlat Sabateyn, the sea was a sea of sand.

Two thousand and more years before the time of the queen of Sheba, a resourceful people lived on the edge of the Ramlat Sabateyn; its sands were no obstacle to their movement and trade—and in due time no deterrent to the rise of their civilization.

A day later we were on our way home to the greener climes of Brazil and California. We would not forget—for we had enjoyed—the scorched sands of Arabia.

Ours was the fortune to visit Yemen in a time (hard to believe) of relative calm and to roam parts of the country closed to outsiders before and since. For all the weaponry, not a shot had been fired, at least at us. We were fortunate to have happened upon the sites of Luqman and al-Alam, both of which, we learned, were unfamiliar to archaeologists.[2]

Further, we had traveled Arabia's Incense Road at a turning point, when old ideas were yielding to new perceptions. A new chronology was displacing the old:

HORIZON	THEORY IN THE EARLY 1990S	THEORY TODAY
Neolithic settlement and local trade	Suspected but not substantiated	3000–5000 B.C.
Development of artificial irrigation	800–1000 B.C.	c. 2400 B.C.
Distinctive ESA alphabet and rise of civilization	500–600 B.C.	1200–1500 B.C.
Beginning of long-range trade	c. 800 B.C.	c. 1000 B.C.
Journey of biblical queen of Sheba (Saba)	Unlikely; there was no writing and thus no civilization	c. 950 B.C.

Best of all, a queen of Sheba stood to be a viable historical character as the kingdom of Saba came of age and was reaching north to establish a lucrative trade.

As we returned from our Arabian adventures, my sole regret was for a road untaken: the mountain road to Sirwah, if there was anything left after the bombing and siege. At present it was the lair of a renegade tribe. Was it once the city of a fabled queen?

At the end of a month back in Los Angeles, I faxed our man in Sa'ana, Mohammed Osman. Was the smoke in Sirwah clearing? How about another try? The typographically expressive reply:

Thanks for your fax!!! It is a real **DIFFICULT QUESTION!!!!!** !!!!!!! **Because you never know when it is open!!!!** For JUNE program we confirmed that you will visit the place!!! **BUT THE WAR SUDDENLY STARTED BETWEEN THE TRIBES!!!!!** And this is something you <u>can not predict, never ever!!!!!</u>

I am really very sorry, but I can not promise such a thing, as it could happen just ONE DAY before or after the arrival that war starts!!!!!

Inshallah. . .

 A Journey Reveals
the Power and Dominion
of the Queen of Sheba

17

The Glory of Kings

WAKING UP AT NIGHT or inching along in traffic blinking with taillights, I did sometimes wonder, as I am sure my family and friends did: was looking for the queen of Sheba more than a little eccentric? Of course it was, and the strange part was that it seemed the most natural, logical, compelling, and necessary quest in the world.

Not making it to Sirwah had been a disappointment, and a small voice whispered that I wouldn't rest until I tried again. And still to be investigated was an African land whose men, women, and children look to the queen of Sheba as an icon of their heritage. Ethiopians have little doubt of the truth of their treasured *Kebra Nagast*—"The Glory of Kings"—a national epic that credits Sheba with establishing a dynasty that ended with the twentieth-century reign of Haile Selassie, King of Kings, Conquering Lion of Judah—and 235th in a line of direct descent from the queen. Ethiopia's 1955 *Revised Constitution* claims that this royal line "descends without interruption from the dynasty of Menelik I, son of the queen of Ethiopia [who is] the queen of Sheba, and King Solomon of Jerusalem."

I recruited companions for a journey through Ethiopia: daughter Cristina; her friend Susan Mathieson, a stage and screen costume designer; and psychoanalyst David Meltzer, ever game for an excursion to exotic lands. Ricardo de Monte Rosa, stalwart of our Yemeni adventure, regretted that he couldn't join us; the old roué was getting married.

We flew to Frankfurt, Germany, and then on to Ethiopia's capital,

Addis Ababa, where we linked up with guide Dawit Alemayehu. In the Hilton's Queen of Sheba Lounge (arguably the best bar in Africa) we laid our plans. Dawit, the same age as Cristina and Susan, held his own as to the coolest running shoes and the future of Detroit Techno, but he was equally well versed in the Ethiopian perception of the queen of Sheba. In pursuit of her, he would take us to places he had heard of but had not seen.

Early the next morning, an Air Ethiopia turboprop dropped us off at a strip well north of Addis Ababa in the remote Lasta Mountains. A season of cold, driving downpours was nearly over, and flights could again get in and out. "Africa!" exclaimed Cristina, taking in a breath of crystal clear air and gazing across a landscape of gentle peaks and verdant pastures, with women and children tending their flocks in the distance. The precipitous, rutted road to the nearest town had yet to recover from the rainy season. Our wheels spun, rooster tails of mud flew skyward, and our van periodically faltered and slipped sideways, prompting Susan to murmur more than once, "I would rather not die just now, if no one minds."

"Sing," Cristina suggested. "Distract yourself."

With a sharp intake of breath, Susan began, "Country road, take me home . . ." Dawit knew a few phrases of this and joined in. Both knew all the words of Bob Marley's "Get up, stand up, stand up for your rights!"

Though no other vehicles came or went our way, we passed people on foot, a few at first, then many, streaming across the countryside to the shoulder of a green-cloaked mountain, where smoke rose from a mantle of huts. Today was market day in the town of Lalibela.

The market, held on a hard-packed plateau just north of town, could have been taking place before the time of Christ. Sheep and goats had been driven from distant valleys; food and produce were borne on the backs of donkeys and carried by men, women, and children. No horns honked; we saw only one other vehicle in Lalibela.

There was no advertising, nothing electrical, not a soul selling cassette tapes. It was the necessities for survival that were for sale or barter: chickens, grains, hand-hammered tools, blankets. The market was alive with haggling, shouts, and laughter; there was the pathos of beggars murmuring, "Christo . . . Christo . . . money."

A long shadow of the past fell on a scattering of merchants who were exiled to a spot beyond the market's perimeter. They were potters and thus pariahs, Dawit explained, for they crafted their wares with fire, an instrument of the devil. They could not intermarry or even touch other villagers. They were heirs of the biblical Tubal-cain.

The ties that bind Lalibela to an Old Testament past are codified in the *Kebra Nagast*, a document claimed to have been discovered in the library of Constantinople's cathedral of Santa Sofia in the third century A.D., but it is more likely a fourteenth-century compilation of Ethiopian oral history. The *Kebra Nagast* tells of the journey of Makeda, virgin queen of Sheba, to the holy city of Jerusalem. There, with a certain crafty deviousness, Solomon insinuates himself into her bed and has his way with her. Later that night Solomon prophetically dreams of

a brilliant sun, and it came down from heaven and shed exceedingly great splendor over Israel. And when it had tarried there for a time it suddenly withdrew itself, and flew away to the country of Ethiopia, and it shone there with exceedingly great brightness forever, for it desired to dwell there. And the King said: 'I waited to see if it would come back to Israel, but it did not return . . .'

When Solomon the King saw this vision in his sleep his soul became disturbed, but his understanding was snatched away by a flash of lightning, and he woke up with an agitated mind . . . Moreover Solomon marvelled concerning the Queen, for she was vigorous in strength and beautiful of form.[1]

In the *Kebra Nagast* Solomon is alarmed by this dream but eventually concedes that Ethiopia rather than Israel is now God's chosen land.

An African Zion.[2]

And this concept, this vision, is nowhere more powerfully and intricately expressed than in a complex of churches hewn from Lalibela's bedrock in the late twelfth century A.D. These churches are so wondrous that the Portuguese friar Francisco Alvares related, "It wearies me to write more of these works, because it seems to me they will not believe me if I write more."

"Look. What do you see?" asked Dawit. After a morning at the market, we were walking back through the village.

"A stream—or at least it would be a stream in the rainy season?" Cristina ventured.

The near-dry watercourse ran through a twenty-foot-deep cut in the brick-red soil and gray rock. It began somewhere uphill to the east, crossed the road, and disappeared downhill to the west.

"The River Jordan. Dug by hand, so Ethiopia too could have such a river. Come."

He led us up a worn path to where the ground sheered away, and there, in the midst of a great pit, rose a church—constructed not of successive courses of masonry but excavated by hand from the bedrock underlying Lalibela. The entire edifice had been shaped the way a sculptor frees a figure from a raw block of stone. Before us was a feat of hope, faith, and a staggering amount of backbreaking labor. A prayer in stone.

"It is said," Dawit recounted, "that side by side, men and angels worked together and created this and more in the rule of King Lalibela. It took them just twenty-five years."

A rock-cut stair descended more than fifty feet to where we could walk around the church and marvel.

"Up ahead," Dawit pointed out, "hermit people."

The sheer wall encircling the church was pocked by a half-dozen tiny caves, each the shelter of a bent-over yellow-robed monk. I had read of such anchorites and had assumed that after a hurrah of pillar-top vigils at the close of the first millennium, they had vanished from the religious landscape. Here they were, renouncing the ways of the flesh, giving their lives but to God.

One anchorite was totally lost to the world; another smiled and waved as we passed by. Lalibela had many such caves, some claimed by the living, some by the skulls and bones of past tenants.

Dawit asked us to remove our shoes and so shake off "the dust of this world" before entering the church. The rock floor glistened with the tread of centuries of bare feet. The walls were dark, smoke stained with incense. Little light filtered through four small windows high above.

A richly robed guardian priest emerged from the gloom and held aloft a large silver filigree cross to bless us. It was a rite that was repeated throughout the afternoon and the next morning as we visited Lalibela's thirteen sunken, rock-cut churches. We saw how, taken as a whole, the churches portrayed a new Jerusalem ordained when the sun in Solomon's sky "flew away to the country of Ethiopia, and it shone there with exceeding great brightness forever." There was the straw-strewn shrine of Bet Lehem (Bethlehem) and the church of Bet Golgota (the House of Golgotha), which in turn enshrined the Iyasus-Cell, the tomb of Jesus. Just beyond was a hollowed rock tower, Adam's tomb. Lalibela's African Zion was connected—both geographically and symbolically—by a maze of tunnels, stairs, and plank bridges that had meanings all their own. Outside the Bet Gabriel-Rufa'el (the House of Archangels Gabriel and Rafael), a steep ramp beckoned the faithful to scale "the path to heaven." With a running start, Dawit made it up and back. On the other hand, as we groped our way deep underground, he was careful to avoid tunnels that might dead-end; they were passages to hell.

Lalibela's churches were intact, living relics of the past. Of the town's population of 2,500, fully 500 were Coptic monks, priests, or nuns. A little after dawn on our second day, we watched as a Bet Lehem priest ritually tapped a little girl's back with a cross to drive away the demons that had made her wan and feverish. The newly risen sun filtered in to highlight the red and gold of the priest's chasuble and edge his deeply lined yet serene features and the child's wide-eyed trust and innocence. The sun illuminated the church's iconography, which had been lost in the shadows the afternoon before. Jesus, Mary, and a host of saints and angels witnessed the exorcism. Snakes slithered beneath the heavenly host and in one case corkscrewed around a saint, whether protecting or crushing him it was hard to say. Serpents both good and evil are intertwined in the Ethiopian Copts' synthesis of Judaism, Christianity, and African animism. The ceremony over, the priest patted the child and chatted amiably with her parents. We took our leave and followed the throb of drums to Bet Giorgis (the House of St. George), the last-built of Lalibela's rock churches.

We recrossed the Jordan River with the realization that all that was Lalibela had sprung from a dream that troubled King Solomon as he slept with the queen of Sheba.

Dawit related that when a dozen of the town's churches were near completion, an indignant St. George appeared in full armor on a white horse to reproach King Lalibela for not constructing a church in his honor, considering that he was not only a Holy Land figure but Ethiopia's patron saint. The king promised him the most beautiful of churches and, just to be sure, St. George lingered to supervise its construction (or, rather, the chiseling away of the rock).

The approach to Bet Giorgis was down an open slope dotted with white-robed figures, many of them lepers. Beyond and below, set in the hollowed earth, was a great, cruciform rock church (see plate 25). Passing a hoof print in the rock, said to have been left by the saint's steed, we descended a stair into a cave facing the church's portal, where devotions were under way. We watched and listened as, to the apocalyptic beat of two enormous drums, monks chanted in Ge'ez, the ritual language of the Ethiopian church (different from everyday Amharic), and shuffled back and forth in a solemn dance they believed to be that of King David before the Ark of the Covenant. With their right hands they grasped prayer staffs; with their left hands they shook sistrums, rattles that filled the cave with silver shimmers. Dawit whispered that a service like this might last all day and through the night.

I was moved by the certainty of belief and fervor that sustained this congregation and thirty-two thousand others throughout Ethiopia. A world fanned by the beat of the wings of angels, a world inspired by an ancient queen, a world that transcended the earthly world of pervasive poverty, frequent drought, and civil revolt. For those who embrace their faith without reservation, the Ethiopian Copts hold that the weaker the body, the stronger the spirit. To this end, many monks debilitate their bodies by rigorous fasting and standing in prayer for days at a time, propped on their T-shaped staffs. The supplicant is rewarded with visions that allow him to communicate directly with God, or God may choose to appear in the guise of a mysterious messenger.

Two hours later, as Cristina and I walked to our hotel in the countryside a few miles west of Lalibela, we were approached by two beggars. Like Coptic snakes, one was virtuous, one sinister. "I will pray for you," said the first, "and God will answer, for Lalibela is the center of the world." I dug into my pocket for a handful of bir. We never saw the second beggar, for he was hidden in the dense brush edging the road. "You, you," he hissed, "listen, listen. I have been to Chicago. I stay Sheraton. Given me one hundred dollars."

While Cristina and I lingered at Bet Giorgis, Dawit, David, and Susan had accepted an invitation to stop by the hut of the guardian priest of the church of Bet Golgota. They were greeted by the priest's wife, Getachew, who supplemented his income (the alms of visitors and pilgrims) by cooking fermented millet in a primitive still crafted of clay pots, bamboo, and bits of copper tubing to produce a milky, vodkalike liquor. She lamented that she had been "burnt by the flame." Her eyes and skin were blistered and fire-darkened and, like the potters beyond the pale of the marketplace, she was a pariah. Her lot, she explained, was what life had forced upon her so that she could feed her children and offer them some hope for the future. She held out little, for she could not remember a time when drought, plague, and war had not stalked her land: "I have seen hell on earth."

The liquor she bottled was sold in a thatch-roofed bar down the lane. When Dawit, David, and Susan went there, the sole customer was a seated woman with her feet submerged in pots of henna. She did this one day a month, she said, for reasons cosmetic and magical (demons, keep your distance). After a time, she was joined by her daughter, a strikingly beautiful young woman. A model for the queen of Sheba, Susan thought, except that she was clearly troubled. She was painfully shy, and too frightened to go to school anymore, her mother said.

"Did something bad happen?" Susan asked. Dawit translated the question into Amharic.

"Yes," her mother replied, explaining that her daughter had managed to save 3,000 bir (almost $500) and had been cheated out of it by people she believed to be friends. At this point Dawit confided to mother and daughter that David was a doctor, a famous doctor, who could tell you the meaning of your dreams.

Before David could protest, the young woman blurted, "I dream about terrible people. Dead people."

"What do they do?" asked David uncomfortably, though he sensed that he might be able to help. In his previous travels in Arabia, he had dispensed medical aid to the bedouin and had counseled them on family and psychological problems.

"They . . . the dead people . . . try to feed me. But I can't . . . I won't eat."

David thought the dead people might be incarnations of her scheming friends. "The bad people in your life. Do you want to kill them?"

"Yes," she said, trembling.

David explained to her at length that thoughts could not kill people—a difficult point to get across in a culture that considers curses and spells everyday matters. He and Susan encouraged her to look to the future rather than be trapped in the past. He offered a prescription, appropriate, he hoped, for her condition and her Ethiopian perception of the natural and supernatural.

"Can you write?"

"Yes, I can."

"Then every day write down the dreams that come to you in the night. Do this for one week, then put away what you've written. Do you understand?"

"Yes."

"Wait a month, then take out your dreams and think about them. You'll know more about yourself. Does that make sense to you?"

"Yes."

"Then burn your dreams."

"Yes," she said softly. "I will do that."

Her mother moved to rise but couldn't, her feet trapped in pools of henna. Tears streamed down her cheeks. "You are a messenger of God. God sent you. God bless you."

18

The Holy City of Aksum

A STORM GATHERED in the Lasta Mountains and followed us to the holy city of Aksum, where Ethiopians believe the queen of Sheba was crowned and reigned.

Our turboprop dodged leaden clouds and bumped down onto a dirt strip just as the skies opened and the rains began to fall. This was not good, Dawit said, for out-of-season rains could delay and rot the upcoming harvest. We drove into Aksum, which was considerably larger and more developed than Lalibela. To the scrape and beat of worn windshield wipers, we glimpsed the Queen of Sheba Elementary School and, several doors farther down, the Queen of Sheba's Video. This was next to the Famous Barber, not to be confused with the Smart Barber down the street. "Aksum is a bigger city than you think," Dawit informed us, "except there is one thing you won't see. A mosque. No mosques allowed in Aksum. When churches are allowed in Mecca, then maybe there might be a mosque in Aksum."

Aksum's first step to holiness came when, long ago and in legend, the city cringed in terror of a serpent king, sometimes called Awre, sometimes Wainaba.

And his eyes resembled a fiery flame, and his eyebrows are black as a raven, and his whole body is like lead and iron . . . and they bring him food every day, ten cows and ten bulls, a thousand goats, one hundred sheep and ten thousand of ten thousand of birds, and he has a horn on him three cubits long.[1]

The day came, it is told, when a courageous and beautiful young woman named Makeda approached Awre-Wainaba, calmly took his measure, and cut off his head. Joyous and grateful, Aksum's population proclaimed Makeda their queen, their queen of Sheba.[2] Soon she was to journey to Jerusalem, there to hold her own with King Solomon—that is, until he tricked his way into her bed and, as previously described, caused God's sun to abandon Jerusalem and "fly away to Ethiopia." On her return journey to Ethiopia, Makeda gave birth to a son at a spring in Maibella (in present-day Eritrea). She named him Menelik, literally "the son of the king." Menelik grew up in Aksum, and when he was of age he was as handsome as his mother was beautiful. At the age of twenty-two he went off to Jerusalem, there to meet his father and recruit advisers and craftsmen so that Ethiopia might flourish as a civilized nation.

But that was not all he did in Jerusalem. With the complicity of his companion, Azirah, young Menelik had the temerity to make off with the Ark of the Covenant: "It was taken by them forthwith, in the twinkling of an eye, the Angel of the Lord being present and directing."[3]

Mighty and many were the reported lamentations of Solomon when he learned that the Ark had been filched. He was sad, he was inconsolable, and he lost precious time pursuing Menelik to Egypt, there to learn that the Ark was well ahead of him and on its way to Aksum.

Then Solomon beheld the angel of the lord, who assured him that no common thief, but rather his own son, had taken the Ark. Solomon dejectedly accepted this news and warned those with him, if they valued their lives, to hold their tongues as to what had happened.[4] He returned to Jerusalem.

On the day Menelik triumphantly brought the Ark to Aksum, relates the *Kebra Nagast*, the queen of Sheba invited everyone to a sumptuous feast—which has been celebrated in late November every year thereafter to this day.

The downpour had slacked to a heavy drizzle as we entered a compound that includes the large circular church of St. Mary of Zion, the much older monastery church of the House of Zion, and the Chapel of the Tablet, an unimposing, weather-worn outbuilding, reminiscent of a kiosk abandoned after a World's Fair. Its metal trim was rusted, its paint faded and flaking, and its roof surely shot with leaks. Inside, Ethiopia's Copts believe, the original Ark of the Covenant is enshrined in an inner sanctum, a Holy of Holies. A lone monk, both hermit and guardian, watches over this relic of relics. That night at midnight, as on every night of the year, he would burn incense and commence a vigil. He dares not doze in the Ark's presence. Only at three the next afternoon, after fifteen hours, does the guardian monk have a respite from his daily devotions.

On rare occasions a select few priests and monks are allowed to enter the shrine to recite psalms and read scriptures. They have described the Ark as a single polished stone tablet on which the Ten Commandments are inscribed in Hebrew. The tablet is two and a half feet long and one and a half inches thick; it rests in an unadorned hinged box, three inches thick, of solid hammered gold. Sometimes the Ark brightens and glows, striking fear into the heart of the guardian and anyone else present. No one dares touch it. Even when the light of day seeps into this Holy of Holies, it is difficult to look at the Ark; it is eerily smooth, like a mirror, like water.

We walked the perimeter of the Ark's shrine; closer approach was forbidden. Our feet sank into the sodden, sacred Ethiopian earth. The rain had discouraged the prudent, and we were alone in the compound. We stopped short as a curtain parted and a gaunt lemon yellow–robed figure stepped from the Chapel of the Tablet—the guardian monk who knew the secrets of Aksum's Ark if anyone did. He looked skyward, rubbed his eyes, and appeared to enjoy the fresh damp air. At first he didn't see us, but when he did he darted back inside. We lingered, even as drizzle reverted to rain.

Hidden in the Chapel of the Tablet was either a great mystery or a great hoax. It was difficult to imagine anything in between. If Aksum's Ark could be shown to have an unexplainable power or even if its lettering could be paleographically dated to before the first millennium B.C., here might—or might not—be the foundation stone of the world's major Western religions, whether it found its way here through the daring of Menelik, son of Solomon and Sheba, or by other hands in later times.

Sentiment dictated that I (if no one else) should stay at Aksum's Queen of Sheba Hotel, listed in a British guidebook in the category of "if cheap and grotty is what you want."

"Five dollars?" Dawit protested in Amharic on my behalf. "His book says a dollar fifty!" Woldo, master of the Queen of Sheba, shrugged and said something to the effect that cheap and grotty evidently had its appeal, prompting the price to soar. He pointed out that for five dollars I would get Room #1, definitely a step up from lesser-priced accommodations out in the hallway with the goats. He led the way through a beaded curtain behind the bar, across a courtyard hung with tattered laundry, and up a concrete staircase, from time to time stepping over sleeping bodies. Room #1 had a sagging bed and a wobbly stool and was painted a sickly green, but what cheered the place up, Woldo pointed out, was a brightly painted plastic circus horse prancing on the balcony outside the single small window. I wrinkled my nose. Room #1 had been freshly sprayed with insecticide. Woldo said in Amharic, and Dawit translated, "For my guests, anything." The two left.

Across the way I could see, over the mane of the circus horse, a last customer taking leave of the Smart Barber. The Smart Barber switched off his shop's dangling bare bulb, casting the street into darkness. Yet Aksum tossed and turned and never quite slept. Somewhere a woman laughed, and the clinks and ricochets of a pool

game lasted far into the night. From time to time, headlights re-
fracted across the ceiling, and trucks ground off to Addis Ababa,
Asmara, and the Sudan. As ever, trade routes radiated from Aksum.

Toward dawn, the throb of drums from the compound of St. Mary
Zion signaled a new day.

I rejoined the others, who had opted for a fancier hotel, and we
further investigated Aksum. At the edge of town was a reservoir reputedly built by the queen of Sheba and, a mile south, a hundred-room
palace where she allegedly had lived, across from a field of monumental fallen stelae. "That one," Dawit pointed out, "is where she
was buried. Maybe." The sticking point was that everything we saw
was the handiwork of an Aksumite empire that flourished well after
the time of Christ, though its roots reached back to 600 B.C. Could
its genesis be even earlier? Archaeologists are doubtful, though not
sure; they've probed no more than 3 percent of ancient Aksum.

What caught our attention later that afternoon was the least prepossessing of Aksum's sites; protected by a corrugated iron shack, it
was a muddy walk across a farmer's field. The farmer's plow had
struck an elongated tablet inscribed in both Ge'ez and Epigraphic
South Arabic, the script of the Sabeans. Still partially buried, the
stone lay where it had been found, for its text, after heralding the exploits of the Aksumite King Ezana, promised an untimely death to
anyone who dared move it. Here, we saw, was tangible evidence of a
link between Arabia and Ethiopia. The scripts of these lands not only
shared the stela but were graphically related. In ESA "the queen of
Sheba" would be written

ℎⵌⵁⵝ𐩵ⵁ𐩵𐩳

In Ge'ez the phrase is

ሳበሳ፥ፈበግን

The explanation for this similarity is that at an undetermined time in the first millennium B.C., the ESA alphabet made its way to Ethiopia, where it was subsequently rounded and embellished. The Arabian version of the script had no provision for vowels, and it is anyone's guess how individual words were pronounced. In Ethiopia this problem was remedied by tagging ESA consonants with vowels in the form of ingenious spurs and tiny circles.

The next morning, on the trail of an Arabian-Ethiopian connection, we drove east toward the Red Sea. Dawit, unfamiliar with the territory, had recruited an Aksumite friend, Nekahiwot Tsehaya, to guide us. Everyone was in good spirits. Susan entertained us with a medley of Broadway show tunes. David and Dawit joined in the refrains. Cristina and I couldn't carry a tune in a bucket. Under a cloudless sky, we threaded our way through ranges of increasingly jagged peaks. Two hours along a well-paved road to Asmara, we turned off onto a dirt track and made for a distant low hill and the archaeological site of Yeha. A small village climbed partway up the hill to a dusty plaza and a church dating to no earlier than the 1950s—with the exception of a single ancient block set high in its façade. On it six ibexes were carved in high relief, ibexes with proudly curved horns, baleful, reindeerlike eyes and snouts, and tiny hooves. They

Sabean ibex at Yeha, Ethiopia (left), and at Ma'rib, Yemen (right)

matched similar rows of ibexes at Ma'rib and elsewhere in the kingdom of Saba.

That this fragment was carefully saved, not smashed or thrown in a ditch, speaks of a people looking with favor rather than anger at what has come before. In Ethiopia, God and his saints and his creatures are at once Christian, Old Testament Jewish, and whatever preceded those beliefs. Thus the ibexes—religiously revered ibexes from Arabia.

Just beyond the church we saw that the ibexes (and many other architectural fragments scattered on the slopes of the hill) had been part of the fabric of a temple that was still standing. With red masonry walls intact to a height of forty feet, it was a grand stone box, once filled with incense and prayer.

The Yeha temple is the oldest major structure in Ethiopia. An initial reading of ESA inscriptions recovered here dated the site to 600 B.C., but that estimate may be pushed back as much as two centuries in the light of a revised chronology for ancient Arabia and its script. The building's style and the skilled construction—its positioning of columns, its mortise and tenon joints—were clearly not only Arabian

Ruins and conjectural restoration of Yeha temple

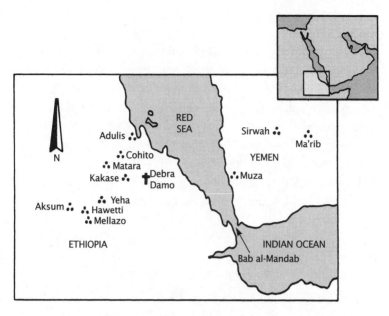

Sabean settlements in Ethiopia

but Sabean. For its period in Ethiopia it was unique: a monumental stone edifice in a land that had known only small brick and wood structures.

I later learned that there are rival scenarios for how such a temple came to be built in the Ethiopian wilderness. One theory holds that an indigenous culture became enamored of Arabian innovations in architecture, iconography, and writing, which it slavishly imitated. A second, and for me more convincing, theory holds that Yeha's temple was a centerpiece of a Sabean outpost established for the same reason the queen of Sheba may have journeyed to Jerusalem: to further trade in incense and spices. And this was not the only evidence of a Sabean incursion into Ethiopia. Not far away at Cohito was a dam constructed along the lines of the Great Dam at Ma'rib. At other sites, inscriptions and altars were dedicated to 'Ilumqah, the moon god of the Sabeans.

From Yeha we returned to the main road and drove east for an hour or so to the foot of the sheer cliffs of a tabletop mesa. High above was Debra Damo, the oldest monastery in Ethiopia. The customary—the only—way up is by climbing a sixty-foot rope dangling from a narrow ledge. A reverse rappel. Long ago I'd enjoyed rock climbing. Was I up for this? No harm in trying, I thought. Aided by fleeting footholds in the rock face, I worked my way ten or twelve feet up the cliff, then stopped to catch my breath.

"You okay?" Dawit asked from the ground.

"So far. Is this safe?"

"No. Not too," volunteered Nekahiwot. "People make pilgrimages here, fall down, get broken."

Hand over hand, I ascended another few feet.

"Lots of people," he elucidated. "Dead."

Not with the best of judgment, I continued up and on until, as exhausted as I've ever been in my life, I pulled myself onto the ledge high on the cliff, not with the thought "I made it!" but "Oh, Lord, how do I get back down?"

A monk helped me to my feet and guided me along the ledge to a flight of stone stairs that led to where some sixty monks dwelt in a time capsule of early Christianity. In Debra Damo's spare, simple church, the only change from the days of Byzantium was an incongruous "Tome Fanta! Mucho gusto!" battery clock that reminded the monks when and how long to pray. Once a monk climbed that rope, he rarely, if ever, went back down. In centuries past, the question had been raised: how did the very first monk attain the precipitous mesa? The traditional explanation was that a kindly disposed serpent slithered over the edge and acted as the next best thing to a rope. (How the snake got up there was not explained.)

The monks at Debra Damo were self-sufficient. They tended gardens and looked after a modest herd of cattle. Their life was austere, as was their church—unadorned but for a distinctive pattern in its exterior masonry. This was in the style of the Mahram Bilqis at Ma'rib.

Some monks lived and prayed apart from the church. Forgoing all human contact, they holed up in caves on the mesa's cliffs, surviving on meager rations lowered over the edge. When a basket was hauled up with its bread and water untouched, fellow monks knew that one of their number had died. There was no other way to know. The monastery, I realized, must have a spiritual life beyond anything I could imagine or witness. Their only earthly compensation was a splendid view eastward across range after range, ending in a haze of humidity cast up by the Red Sea. To the west were the half-dozen ranges we had crossed on our way here from the ruined Sabean temple of Yeha.

The view prompted a realization bearing upon the queen of Sheba. If Yeha off in the distance dated to the seventh or eighth century B.C., how long did it take the Sabeans to establish an African beachhead, reconnoiter the territory inland, subdue its indigenous population, and finally bend them to the task of raising a colonial settlement and masonry temple? Long enough, quite possibly, for the Sabeans to have been in Ethiopia in the tenth century B.C.

If archaeology bore this theory out, it would be possible for *both* Yemen and Ethiopia to claim a tenth-century biblical queen of Sheba.[5] Though based in Yemen, she would have had dominion over Ethiopia. And here would be an answer to the oft-posed question "Was she black?" The answer would be "She—from Arabia—probably not. Many of her people—in Ethiopia—yes."

From Debra Damo's church I walked back—a walk of dread—to the monastery's clifftop portal. Two monks held me as, with one hand, I reached out into space for the rope that was the only way in or out of their world. I grasped the rope with one white-knuckled hand, then let go of the monks with the other and swung out onto the rock face.

"Amuhseguhnalhoo!" I said, assuredly mispronouncing an Amharic thank you. Benevolently, they smiled and faded from sight.

Going down was more nerve-rattling than going up. My feet flailed in midair, finding a toehold only every so often.

I slid. My palms burned, bled.

"How far?"

"Halfway," Cristina shouted, and then everyone joined in a chorus. "Twenty! Just fifteen! Ten, nine, eight, seven, six! Jump! You can jump!"

Shadows swept across eastern Ethiopia's valleys and mountains, as we drove back to Aksum. By night the road seemed more precipitous than it had in the morning. A little past the turnoff to Yeha, Susan had an operatic turn of mind and sang, quite well, Rossini's "Due Gatti." Dawit and Nekahiwot, in the meantime, had fallen into an argument as to *just how* Solomon had seduced the queen of Sheba and begotten Menelik, their country's first king.

Solomon, Dawit asserted, had in his harem seven hundred wives and three hundred concubines.

Susan broke off the Rossini in midphrase. "That pig!" she exclaimed. She returned to the song, but not for long. "That pig!" she repeated with rising indignation.

Dawit nodded. According to the *Kebra Nagast*, he said, the Sheba seduction was a setup. Earlier in the evening, Solomon had served her a highly spiced and salted dinner and, feigning suspicion that she might be untrustworthy, made her promise not to take anything he owned. If she did, Solomon asserted, he would be free to take her by force. Sheba was puzzled but nevertheless went along with this, knowing in her heart that she was an honest and, in any case, a rich queen. She went to bed, but before long she awoke, her throat parched. She reached for a glass of water, drank it down, and felt a hand grasp her wrist. It was Solomon, who lost no time insisting that *the water was his*—and Sheba as well.

"But," said Dawit, "don't go getting the idea that she was so innocent. That glass of water was in Solomon's room down the hall."

"No," objected Nekahiwot, "not so. She didn't leave her own bed. They were sleeping in the same room, and that glass was on the table between them."

"It was not! The glass was down the hall."

"No, no, you've got it wrong."

"Then answer me this. If she was so taken advantage of, how come the queen of Sheba stayed in Jerusalem for another six months before going home?"

"He made her stay."

"Dawit, not so."

So it went, the embers of a fateful evening glowing thirty centuries later.

19
By Dhow from Djibouti

THE MONOGRAM was an artfully entwined *FE*, the logo of the Chemin de Fer Franco-Ethiopien. The train itself was a wreck. Sandblasted, windows cracked and broken, horsehair stuffing weeping from cracked vinyl seats.

I could still decide not to go ahead with this and instead board tonight's Air Ethiopia flight to Germany, then home, but the queen of incense and spices beckoned me on. I had sought her in the far reaches of the biblical world—except I had never made it to Sirwah, our excursion cut short by a government bombing run. Was it worth another try? From Addis Ababa I had faxed Mohammed Osman in nearby Yemen. His terse reply:

> I talked to Mr. Naser about Sirwah. IT IS STILL **NOT POSSI-BLE** TO GO THERE. I am sorry for that but we can't help.

Nevertheless, I had phoned Mohammed. I wasn't far away; what if I came to Yemen on the chance that minds and conditions might change? I pictured him taking the phone from his ear and looking at it in disbelief; doesn't this fellow get it? "Mr. Nicholas, THEY BOMB SIRWAH!!!"

"Maybe we could ask, one last time?"

"I'll see what I can do," sighed Mohammed.

A whistle that had trouble clearing its throat announced the train's imminent departure from the Addis Ababa station. On the platform, I thanked Cristina, Susan, and David for their good company and regretted that it seemed best for me to continue alone. If anything went amiss, it was one thing to risk my own neck, another to risk anyone else's. We exchanged hugs and farewells. I swung aboard the lead car, a combination engine and passenger car. With an adagio of groans, hisses, and chronic mechanical complaints, the train crept on its way.

The track ahead, laid just after World War II, had at the time been billed as the costliest in the world, for it snaked through 10,000-foot-plus mountains, then descended to traverse a blistering, heartless desert riven by deep canyons. The line ended at Djibouti, on the Indian Ocean, the closest African port to Yemen. With luck, it would be a twenty-four-hour run.

"Bonjour," wished the swaying conductor. "Je vous souhaite la bienvenue."

"Merci."

Switching to English, he informed me, "This is the worst train in the world."

"Oh, it couldn't be," I answered. I had long believed that there were no bad trains. (True, some trains deserved to be scrapped, but that makes them in-the-face-of-death survivors. And gallant for that.)

He took no notice of a violent lurch, cascading luggage. "Then tell me, where is there a worse train?"

"In China maybe? Or India? I don't know . . ." I trailed off.

"Attendez . . . ," he said, moving on through the car.

Cristina and Susan had sent me on my way with half a cardboard box of Balance energy bars. I munched one, then another. Dinner. Out the window the last rays of the sun rippled across scattered edge-of-the-city corrugated iron shanties. From their doorways somber children half-heartedly waved. The Franco-Ethiopien rattled over a series of high trestles and plunged into the night. I dozed. As the train slowed and shuddered to a stop at a succession of tiny stations, I would half wake and, in the darkness (there being no light in the car), perceive an ever-shifting tableau of passengers. In the facing seat, an aged woman with a little girl in her lap became a one-legged holy man (priest or mullah, I couldn't tell) toting a plastic bag advertising a modeling service in Dubai. My foot cramped. Wiggling it, I inadvertently bumped a gaunt man who had stretched out under my seat.

Sometime after eleven o'clock, it occurred to me that the train was not moving and hadn't been for quite a while. Resigned passengers quietly conversed in Amharic, French, Arabic, and Portuguese. But not Danish; the three Danish students who had been chattering away down the aisle had vanished. I was now the sole *faranji* in the car and probably on the train. I shook myself awake and stepped out onto a kerosene-lit platform. The conductor there explained that the engine had run dry, which was why a procession of villagers was climbing up and down a rickety ladder with bucket after bucket of water.

"Voilà, two hundred liters," he concluded and hustled everyone back on the train.

There was a *squish, splash, squish* as I returned to my seat. Voilà, the two hundred liters had passed through the engine to flood the passenger compartment. Passengers took off their shoes; mutterings in a language unknown rose from below my seat. A pump had failed. A replacement would have to be scavenged from a derelict engine back in the Addis Ababa yards.

Many hours, one pump, and another two hundred liters of water later, the engine lurched onward. I drifted off to sleep, only to be awakened by gunshot. The one-legged holy man opposite me had been replaced by a fatigue-clad soldier, blazing out the window with an M-1 rifle.

"Shifta bandits from Somalia," explained the conductor on his next pass through. "Vous êtes fatigué?" He pointed out the early morning shadows cast on the scrubby trackside brush, the shadows of soldiers up on the roof.

Every few hours I ate a Balance bar but didn't dare lick my sticky, grubby fingers. The compartment was jammed, cramped, stifling. A little after seven in the evening, ten hours behind schedule, we rolled into Diredawa, where it was announced that the engine and passengers would have an overnight break before braving the desert beyond. I found a cheap but comfortable hotel and gloried in the space to wildly thrash my arms and keel over backward into a clean-sheeted, lumpy bed.

It was still dark when I walked back to the train station, and the journey resumed. Not long after dawn I debated whether to keep my window closed and swelter in the desert heat or open it and be caked in billowing red dust. I opted for the dust, for it cut the stench of diesel and the acrid ammonia fumes from the sole, clogged toilet. (As it was, my throat became so sore I could hardly swallow.) Giant anthills dotted the otherwise lifeless landscape crawling by. The two seats opposite me had been commandeered by a single enormous woman; her legs and feet stuck straight out and claimed the seat to my left.

We took on water at the flyspeck settlement of Aysha. A crazed, ragged man, drooling green (qat, I guessed), got on and pushed his way up and down the crowded aisle, shouting at no one in particular with great urgency. At Dewele a strikingly beautiful woman boarded. She was dark-eyed, slender, and dressed in a simple black-and-white print dress, with a black shawl over her shoulders. She had no luggage, only a shopping bag. The enormous woman grumped and glowered at her, staking her claim to two seats and one more for her feet. The dark-eyed young woman met her stare, but without hostility, then squeezed in across the aisle and gazed out across the barren landscape from which she had sprung. She seemed like one of its creatures, the oryx or the addax: delicate to the eye but resilient and resourceful. Like a queen, perhaps, of Sheba?

I would have to cut back on relating everything to the queen of Sheba, I decided.

It was late afternoon when we stopped at what a crude sign said was Nazaret. It was nowhere on my Michelin map. We had apparently left Ethiopia and crossed into Djibouti, which had been a French colony until 1977. Even now French soldiers sauntered back and forth on the platform.

Surly local police boarded the train and walked its length, checking documents. They questioned the woman in the black shawl and abruptly took her away. Where? Why? Could I do anything? On a bluff by the tracks I saw two large chain-link cages filled with men, women, and children. Were they refugees? Prisoners? A half hour passed. The whistle sounded; we were about to leave. At the last minute the Djibouti police escorted the woman in the black shawl back to her seat and, with new-found deference, returned her papers, apologizing for any inconvenience. Blaming her for the train's delay, the enormous woman opposite me quivered and sputtered with rage. A gold-toothed crone joined in. The queen of Sheba looked calmly at one, then the other, and spoke to them quietly with measured self-assurance. A departing policeman tapped his lips with his finger and advised, "Mesdames, ça suffit!"

The train rattled on into gathering gloom. A row of telephone poles paralleled the tracks, nearly every one capped by a funereal snake eagle.

Several hours later, twelve hours behind schedule, the conductor made his final pass through the car. "Oui?" he asked me, meaning, wasn't this truly the world's worst train? "Non," I said, though not without a twinge of hesitation. He nodded, pleased or disappointed I couldn't tell. He ordered windows rolled up to deflect the rocks and bricks customarily thrown as the train rumbled through the Bender Jilid district to Djibouti's main station.

The train quickly emptied. Within the month, I later learned, faranjis would be forbidden on the Chemin de Fer Franco-Ethiopien, and its further fate would be unrecorded.

Au revoir, père chemin.

I lost sight of the queen of Sheba as the crowd surged past the shanty housing the "Sous-Chef du Gard." Reaching the street, I was hailed, "Monsieur . . . votre charabanc," by a voice at once squeaky and gravelly. This was Moussie, a cab driver, who within a few minutes had offered his services as agent for a sea passage to Arabia. After some discussion we agreed that first thing the next morning he, I, and his salt-corroded Peugeot would make the rounds of Djibouti's docks.

A dozen listless tramp freighters were in port, but none were bound for anywhere in Arabia, though one captain said he could offload a dinghy and have a sailor run me to an isolated Yemeni beach. It would be expensive, as the dinghy required certain repairs.

Moussie and I paid a call on the harbormaster, who held out some hope. "You come Saturday. There will be pirates then. We do papers. You go off with them."

Pirates? He was joking. I was sure he was joking. Even so, Saturday was four days away, four very long days if you happen to be in Djibouti. Moussie and I resolved to keep looking, twice a day. Of course, I could still forget all this and head home; there was a Thursday flight to Paris. But no, if need be I would wait for Saturday and the pirates, for two not terribly good reasons. One, I was resolved to go on to Yemen, even though my chances of reaching Sirwah were nearly nil. Two, I wanted to experience for myself how easy it would have been for the Sabeans to cross the Red Sea in the course of their colonization of Ethiopia. As the classical historian Artemidorus tells us, the Sabeans engaged "in the traffic in aromatics, both the local kind and those from Ethiopia; to get the latter they sail across the straits in leather boats." My boat, I hoped, would be wooden, a traditional dhow.

No luck that afternoon or the next morning. Moussie and I had stopped for coffee and were planning a lookabout later in the day when something told me we should have another look, right now.

"Moussie, le Peugeot cherche les pirates?"

"Encore une fois? . . . again?"

"Oui."

"Fou."

We retraced our rounds and found that in on the morning tide had come the *Fatah Alkyar* ("Bringer of Good Things"), a fifty-foot dhow dwarfed by the nearby tramp steamers. Bound next for Yemen!

The boat's taciturn captain, Mohammed Ali, told us his crew would cast off for the Red Sea port of Mokha as soon as they took aboard 1,600 sacks of Ethiopian sesame seeds. Could I go along? Captain Ali arched his eyebrows and squinted. Moussie asked me for the equivalent of twenty dollars in Djibouti rials, neatly folded the bills, and handed them to Captain Ali, who, without a word and hardly a glance, handed them back. We added another five dollars' worth. With an almost imperceptible nod, he pocketed the fare and turned to loading the boat.

Its wooden planking blackened not by paint but by age, the *Fatah Alkyar* had a peaked prow and stern and was built to run under sail, but at some point the mast had been removed and a primitive diesel installed amidships. The crew's tattered and grease-stained T-shirts were of the late 1990s. Two read "High Traffic Area"; there was one each of "Chattanooga Billiards," "Emerald Printing, San Diego," and "Who Else?"

The *Fatah Alkyar* sank ever deeper into the harbor as more and more sacks were shouldered aboard; in all, I calculated seventy-two tons of sesame seeds. Moussie looked at me and then at the boat. I should expect, he advised, "un voyage difficile."

It was a fine day. Clear, no clouds.

Moussie eased into his Peugeot and, before rolling up his window, repeated, "Un voyage difficile." He drove off.

I was not the *Fatah Alkyar*'s only passenger. A fleshy, dyspeptic Somali merchant slouched aboard; "Jazz It" said his T-shirt, riding high over his belly. In tow he had two veiled ladies and a personal cargo of a dozen greasy yellow plastic five-gallon containers. "Tequila," I

heard him confide to Captain Ali, though he may have been utter-
ing a sound-alike Arabic warning to watch out for Allah.

A little after three that afternoon, the alarmingly low-in-the-water
dhow cast off in the direction of the headland of Ras el Bir. We four
passengers were confined to a low-roofed alcove tucked under an upper deck spanning the stern. With pillows, rugs, and rags, the merchant of "Jazz It" had made a nest for himself on a low bench and sat
twirling a branch of qat, selecting succulent leaves with his pudgy
fingers and popping them into his mouth. His qat, from Somalia,
was said to be quite inferior to the Yemeni qat. His women were at
his feet, as were his dozen yellow containers of "cooking oil" (his
only two words of English). On the deck above us, Captain Mohammed Ali sat cross-legged, directing his crew with whistles and curt,
small gestures. Behind him, the first mate steered the *Fatah Alkyar*,
hopping back and forth on his left foot as he guided the tiller with his
right. Behind us, the sun was sinking into a bank of rather ominous
clouds. Rounding Ras el Bir, we bore north to the Bab Al-Mandab
(the "Gate of Tears"), the strait into the Red Sea. We were sailing
without a chart, without sextant or life preservers. The first mate,
who had a smattering of English, assured, "Captain Ali, he very
goody. Never study. No school. Can still take the boat all way to India. Like old days."

In the enveloping darkness, a large, slippery fish flew through the
air, glanced off the side of my head, and was reeled in to where two
of the crew were tending a small stove. They had set out lines, and
now had dinner and breakfast for all.

A following wind corrugated the sea, and before long had it churn-
ing with whitecaps. The *Fatah Alkyar* rolled and bobbed; every so
often a wave broke over its sideboards. From time to time, we saw the
lights and bulk of freighters and tankers as they plied one of the most
heavily traveled shipping lanes on earth. I trusted they could see our
low-watt, low-to-the-water running lights.

A light, then not so light, rain began to fall. Rolled up in a tattered blanket, I tried as best I could to sleep, wedged into a corner so I wouldn't slide about in the choppy seas.

A wave, larger than any before, crashed upon us. The Somali merchant's women shrieked as they were pitched across the deck. I broke loose as well, and we collided. I jumped to my feet and, forgetting the low clearance between decks, gashed the top of my head on an overhead beam.

The little boat was out of control. The engine room was flooded, the diesel knocked out. Blood streamed down my forehead. I wiped it from my eyes and checked my watch: 12:15 A.M. The crew rushed to rig hoses and a pump.

Thank God the crew had light to work by. Light? Our power was out and the moon obscured by the storm. Yet every few seconds, a bright light swept the deck of the *Fatah Alkyar*.

"Jazirat?" I asked the nearest of the crew.

"Jazirat, nam!" he replied. "An island, yes!" Its lighthouse was off the port bow.

There were rocks ahead. And behind me a violent thumping. I turned to see the merchant of Jazz It face down on the deck, convulsed with spasms. His arms and legs jerked uncontrollably. Either he'd had too much qat, or the qat had been laced with pesticide. The prospect of shipwreck didn't help.

Over and over and over again, he battered the deck with his head.

20

The Road to Sirwah

THE LITTLE SHIP'S DIESEL coughed, sputtered—and quit.

A *Moby Dick* phrase flashed through my mind: "Consider the sharks of the sea . . ." And then the title of an English-language book I'd leafed through in Djibouti: *The Forty-Seven Species of Sharks in the Red Sea.*

What could I do? For the moment, not much, except trust that the *Fatah Alkyar*'s crew would pull us through. The first mate kept us headed into the wind. The overloaded boat would surely capsize if it took a big wave broadside.

As the engine room was pumped clear of water, the crew again coaxed the diesel to life, and this time it throbbed on, angling us away from the lighthouse and its rocky isle.

The storm lasted the night through, and the diesel quit—and was restarted—twice more. Finally, at dawn, we hove to in the protection of a breakwater at the Yemeni port of Mokha. It was in the blood of captain and crew—and of many Yemenis, I thought—to range over long distances, by sea or land, and outwit the elements. It was also in their blood to cut hard, even merciless, bargains. As lines were secured fore and aft, the dhow's four passengers were greeted by men who appeared to be customs agents but who turned out to be volunteer personal assistants for dealing with the *actual* customs officials, who were not at present on the dock.

"Just you ride on my motorcycle."

"Just wait a minute."

"You pay me nothing, *sadik* (friend), as you wish."

With not much choice in the matter, I was soon whizzing, with my new friend, past the ruined white villas of the seventeenth-century Dutch coffee merchants who had been drawn to Mokha (and had given us "mocha-java"). Our destination was a squat, unpainted concrete-block building, the lair of two baggy-eyed officials seated at two cigarette-burned desks. Broken glass littered the floor. The shards were dusty; nobody had thought to sweep them up.

"Where from you?" asked the first.

"The U.S."

"Where is this U.S.? I do not know this place!" demanded the second.

"America . . ."

"Ah, ah," broke in the first, astonished that I knew so little of my own country. "You mean U.S.A.! You must say U.S.A.! That is what you must say!"

With surly finger-twitching, he signaled for my passport, which, after much examination and the equivalent of a ten-dollar fee, he stamped. He tossed it to his partner.

"Now, you must pay us three hundred and fifty rials [seven dollars]," demanded the second official, "for taking the picture."

"Oh, no problem. You see," I said, rustling in my wallet for visa-sized snapshots, "I have pictures. For you."

"No, no." He waved his hands in exasperation. "We take the picture."

This proved untenable, as they had no camera. And so it was that I cleared customs: ten dollars for the rubber stamp and seven dollars for *not* taking my picture. "And what more have you got in there?" inquired my personal assistant, peering into my wallet, at the same time reassuring, "Sadik, sadik, I do *this*"—do *what*, I wondered— "just for you and for U.S.A." We settled on four dollars for the motor-cycle ride.

All this was nothing compared to the working over of Jazz It, he of the two questionable ladies and the even more questionable "cooking oil." The two customs agents roused themselves from their desks and stepped outside to inspect his yellow containers, murmur ominously, and shake their heads. Placing a solicitous arm around the merchant's shoulder, the first suggested a walk around the building. Out of everyone's sight. On their return, the merchant was visibly shaken and the customs agent wreathed in smiles. The merchant shuddered as the second agent, eyes atwinkle, invited Jazz It on a second stroll. My God, I thought, such mischief, and at six-thirty in the morning. Here were people to hold their own with Solomon.

The shared serial intercity taxis that took me from Mokha inland to Taiz and then on to Sana'a were a bargain, the fare working out to a dollar per hundred miles. The scenery was grand and the company good, if you discounted qat drool and clouds of cigarette smoke. In Sana'a I hastened to Mohammed Osman's office. He was away, I was told, but soon would return from the Ministry of Tourism. Hoping that he might have gone there on my behalf, I waited. My head hurt, and not just from having smashed it on the dhow. Was I coming down with something, the flu? Or was I just agitated from too much Yemeni coffee on the road? I leafed through the latest issue of the *Yemen Times*, an English-language weekly with a reputation for excoriating government officials—indeed, all of Yemen—for qat chewing, foreigner snatching, and generalized medieval behavior. Page two had the following Q & A:

Q: How do people in Yemen view lepers?
A: A leprosy-infected person in Yemen is forced to divorce his wife, denied inheritance, prevented from entering a mosque, and is even greeted with a handshake by a long stick. There are weird stories of lepers being prevented from going out in the rain. Some people really believe that the disease would go through the rain water into the ground, be absorbed by plants, and infect humans

who eat these plants. In some areas of Yemen, lepers are not allowed to switch the light on for fear of transmitting the disease via electricity.

"Ah, Nicholas, you're here," cried Mohammed. "And it's okay! The papers for you, I will have them in the morning. Yes, you can go to Sirwah."

I was stunned and elated. And feverish, I realized, with burning eyes and, later on, chills. For dinner I ate only half of my Bilqis Burger in the café of the Taj Sheba hotel. I was ill, but whatever it was could wait, as could the gash on my head, doctored for the time being with splashes from an airplane gin bottle.

True to his word, Mohammed Osman was at my hotel early the next morning with the ministry paperwork and word that the provincial governor, headquartered at Ma'rib, would grant me further clearance. On such short notice, neither desert nor highland Hussein was available to accompany me; instead Mohammed introduced me to Absalom, a cheerful individual who spoke only a few words of English. His name gave me pause. In the Bible, Absalom was Solomon's treacherous brother, and if he'd had his way, it would have been Absalom and Sheba. Only later did I discover that my guide's name was actually Abu Salem, "the Father of Peace." Much better. We agreed that the best plan was to immediately drive to Ma'rib, where Sheik Naser Zaid would provide an additional local guide and secure the governor's written permission; by midafternoon at the latest we would be on the road to Sirwah.

This, alas, was not to be. In Ma'rib, Sheik Naser shrugged. The governor's clearance for Sirwah hadn't come through and probably wouldn't. *It just wasn't a good idea to go there.* But if I liked, the sheik could explore one or two possibilities, with Abu Salem on loan as an intermediary.

I checked into the familiar Garden of the Two Paradises hotel. Still feverish, I paced its stained and matted carpeting, its gloomy halls, and thought and waited and paced. Sirwah wasn't so important, I told myself. I'd live if I couldn't get to the last possible place on earth that might have a bearing on the queen of Sheba.

Seven o'clock. The sole occupant of the hotel's gloomy, cavernous dining room, I ordered a nonalcoholic Amstel and fries.

Eight o'clock. In the lobby I studied a Xerox of Egyptian archaeologist Ahmed Fakhry's 1947 account of his journey to Sirwah, and imagined where I would walk, what I would photograph.[1] I rested my forehead, still baking but maybe cooling, on my hand. I folded the report and returned to my room.

A little after nine o'clock, I jumped up to answer a knock at the door. It was Abu Salem, and he was smiling. "Peek-neek," he said. "Peek-neek." We rushed out into the night to buy biscuits, bananas, and Fantas, for we would be picnicking at Sirwah!

At five-thirty in the morning, we left Ma'rib by a roundabout route through alleys and up a dry wash to evade troublesome checkpoints. Five of us were aboard a blue-and-rust pickup driven by Ali—not Ali al-Sharif of previous adventures but a stocky, stubble-jowled Ali with black, piratical eyes. Abu Salem was in back, hanging on to the cab, along with two bodyguards, English-speaking Najib and a man whose name I don't recall. They were from the Sirwah area and had been called to Ma'rib and hired on my behalf by Sheik Naser. The idea was that it would be awkward if not daunting for their fellow Sirwahites to shoot at or kidnap someone under their own tribe's protection.

Our route led away from the desert into a field of dead volcanoes silhouetted against a predawn sky shaded purple to rose.

"Here for you," said piratical Ali. "You may need." He handed me a Kalashnikov. The pickup swerved as he rustled around for an extra clip and a beer can–sized cylinder. "And you have this." He swerved again as he handed it to me. Abu Salem and the bodyguards banged on the roof.

The cylinder had a four-inch neck capped by a screw top. Baffling. Ali grinned as though I should grin, too, to be holding whatever it was. The only way to find out, I witlessly decided, was to unscrew the cap and see what was inside. I was less than a turn into this when, yelling "La! La! La!" Ali slammed on the brakes, fishtailing the pickup and setting off a chorus of shouts and more banging on the roof. He seized the canister and made a theatrical display of tightly screwing the cap clockwise. He thrust the device into my pants pocket, shifted down into first, and was off again.

Now it came to me what the canister might be. From my army days, I recalled a U.S. hand grenade, which I sketched on a scrap of paper and showed to Ali.

"Same-same?" I asked.

"Same-same," he confirmed, at first grimly shaking his head, then darkly chortling, and finally laughing. Indeed, what had almost happened so amused him that he again hit the brakes, again sent the trio in back careening, and leapt out to act out how the Nazrani had nearly triggered the detonator of his Czech grenade and, if it had not been for Ali's alacrity, would have dispatched them all directly to Paradise. "Boom! Aieee! Khalas!" Exclaimed Najib, "Almost blow up whole truck bedu! Ha! Ha!" He and his co-bodyguard (though not ashen-faced Abu Salem) agreed that the idea of this was hilarious and pantomimed further detonations by further grenades, as they would continue to do from time to time throughout the day.

Piratical Ali swung back into the cab, slapped me on the back, patted the grenade in my pocket, made sure the safety on my Kalashnikov was on, and drove on down the road to Sirwah, scarred tires crinkling on broken basalt.

The sun peered over a volcano's shoulder and cast roadside shadows of our mini-militia and automatic weapons rippling over a landscape greener and less spiky than Ma'rib's. We had gained altitude; the day would be cooler, refreshed by a light breeze. At 5,300 feet above sea level, we crested a low pass into a broad valley nestled in an almost perfect circle of mountains. Away off in the center of the valley, the sun highlighted a small mesa. I wasn't sure, but the mesa looked to be crowned with walls and parapets.

"Sirwah?" I asked.

"Sirwah," said Ali.

21

In the House of the South Wind

SIRWAH VANISHED FROM VIEW as we descended from the pass. I wondered what shape the site would be in. Photographs taken in 1947 by Ahmed Fakhry were blurry but impressive. Since then Sirwah had been the scene of a major battle between royalists and rebels in 1962 and, just a few months before, had been battered by the government air strike we had witnessed at a distance.

A suspenseful fifteen minutes later, quite suddenly, Sirwah rose up before us as a hill on the left and a mesa on the right. A structure called the al-Qasr (the castle) had once surmounted the hill. All that survived of it was a few feet of wall; the rest was rubble. "Khalas," said piratical Ali. Finished.

The mesa—al-Kharibeh (simply, Place of Ruins)—looked much as it had in Fakhry's photographs, still guarded by soaring pale yellow masonry walls. More imposing than I'd imagined. But we couldn't go there just yet, not without the consent of Sirwah's Sheik Ahmed, a "bad man, a very bad man," a government official had warned me, describing how the sheik had indiscriminately kidnapped foreigners and Yemenis by the dozen. As the spirit moved them, he and his tribe had dynamited oil pipelines and at one point had mustered enough weaponry to block the main highway from Sana'a to Ma'rib.

A mile beyond the ruins, quite alone, Sheik Ahmed now stepped from a modest white-plastered house. Though he was not in any definable way prepossessing, his dark eyes set beneath a heavy brow gave him an aura of brooding intensity. Yet from time to time he would chuckle and even laugh, and he was ever considerate. Having anticipated my arrival, he invited me to join him for breakfast on a carpet spread in the shade of a large acacia. Small children brought out coffee, freshly baked bread, and a flavorful pudding.

Was this the scariest man in Yemen? I recalled that the accusation "He kidnaps foreigners . . ." usually ended, even in the words of his detractors, with ". . . but he never harms them," for what he wanted was to exchange them for a new clinic, school, or road. "How you say, a Robin Hood?" one person told me and allowed that though a fortune in oil flowed through the pipeline that traversed Sheik Ahmed's territory, few government funds flowed back to him.[1]

With bodyguard Najib as interpreter, I conversed with Sheik Ahmed, avoiding the present in favor of the past. I asked about routes in and out of his valley, and he confirmed that the Incense Road may have once bypassed Ma'rib in favor of Sirwah—an argument for Sirwah as an earlier capital of the Sabeans. He stirred at the mention of Malkat ("queen of") Saba and invited me to stroll through a well-tended orchard to have a look at a pile of a dozen inscriptions in Epigraphic South Arabic. The mark of the mason's chisel was as sharp-edged as it had been two thousand and more years ago, in part because Sirwah is beyond the reach of the desert's scouring sand. Sheik Ahmed pointed out different styles of lettering, perhaps from different periods.

I asked if he thought Sirwah had been the capital of the Sabeans before Ma'rib—and was therefore the city of Malkat Saba. To my surprise, he shook his head and, through Najib, said no, the two cities had flourished at the same time. Ma'rib was the location of the winter palace of the kings and queens of Saba; the palace at Sirwah was where they escaped for the summer.

Which made considerable sense.

Ma'rib would have been the market and trading town, filled with the cries of merchants and the curses of cameleers, and Sirwah the royal retreat—a "place of joy," the chronicler Abu Mohammed al-Hamdani called it.[2] It may also have been a religious center, a home of the gods, like Delphi; an inscription recorded by Fakhry describes the site as "the sacred enclave of the Lord of the Ibexes of Sirwah" (that lord being the omnipresent moon god 'Ilumqah).

"Sirwah number one," proclaimed Sheik Ahmed with a thumbs up, "and now you must see for yourself." He entrusted me to his bright-eyed nephew, Mana al-Nasirah, and the two of us were off to the ruins. My retinue elected to stay behind to laze, sip coffee, perchance to plot.

"Al-Bina?" I asked Mana, repeating Fakhry's name for what remained of Sirwah's ancient reservoir. Mana knew of this, and we hiked to an acre-sized low-walled enclosure northwest of the mesa. With its severely limited watershed, Sirwah could never support a population of more than a few thousand and thus was fated to be overshadowed by Ma'rib and that city's vast waterworks.

Now for the mesa, al-Kharibeh. To my knowledge there was no accurate surveyed site plan; all that existed were sketches, hastily drawn. Sirwah's first Westerner—Joseph Halevy, in 1869—had been waylaid and beaten, and the visits of explorers thereafter were measured in days, even hours. From their jottings I had drawn a plan to guide my tour of the site. We would see as much as possible in the morning and, if no problems arose, return for a further, more detailed look in the afternoon.

"Look you here! Very, very old I think," called Mana as we scrambled up the mesa.

He pointed out an inscription on a half-buried section of al-Kharibeh's northern wall. It was unusually weatherbeaten and worn; only a few letters were legible. What caught my eye was the sunburst symbol in a scattering of graffiti above the formal inscription. I

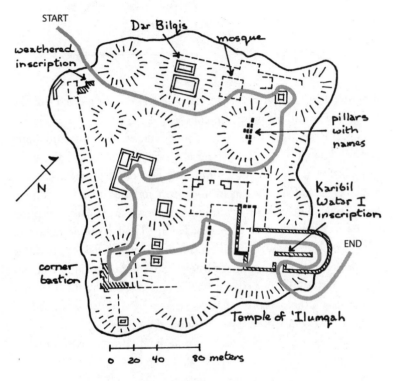

START

Dar Bilqis

mosque

weathered
inscription

N

pillars
with
names

Karibil
Watar I
inscription

END

corner
bastion

Temple of 'Ilumqah

0   20   40   80 meters

Sketch plan of Sirwah

Sirwah inscription

thought it just might be a very early letter—later dropped—of the Epigraphic South Arabian alphabet.

Gaining the top of the mesa, we made our way to a structure traditionally known as the Dar [House of] Bilqis. In 1947, Fakhry described this as being in an almost perfect state of preservation. Regrettably, it had in the meantime been reduced to an ill-defined heap, most likely during Yemen's 1962 civil war. An inscription (which I couldn't locate) copied by Fakhry dated the building to A.D. 300—which undercut a tradition (reported also by Fakhry) that this was the palace of the queen of Sheba. Still, the date didn't rule out the possibility that her palace had been overbuilt by this or other structures on the mesa.

Next along our path was an abandoned mosque.

"Not very old. My grandfather pray here. People lived up here then, but no longer. Water go salt. Water go bad."

Near the mosque was a deep, masonry-lined well dating to Sabean times. Thousands of ropes hauling thousands of buckets had worn deep grooves in the lip of the well, once a protected, reliable water supply in the event the mesa was besieged.

As we worked our way south, Sirwah became less a forlorn ruin and more a remarkably well preserved evocation of Sabean splendor, superior to anything that has survived in southern Arabia. To me, its magic rivaled that of Petra in Jordan or Palmyra in Syria.

Not watching where I was going, I tripped and banged my knee.

"You be okay?"

"Most certainly!"

I'd been distracted by two pillars rising from what may have been a fallen temple. Fakhry had counted eight pillars, each inscribed with a single proper name. All I immediately saw was a single letter W, just below the point where a pillar had been fractured; it was likely a remnant of Fakhry's reported Afrawn pillar (pillar B). I recalled another, well-known case of named pillars in the Middle East. As described in I Kings, the entrance of Solomon's temple was flanked by "two bronze pillars . . . he set up the right-hand pillar and named it Jacin; he set up the left-hand pillar and named it Boaz."[3]

In the afternoon I would look for further fragments of pillars with names.

We walked across to a surviving corner bastion of the wall that had once encircled and protected the mesa. We inched our way to the edge. The bastion rose fifty feet from the valley floor, twenty-seven courses of finely fitted masonry topped by fifteen courses of crude rebuilding (in medieval times or later).

Turning east, Mana and I crossed the mesa to Sirwah's monumental Temple of 'Ilumqah. He scampered ahead; I paused, then paused again to take pictures and pencil notes. This was the grandest ancient structure I'd seen in all Arabia.

I passed pillars that once may have delineated an extended fore-

Southwest bastion

Temple of 'Ilumqah from the west

court and, skirting a second row of pillars, entered the temple's sanctuary. There was a sense of something indefinably awesome once here: solemn ritual, songs in a language we can read but cannot speak, oracles and divination, the offering of incense. Long rows of stone ibexes, the Sabeans' totemic animal, stood as mute witnesses.

The temple was a complex structure; it would take hours to grasp its design and layers of construction and use. What was immediately evident was that the eastern wall formed an imposing stone semicircle.

"Like moon?" I asked Mana, following the wall's curve with my outstretched hand.

"Moon, yes, I think so. And you see the moon too in the animals," he said pointing to the ibexes' crescent horns.

"Roof?" I wondered.

"No roof, so can see sky. The moon."

Here the Sabeans looked to the heavens and their astral gods. And here they commemorated the earthly and the brutal. An enormous stone slab—carved with the largest and longest known Sabean inscription—bisects the temple of 'Ilumqah. A "Text of Victory," it cat-

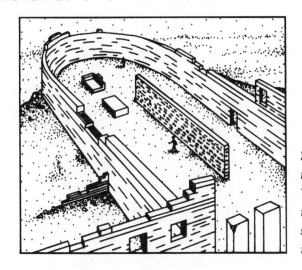

Sanctuary of the temple of 'Ilumqah (with medieval structures removed)

alogues the rapacious exploits of the mukarrib Karibil Watar I as he expanded the Sabean state in the late fifth century B.C. The inscription boasts of the looting and burning of far-flung towns and the wholesale killing and capture of their inhabitants.

Beyond its gruesome message, there was the question of the inscription's date. I reminded myself: the temple as I saw it was built in or shortly after Karibil I's reign, at least three hundred years after the biblical queen of Sheba. Nevertheless, the temple testified to the existence of an advanced civilization in an earlier era, for the skills needed to raise this monumental structure—quarrying and fitting great ashlars, engineering a curved casemate wall—were not easily or quickly acquired. Standing where I now stood, Ahmed Fakhry surmised that "if we examine the construction of the Temple, we see clearly that its builders had by that time mastered the art of building in stone, and before being able to erect such monuments they must have had long experience behind them, and their civilization must have been developing for several centuries."[4]

In the afternoon I'd return and spend several hours here. In this temple, better than anywhere else, I could touch the world of the Sabeans.

Overdue now at Sheik Ahmed's house, Mana and I left 'Ilumqah's sanctuary and walked from the mesa down to the valley floor. Looking up, I was able to grasp the temple's scale and appreciate its architectural integrity. Its great masonry curve had not a sag or crack, though shaken by countless rift-zone earthquakes (see plate 30).

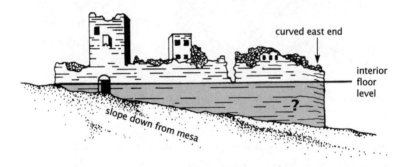

West-east cross-section of Sirwah's temple of 'Ilumqah

What struck me was that the temple's eastern wall was much higher than I had expected, for the sanctuary extended out over the sloping edge of the mesa. I counted eighteen courses of *exterior* masonry compared to four courses of *interior* masonry. That is to say: below the temple's floor level were fourteen courses . . . of what?

What was down in there, unseen? A shrine, a cave, a grave? Or just dirt and rubble fill? Back in 1947, Sirwahites confided to Fakhry that, though partly formed of natural rock, the al-Kharibeh mesa

. . . was made by magic in order to hide the treasures of Queen Bilqis; and I was told some stories of persons who had come especially to search for this treasure, using magic to help them, but had failed. As in other parts of the East, such stories usually end by relating that such treasures are decreed to await the coming of a certain lucky person, and can never by acquired by anyone else, either by force or by magic. They also say that some of the seekers come to actual harm, because the magic of the ancients, which protects the treasure, is more powerful than the magic of the present day.

I hoped that the certain lucky person would be an archaeologist, not a looter. And the treasure need not be gold and pearls; enlightenment would be reward enough.

Beyond what I saw and sensed in my morning at Sirwah, I knew of historical allusions to the site's glory. In *Al-Iklil* ("The Crown"), written circa 930 by Abu Mohammed al-Hasan al-Hamdani, a discourse on Sana'a and Ma'rib is interrupted with this claim: "None of their public buildings could be compared to Sirwah. Its fame has spread far and wide in Arab poetry. Little of it, however, has survived." Al-Hamdani quotes the earlier poet Amir al-Khaisey: "There were kings for the duration of one thousand months, and they built over Sirwah the 'House of the South Wind.' When the wind moves, this house moves with it. It is circular in shape, and has panes set in wooden frames. They glitter, a delight to the eye."

The House of the South Wind. How dazzling it must have been—and what a metaphor for the legend of the queen of Sheba, a legend that at once defines and obscures her. Tales upon tales offer glimpses of someone who may have been a historical figure, but they are clad, every one, with glittering panes—panes of wonder and imagination—that with their glare dazzle the eye, and in the cool shadows of the House, conceal her. We look in and can almost—but not quite—see her upon her renowned throne.

The House of the South Wind, indeed, is not a bad metaphor for all myth—and for the value of myth. Though "glittering panes" may distort and obscure the myth's underlying reality, they preserve that reality by wrapping it in fantasy, making it an entertainment. If it weren't for the appealing story—embellished by djinns, a talking bird, a glass floor—of the queen of Sheba and her journey to Solomon, she probably would have been lost to memory in a few generations, displaced, say, by the boasts of a later ruler, the lout Karibil Watar I. As it is, he's remembered only in a self-aggrandizing slab at Sirwah; she is known the world over, for hers is the better story.

At Sirwah there is nothing to be seen of the House of the South Wind, though traces of it may lie buried, as may more inscriptions, even a royal archive. Even a throne, an artifact at once impossibly romantic and quite to be expected. The mukarribs and kings of Saba certainly had one or more thrones, and either here or at Ma'rib one could lie hidden. In legend, the queen of Sheba's throne is described as carved with garlands of flowers bursting with countless jewels, its canopy soaring to the heavens. In reality—as suggested by archaeological fragments—it would have been an impressive symbol of her rich, powerful, and opulent civilization.[5]

As we shall see in the next and final chapter of this story, a queen

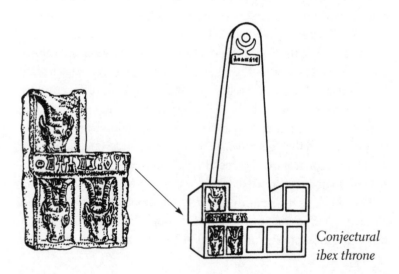

Conjectural ibex throne

of Ma'rib and Sirwah would have had good cause to arise from her throne and set out on a great journey. It would not have been the dreamy, mystical quest of which myth is so fond. Rather, it would be ordained by a sequence of very real, down-to-earth economic factors having to do with incense, camels, saddles, and ships.

Imbued with the power of her throne and kingdom, a queen of Sheba would emerge from a House of the South Wind (whether real, metaphorical, or both) and become that very wind, the desert wind rushing north to Jerusalem.

"Yellah, yellah . . . [We'd better get on with it]," urged Mana al-Nasirah. We had wandered through Sirwah long enough, and I had pushed my luck taking a great many pictures. I regretted this as, back at Sheik Ahmed's house, piratical Ali (supposedly on my side) confiscated my camera.

With a wave of his hand, the sheik indicated that I should come inside and join a half-dozen waiting Sirwahite tribesmen, their weapons leaning against his mifraj's white-plastered walls.

A goat had been slaughtered.

Lunch was tense.

Incidental small talk was punctuated by long pauses. I managed a few words complimenting Mana al-Nasirah and suggesting that he could have a role in what archaeology might do for Sirwah's ruins, which in turn could benefit the valley's economy. I have to admit I was distracted by framed photographs of Moammar Khadafy and Saddam Hussein hanging above my white-robed, cross-legged host. Following my gaze, Sheik Ahmed intoned "Saddam" and made a gesture as if Saddam were cutting someone's throat.

"Bill Clin-ton." He again drew his hand across an imagined throat. "Bill Clin-ton."

"La [no]," I gulped and continued, as offhandedly as I could, "Bill Clinton okay."

"Saddam Hussein number one! Bill Clin-ton number two!"

"La," I objected. "Bill Clinton number one!"

To my left Abu Salem visibly cringed. Had I really said that, when I could just as well have weasel-worded an innocuous reply? I detected, or hoped I detected, the sheik's flicker of a smile.

A young boy brought in an armload of qat branches. Wordlessly, Sheik Ahmed selected a first branch.

For the longest time there was only the rustle and tearing of leaves, the smacking of lips, the grinding of teeth.

Sheik Ahmed, a glaze stealing across his eyes, broke the silence to slowly and deliberately ask me, "Mr. Nich-olas, how *you* like to be *number one*, malik [king of] Sirwah? Stay here a week. More. Spend all the time you want up at the ruins."

"La, la," I replied, "I cannot be malik Sirwah. You are kind, too kind. There is only one malik Sirwah. You, Sheik Ahmed, you are malik Sirwah. Number one."

The most notorious kidnapper in all Yemen raised my 35-mm camera and, for seconds that seemed like minutes, peered at me through the viewfinder. He then lowered the camera and handed it to me. Immediately, guide Abu Salem was at my ear. "Khalas Sirwah?" he whispered.

"Khalas Sirwah," I agreed. I rose and shook hands with Sheik Ahmed. I thanked him for his hospitality, thinking he might not be that bad a man for a bad man (though I wouldn't suggest that Mr. Clinton go calling at his ruins).

By midafternoon, Abu Salem and I had made it back to Ma'rib and dropped off piratical Ali and our bodyguards. Soon thereafter we were on a paved highway hellbent for the Yemeni highlands, the Sana'a airport, and my flight home. We should have waited to join an armed convoy, but we didn't, for who, other than our host for breakfast and lunch, might we fear? In a little under an hour, we slowed, but not much, for a fork in the road where the Queen of the South would have headed north, bound for her fateful encounter with Solomon. Today the way she would have taken was blocked by two tanks and a dozen qat-stupefied soldiers. The tribes beyond, according to Abu Salem, seethed with discontent.

We veered left and, forsaking Sheba's route, raced on to the west. In silence, for I had no wish to distract Abu Salem from his driving.

As the Ramlat Sabateyn faded in the rear-view mirror and we switchbacked up to the Yemeni highlands, Abu Salem asked, "Habiby?"

"Habiby? What means 'habiby'?"

"Sirwah. You habiby this trip, go Sirwah?"

"I habiby . . ."

22

Sheba and Solomon

THE LIGHTS OF SANA'A fell away, and a full moon glided through silver-edged clouds as the night flight to Frankfurt headed north; in just over twenty hours I would be in Los Angeles, half a world away. Far below and long ago, Sabeans would have thanked 'Ilumqah if their caravan made it to the next sand-clogged spring.

I was relieved—and fortunate.

I was relieved to not be staying on as an involuntary guest of Sheik Ahmed. I was fortunate to have reached Sirwah and, on a larger scale, to have had the dumb luck to look for the queen of Sheba just when researchers had pushed her civilization back in time to the tenth century, the time of Solomon. With king and queen no longer separated by hundreds of years, their biblical meeting had a newly acquired ring of authenticity.

Clouds clinging to the Yemeni highlands were soon behind us, and below was the moonlit expanse of Saudi Arabia. I flipped on the overhead reading light and brought my tattered pocket notebook up to date. I jotted what nexts, what nows, such as taking a fresh look at I Kings 10 and also rechecking the Bible for allusions to Sheba beyond the confines of Solomon's court, which I did first, and which was to prove enlightening in an unexpected way. In more than a dozen instances, Sabeans are mentioned in genealogies in the book of Genesis, as traders and raiders, as tall, as rich with incense and gold. But they are rarely accorded more than a phrase, an aside. An argument for the Bible's authenticity, I thought: the Book was silent whereof it knew not. Subsequent historians—Herodotus, Strabo, Pliny, and others—gave us glimpses of that distant land, but only glimpses. The Romans may have coined the term *Arabia Felix* ("Happy Arabia"), but their maps were blank concerning how to get there and what to expect. It would fall to archaeologists—now and in coming years—to recover the Sabeans' lost world. Their efforts, still pioneering (a candle to what's been done in the classical world), have sketched in the Sabeans' rise to civilization—which, as we shall see, reached a turning point at the time of Solomon.

It is a story that begins with a blank slate, a slate wiped clean by the hand of nature.

Eight thousand years ago Arabia was a hell on earth. As far as is known, there was not a soul living in the peninsula and only the hardiest of plants and animals, for some twelve thousand years earlier the earth had wobbled on its axis—"Milankovitch forcing," the phenomenon is called—and that wobble had initiated the opposite of an Ice Age. In a swath of savanna lands circling the earth, air temperatures soared to 140 degrees Fahrenheit and higher. Clouds were driven from the sky. Across Arabia, a thousand lakes dissolved to dust, trees cracked and splintered, game died off. Neolithic man, if he was able, fled to the north and the less lethal Fertile Crescent.

Some eight to ten thousand years ago, the earth regained its composure, wobbling back to its former axis and offering the slate on which the Sabeans would in time write their rise to civilization.

The seeds of that rise were cast upon the desert when temperate breezes and seasonal rains encouraged a surprisingly rapid migration from the north of the adventurous, the dispossessed, and the misfits of the Fertile Crescent. Their passage is recorded in petroglyphs of the cattle they drove before them. These people fared well, and in less than two hundred years their campfires glowed across Arabia.

Scholars have tended to shrug off these settlers on the theory that only a much later migration—of considerably brighter stock—could have paved the way for an advanced state. But that is not so, it has recently been shown: the Sabeans were a home-grown civilization, their steps along the way now revealed and documented.

Far out in the dunes of the Ramlat Sabateyn, David Meltzer, Ricardo de Monte Rosa, and I had explored the pre-Sabean necropolis of al-Alam. We were awed by the mass of tombs and intrigued by the rock lines pointing to ancient sites—al-'Uqla, Timna', Ma'in— many miles distant. Dating to 3000–5000 B.C., al-Alam's diverging lines told us that there had been a trade in commodities such as salt, obsidian, and possibly incense through this area—and that its caravaneers were versed in navigating vast and shifting sands.

At desert-edge settlements of this era there is widespread evidence of croplands watered by the harnessing of sudden, frequently violent flash floods. Artificial irrigation was in place in 3200 B.C., and perhaps earlier. Scattered throughout what were in essence cooperative waterworks, individual families dwelt in circular huts built of loosely piled-up rocks, thatch, and unfired mud brick. As time went by, a dozen or so huts would cluster together, share common walls, and become hamlets, each with a population of no more than a hundred and each with an independent chief.[1]

Generation after generation, the forerunners of the Sabeans passed on what they knew of the stars and of survival in an arid land.

Centuries rolled by and little happened, other than a low-key transition from a Neolithic to a Bronze Age marked by the use of pottery and of tools fashioned of metal as well as stone. And at some point southern Arabians came to enjoy the fragrance of the burning sap of the gnarled trees—frankincense—and scrubby bushes—myrrh— that grew wild in surrounding stark hills. These people lived in isolation, but not total isolation, from their origins in the Fertile Crescent. As evidence of overland contact, a probable word for frankincense—*shim.gig*—appears on Sumerian tablets as early as 2350 B.C. Even earlier, a 2500 B.C. inscription tells of contact with *Saba.um* and *Gu.te.bu.um*, a possible first written reference to Saba and neighboring Qataban. By sea, foreigners skirted Arabia's shores, but it is doubtful that they ventured beyond the rugged coastal mountains. If they did obtain inland goods, the ships' crews bartered (or commandeered) them from coastal tribes, principally a group known as the people of Punt.[2]

Then, beginning in approximately 1500 B.C., a sequence of remarkable circumstances and inventions inspired the proto-Sabeans and Sabeans to stir themselves, to shake off their sun-baked somnolence.

A first and admittedly faint hint of change is that Egyptian king Thutmose III (reigned 1482–1450 B.C.) took as a wife Menwai, a foreign-named woman whose features look suspiciously southern Arabian.[3] As was the way of the ancient world, affairs of state and trade could well have prompted the union; the Egyptians may no longer have been able to freely sail down the Red Sea and help themselves to the riches of Arabia, but rather had to reach an accommodation with an indigenous culture that was growing in power and aware of the value of what they possessed—and what the Egyptians didn't.

At this time or soon after, southern Arabians acquired the hallmark of civilization and handmaiden of trade: a written language. Recently demonstrated to have been derived from Egyptian hieroglyphics, with Proto-Sinaitic as an intermediate step,[4] the letters of the Epigraphic South Arabic alphabet may indeed have made the leap from irregular squiggles to classic sophistication at the hand of a single individual, a lone genius calligrapher. The codification of an alphabet allowed accounts to be kept and settled on animal skins or palm stalks and trade goods to be sealed with stamped-in-clay monograms, some of which were quite elaborate.

Most trade would have been over short distances and cumbersome. Horses and asses could carry reasonably heavy loads, but they required near-daily watering. Such caravans couldn't follow a straight line across the desert; rather, they had to laboriously zigzag to take advantage of every possible spring, seep, and well.

As they dreaded the dried-up waterhole that could be their last, caravaneers glimpsed in distant mirages a curious, ungainly beast quite at home in dry lands. Sometime in the thirteenth or twelfth century B.C., the animal was captured and, over noisy objection, domesticated as a source of milk and flesh. It was considered useless as a beast of burden, for its great hump defied pack saddles and up-ended riders.

What revolutionized desert trade was a unique technological achievement: a workable camel saddle, a contraption that shifted the weight of heavy cargo from the beast's hump to its flanks. Where it was invented is unknown, but very quickly traders throughout the Middle East delighted in a creature that could carry five to seven times as much weight as an ass, keep up a steady pace of seven to eight miles an hour, plod on for days and even weeks without water, and then, in as little as ten minutes, replenish itself with upward of thirty gallons (increasing its body weight by a third). A camel's nostrils filtered sand, and the creature sweated only when near death. Caravan routes could now bypass water sources and strike out directly across the desert.[5]

To distant lands. To the great markets of the Fertile Crescent.

To the benefit of the Sabeans, enormous cargoes could now be borne by the cranky, haughty creatures with the terrible breath. A lucrative trade was in the offing—yet there appears to have been a threat. It is strongly implied in I Kings 9: 26–28, just before the arrival of the queen of Sheba. A boastful account relates how the kings of Judah and Tyre, Solomon and Hiram, had established Ezion-geber (near present-day Eilat) as a Red Sea port for their merchant fleet. Its ships could have had little other purpose than sea trade south along the coasts of Africa and Arabia.

The extent and ownership of this fledgling merchant marine is unstated (the ships could have been Hiram's, the port Solomon's). But, large or small, it challenged the Sabeans to reach beyond their borders and establish a rival overland trade route. They had the goods, the transport, the demand. Everything was in place. But if they didn't move quickly, Judah and Tyre could sail to the shores of Arabia and, with agile tongue and heavy hand, undercut Sabean control of trade to the north. Arabia's incense and spices were essentially valueless at their point of origin; fortune would smile on whoever initiated and controlled the trade, either by sea or land.

I Kings 10 tells us it was the queen of Sheba.

Sheba, daughter of the royal cities of Ma'rib and Sirwah, would have ridden north sometime between 955 and 935 B.C. Her caravan would have traveled in the cool of winter or, if urgency required, braved the summer's heat, resting by day and marching the night through by torchlight. The journey, never to be easy, was a journey of heat, thirst, danger, and boredom. The camels rocked interminably, sandstorms shot eyes with blood, and there were lurking jackals four-footed and two. Bandits could appear from nowhere, fall upon a meandering caravan, and be gone.

The journey, though, would not have been unrelentingly grim. As still and lifeless as the desert can be by day, at night all manner of creatures creep out from beneath its stones, from the boles of its shrubs and cacti. Night birds sing; the moon shines upon the dunes. At Yathrib (now Medina), Dedan, Taima', Qurayya, and other oases, there would be shade and dates and cool water—as well as tolls to be negotiated and paid. A single no-account tribe could block the journey, and if they so chose, annihilate a caravan. The raiders would have an advantage of numbers, access to water, and both natural and man-made fortifications. Sheba's caravan was vulnerable. What wit and tenacity she must have had to negotiate the nearly 1,500-mile (2,400-kilometer) length of Arabia.

After sixty or more days in the desert, the queen of Sheba's caravan, heralded by a golden plume of dust, would have been sighted by outlying Israelite settlements, possibly the fortlets of Horvat Halluqim or Mesed Hatia in the southern Negev. Word of the caravan would have been rushed to Jerusalem and the court of King Solomon.

The best and only real guide to what happened next is the account of I Kings 10, its thirteen lines and seven hundred and thirty-three words (quite long compared to inscriptions of the day). At first reading the account is bland, and if one isn't conscientious, it is easy to skim through it. On further examination, the passage has subtle and not so subtle crosscurrents that tell us something of sex, of the art of the biblical deal, and of the era's power and dominion, both temporal and divine.

> 1 The fame of Solomon having reached the queen of Sheba . . .
> she came to test him with difficult questions.

It has been long assumed that the queen's "difficult questions" were riddles, that she might take Solomon's measure. There are precedents for such a reading, going back to a Sumerian account of a trade mission posing riddles to Enmerkar, lord of Aratta. Yet the queen of Sheba would hardly have traveled from afar to engage in the day's equivalent of parlor games. Though she may have tried Solomon with a riddle or two, her "difficult questions" almost certainly bore on long-range trade. Considering the geographical separation between Saba and Israel, what else could have been of issue? To this point, we immediately learn what she brought to the meeting.

> 2A She brought immense riches to Jerusalem with her, camels
> laden with spices, great quantities of gold, and precious stones.

Biblical verse is partial to groupings of three, and here is a precursor of the "gold, frankincense, and myrrh" brought to the infant Jesus by the Wise Men—one or more of whom may have been Sabean.

Note a shift in emphasis: in the tenth century B.C., frankincense had yet to become the most-sought-after and exorbitantly expensive of spices; we can only assume that Sheba's "spices" included incense. A millennium later, however, two of the three precious gifts were without doubt incense.[6] Note as well that the items Sheba brought were raw commodities—trade goods—not finely wrought gifts.

2B   On coming to Solomon she opened her mind freely to him.

It may not be readily apparent, but here is the part about sex. The giveaway is the Hebrew verb evoked in "On coming to." It is בּוֹא (bw'), and in a dozen similar contexts in the Old Testament it describes "entering a tent or house for sexual purposes."[7] Or as one lexicon discreetly defines it, "Coire cum femina." In Jerusalem it would seem that Sheba willingly accepted Solomon's embrace—and it is even possible that the two were overcome by the passion and poetry of the Song of Songs. On a pragmatic level, theirs would have been an affair of state; in the ancient Middle East, tribal alliances were customarily sealed by intimate relations, often by marriage. Whoever credited Solomon (in I Kings 11:3) with eight hundred wives and two hundred concubines (but only two children?) was praising his prowess in the throne room more than in the bedroom.

3   and Solomon had an answer for all her questions, not one of them was too obscure for the king to expound.

Whatever was at stake—riddles, trade, an alliance—was settled, with Solomon taking a remarkably passive role in the proceedings. Did he have nothing to ask or demand of Sheba? Wasn't he the one with the vast territory, power, and panoply? Why, yes, the next lines effuse:

4   When the queen of Sheba saw all the wisdom of Solomon, the
5   palace he had built, •the food at his table, the accommodations

for his officials, the organization of his staff and the way they
were dressed, his cup-bearers, and the holocausts he offered in
6 the Temple of Yahweh, it left her breathless, •and she said to the
king, "What I heard in my own country about you and your wis-
7 dom was true, then! •Until I came and saw it with my own eyes I
could not believe what they told me, but clearly they told me less
than half: for wisdom and prosperity you surpass the report I
8 heard. •How happy your wives are! How happy are these servants
of yours who wait on you always and hear your wisdom!"

What had come over the queen? Or, more to the point, what
came over the passage's writer? Having crossed an immense landscape, at times as harsh as hell itself, all she could do was gush to the
point of breathlessness (or, in the King James translation, "until
there was no life left in her"). Over what? She carried on about what
was for dinner, the palace fashions, cup-bearers, the happiness of
wives, the contentment of the staff.

Something is askew.

There is an agenda at work here, though its precise nature is uncertain. One possibility is that this was not Sheba but the pagan goddess Astarte speaking. The writer—or, more likely, a later redactor—
may have conflated the two women and then put both in their place
by dazzling them with the wonders, real or imagined, of Solomon's
court. (More on this when we consider the next line.)

A further cause for the hyperbole may be an uncertainty, a ner-
vousness on the part of the narrator as to who was the more powerful,
Solomon or Sheba. The lines assert that it was Solomon. But archaeology now suggests it was Sheba—and, as proof, offers a comparison
of their cities.

With daunting mountains to the west and scorched sands to the
east, Saba was a state of secure, splendid isolation. Ma'rib, Sirwah,
and lesser settlements were lush oases watered by elaborate networks

of canals. The Sabean economy rested on a dependable agricultural footing; the trade in incense and spices was a windfall.

Solomon, by contrast, faced enemies large and small: Canaanites, Edomites, the Israelite malcontents Rezon and Hadad, even his brother Absalom. The surrounding Judean hill country had few natural resources and was better suited to goats than to crops.

Though Jerusalem in Solomon's time was a crossroads, it was a backwater crossroads, a cluster of single-story dwellings and tents, with perhaps a palace and temple on a lonely ridge. A town of no more than 12 acres with a population of 900 to 1200.

The walls of Sheba's Ma'rib enclosed 250 or more acres. At the time the "Garden of the Two Paradises" could support a population of 20,000, perhaps more.

The queen of Sheba would have wielded considerable temporal power, the first—and only—woman in the Bible to do so. In contrast, Solomon may have been a king, but he was a king of not all that much—at best a confederation of tribes scraping by in the Judean hills. The phrase "hill-country chieftain" is used more and more to define his role. This comparison may cause some to wince, yet it is supported by an emerging understanding of the tenth-century B.C. archaeology of both Yemen and Israel. Legend as well makes the point: Sheba's Kitor (Ma'rib) is a work of stone and sweat, with its centerpiece an enormous dam; Solomon's Jerusalem is illusory, conjured by storytellers, the construct of djinns.

A queen for whom everyday items are the greatest luxuries.

A king and his people singing of goats and bees, milk and honey.

But how well the Israelites sang—and that was to make an enduring difference. Sheba may have surpassed, even overwhelmed, Solomon in material wealth, but what, we may ask, endures when dams burst and palaces crumble?

The Israelites' tradition of storytelling and reflection on their pastoral world transcends anything in the inscriptions of the Sabeans or,

for that matter, anything else in the world of the first millennium
B.C. Their prose and poetry were—and remain—suspenseful, soaring, scented with imagery. (Just take an hour and read Ecclesiastes
and the Song of Songs.) The Israelites may have lived in mud and
crude stone villages, but they dwelt as well in wondrous cities of
words—words that told of their history, identity, moral travails, and
God, Yahweh.

> 9 "Blessed be Yahweh your God who has granted you his favor,
> setting you on the throne of Israel! Because of Yahweh's ever-
> lasting love for Israel, he has made you king to deal out law and
> justice."

Sheba praised Solomon's God—and that was not as implausible as
it seems, for she may have observed that the Israelites worshipped a
god not unlike her 'Ilumqah, a god ubiquitous in southern Arabia.
The Sabeans, like the Israelites, may have been drawn to the idea of
a single god just as Egyptians in the reign of Akhenaton had been
four centuries earlier. Life in the desert could have fostered such
a belief. Perhaps it is the clarity of the air, the austerity and power
of the landscape—or, conversely, the lack of dells and dark places
haunted by the multiple deities of forest and jungle-evolved religions. The face of Yahweh—and what we know of Sheba's
'Ilumqah—was the face of the desert: angry but also comforting, at
once merciful and unforgiving.

Indeed, Sheba and Solomon's deities share a Semitic source. In
the Old Testament, God is both Yahweh and El (*'el* or *'il(u)*), a word
likely meaning "to be strong," and possibly an ancient designation
for the quarter phase of the moon. 'Ilumqah is derived from the same
root, and may mean "He is strong." There is a distinction, though.
'Ilumqah was never more than a moon god; the God of the Israelites
became the *creator* of heavenly bodies and therefore superior to any
of them, the moon included. This is demonstrated in the book of Job

when Yahweh metaphorically "covers the moon in full, his mists spread over it." There follows a warning against having one's heart stolen by "the glow of the moon as it walked the sky."

Still we should note that, appreciative as Sheba may have been, "your God" did not become "our God." She stood by 'Ilumqah, the moon walking the sky. She arrived and left Jerusalem a pagan, though a "righteous pagan" in the view of later Christian theologians, for she affirmed the worthiness of Yahweh in a world of many gods jostling for power. That affirmation would have been appreciated, for in Solomon's day and for centuries to come, the idea of a single God did not yet have a firm hold on the Israelites; the biblical injunction is "Thou shall have no other gods before [more important than] Me," not "Thou shall have no other gods but Me."

In this stamp-of-approval context, Sheba—by intent or coincidence—may reflect the goddess Astarte (known to the Israelites as Ashtoreth), Yahweh's great rival and ultimately a seducer of Solomon. Sheba-Astarte, then, would be a queen of heaven come to earthly Jerusalem to smile on Solomon and validate both him and his God—even if in so doing she would be coopted and robbed of her power (as investigated in Chapter 11). This is an intriguing theory, for there is something goddesslike about Sheba sweeping into Jerusalem. Nevertheless, the association of Astarte with Sheba as the *prime* motivation for the text is doubtful. An association of queen and goddess makes better sense as an *afterthought*—a gloss or burnish added by a redactor—to a very real meeting, in which the issue at hand was earthly high-stakes trade.

As the story of Sheba and Solomon moves to its conclusion, it is muddled by two non sequitur lines that make far more sense if they are inserted just after I King 9:28 (just prior to Sheba's arrival). It is odd that this apparent transposition was never corrected; perhaps it was left to remind the reader that if Solomon and Hiram of Tyre so chose, their nascent merchant marine could challenge Sheba's caravans. To clarify what was transpiring between Sheba and Solomon, the text in question is crossed out.

10 And she presented the king with a hundred and twenty talents of gold and great quantities of spices and precious stones; no such wealth of spices ever came again as those given to King
11 Solomon by the queen of Sheba. •And the fleet of Hiram, which carried gold from Ophir, also brought great cargoes of
12 almuggim wood and precious stones. •The king made supports with the almuggim wood for the Temple of Yahweh and for the royal palace, and lyres and harps for the musicians; no more of this almuggim wood has since come or been seen to this day
13A •And King Solomon in his turn, presented the queen of Sheba with all she expressed a wish for, besides those presents he made her out of his royal bounty.

With the extraneous lines excised, we see clearly what was in play. The goods Sheba brought to Jerusalem are reiterated, and their value underscored: 120 talents of gold—weighing between 3,000 and 5,000 pounds (experts disagree)—as well as precious stones and more spices than would ever again come the Israelites' way. And these are more than generous gifts; they are commodities in want of distribution. It is in fact doubtful that all the goods stated were from Sheba's own country. There is gold in Yemen, but she could well have acquired more on her way north at the workings of the Mahd al-Dhabab—"the Cradle of Gold"—in the mountains behind Mecca. As for precious stones, there are few in southern Arabia. What Sheba conveyed to Solomon may have come from Ethiopia (amber and garnets) to the west or from as far away as India (agates and emeralds) and Afghanistan (lapis lazuli) to the east.

Even some part of the queen's spices may have been Sabean imports that were then exported. The finest incense trees—those producing "silver" frankincense—grew wild in the Dhofar Mountains of

Oman, east across the desert from Saba. In any case, Sheba rode onto the biblical scene as a consummate merchant queen. Her caravan overflowed with riches—and if they came from somewhere other than her own country, Solomon didn't need to know that.[8]

To counter Sheba's riches, what could Solomon offer? Materially, not a great deal; I Kings 10 mumbles, "those presents he made her out of his royal bounty." But under the category of "all she expressed a wish for," Solomon the hill-country chieftain might have guaranteed her caravans passage through Israelite territory to the lucrative markets of Damascus, Sidon, and Tyre, and to the port of Gaza, with its access to Mediterranean sea lanes. Though the details of their agreement are (and probably always will be) a matter of speculation, we can be sure that if he chose, Solomon could effectively stand in her way, for she was a long way from home.

But he didn't. He acceded to "all she expressed a wish for," words that may have an implication beyond the mercantile. An affair of state could have been sealed by an affair of the heart, as suggested in the earlier overtone of Sheba "coming to Solomon." (And Ethiopian tradition offers us Menelik, a child born of this union in the course of Sheba's journey home.)

13B   Then she went home, she and her servants, to her own country.

The Bible and all but a few legends agree that after she left Jerusalem, the queen of Sheba never again matched wits with the Israelite king or enjoyed his company.

Before returning home, she could have visited other Middle Eastern kingdoms, but perhaps she did not, instead trusting Solomon to be a capable intermediary on her behalf. Already he had initiated a new order in his region, a change from the days of Judges, when "everyone did as he pleased." If he could join a dozen fractious tribes in an alliance, he would be a good, even ideal partner for the Sabeans' designs for long-range trade.

That trade endured and prospered for well over twelve hundred years.

What is striking about all this is a tilt in power from Solomon to Sheba—which really should come as no surprise. In nonbiblical legend, her power and dominion—and their threat to assumed male superiority—was a long-running, ever-present theme. Even in the Bible, I Kings 10 not only states but restates the queen's great wealth. The only discordant note is her slavish praise of Solomon's cup-bearers and his court, an apparent thumb-on-the-scales effort by the narrator to lend weight to Solomon.

What *is* disquieting about Solomon and Sheba has nothing to do with Sabean power; it is the current and noisy assertion of Minimalist scholars that all this—including the very existence of Solomon— is a fantasy created several centuries later to provide a meaningful heritage for the sons and daughters of Israel. Where is there mention of Solomon, they ask, beyond the pages of the Bible? Where is the archaeological record of his Jerusalem? Rationales have been offered in answer: archaeological evidence may have been destroyed by later quarrying or may be concealed beneath private homes whose residents are reluctant to have their living room floors ripped up. But shouldn't there be *something* left of tenth-century Jerusalem, if only a single homely shard?

We must be patient and remember: absence of evidence is not evidence of absence.

A few years ago, the existence of Sheba's Ma'rib (and Sirwah in her era) was equally in question. Yes, there was a Sabean civilization, and yes, it was grand, but it was of no consequence before 600 or 700 B.C. This appraisal was widely agreed on—and, as is now known, totally in error. Ma'rib in the tenth century was a large, prosperous, literate city, with a stock of luxury goods that would sell well in markets to the north, which were accessible through Israel by the grace—and profitable participation—of its king.

In these circumstances, the queen of Sheba would hardly have been a fantasy wafting out of the desert or merely an incarnation of Astarte smiling on Solomon from the heavens (though the biblical passage has an overtone of this). She would have been an earthly emissary pursuing the economic interests of her powerful—and very real—civilization. With that civilization now coming into focus, the biblical account of Sheba and Solomon assumes the markings of a real event—and by association gives Solomon credibility as a historical figure.

It's the age-old story of a good woman redeeming a man of dubious reputation.

There is little question that more information about Sheba and Solomon stands to be revealed. Jerusalem still has its secrets, and serious, long-term excavation in southern Arabia has barely begun. Along the route between the two kingdoms, a fortuitous wind could expose a revelatory cache of caravan dispatches. Or a London auction house could gavel down an artifact "from the Estate of an Anonymous Collector" (that is, looted) that sheds light on king or queen.

And hidden in a desert that looks for all the world like any other desert may be a find that archaeologists dream of.

It is improbable. It could happen tomorrow.

Knifing through sand, a trowel could strike stone—and the tomb of the queen of Sheba.

Epilogue: Sheba's Tomb

At the end of life there is nothing but the whisper of the
desert wind, the tinkling of the camel's bell.

—Bedouin saying, an elegy for the Sabeans

IN THE END, the incense that offered the Sabeans their ascendancy
and glory sealed their fate, in a way that no one could have imagined
or foretold.

In temples from Rome to Babylon, clouds of frankincense had
long risen heavenward as "food for the gods." In marble palaces
and villas its liquefied resin perfumed silk-gowned women; in far-
flung provinces Roman legionaries used frankincense to tend "broken heads . . . and to bind bloody wounds and assuage malignant
ulcers about the seat." In a rite at once sacred and profane, prodigious quantities of frankincense were heaped upon funeral pyres of
the wealthy. Pliny tells us that an entire year's output of Arabian
frankincense bore Poppaea Sabina, Nero's wife, to the gods. Weary
of the indulgences of the imperial world, Pliny sardonically observed, "It is the luxury of man, which is displayed even in the paraphernalia of death, that has rendered Arabia thus happy."[1]

As Pliny wrote this, the new religion of Christianity was infiltrating
the Roman Empire, and with it the idea that the dead should be
committed to the earth intact rather than cremated. The reason for
this change was the new religion's promise of physical resurrection
of the body and life everlasting. Was it not enough to ask God to reas-
semble a jumble of bones? Why make things difficult by reducing
the body to ashes? (And for the impatient, the more intact the body
the swifter the heavenly ascent.)

When the Roman Empire became the Holy Roman Empire, cre-

mation gave way to burial and the demand for frankincense plum-
meted.

In southern Arabia, the Sabeans fell back on their agricultural
economy, but even that was in trouble. At Ma'rib, the silt deposited
by close to three thousand years of yearly flooding had raised the
level of their farmland almost to the level of their highest canals, so
gravity-fed irrigation would soon be impossible. Heavy autumn rains
in A.D. 340 breached the Great Dam at Ma'rib, where a sluice-tower
inscription relates that extensive rebuilding required a work force
of 30,000 laborers. And then, sometime between 600 and 630, the
Great Dam irreparably burst.

Once-shining Ma'rib and Sirwah and the kingdom they ruled became the haunts of lizards, the halls of screech owls. And so wrench-
ing and complete was the demise of the Sabeans' proud civilization
that *the location of their royal tombs—all of them—was lost to memory.* To this day the whereabouts of the graves of one hundred and fifteen mukarribs and kings is a mystery.

Wherever the graves lie hidden, the likelihood is that they were
long ago broken into and looted. Ancient Arabia was rife with grave
robbers. A major calling of the god Attar (an incarnation of Astarte)
was to wreak havoc on disturbers of the dead, and with the advent of
Islam, the Koran curses looters a hundred times over. Despite this,
there was thrill and profit in finding and robbing sepulchers. In
his treatise on the ruins of Yemen, circa 920, Abu Mohammed al-
Hamdani relates:

When my grandfather was governor of al-Yaman he used to ran-
sack the Jahilaya [pre-Islamic] tombs to acquire their treasures . . .

Breaking into what seemed like a cave . . . I came upon a tomb of
ibn al-Yaman on which was an inscribed stone . . .

. . . the spade hit a sealed iron coffin . . . In it lay an old man whose
hair and beard were as white as hyssop and his body decayed. He

was wrapped in a fine garment and by his head was the following inscription, "I am Junaydah ibn al-Junayd . . . I lived a hundred years only to become what you behold. O fie on life and on those who desire it; woe to them who fall victims to its lures."[2]

In these lines al-Hamdani gives us a good idea of what would be found in a Sabean royal tomb: a coffin with accompanying grave goods and a moralizing tablet identifying the deceased. This form of interment has been verified by the discovery of scattered nonroyal Sabean graves, except that their epitaphs favor curses against grave robbers over moralizings. Often there is an indication of the deceased's everyday life in the form of a relief of hunting, plowing, or some such.

In the early 1950s a team headed by Wendell Phillips happened on a first hint of a Sabean royal burial. Under the gaze of hostile officials, they cleared the forecourt of Ma'rib's Mahram Bilqis. No interments there. They then shifted their attention to a small four-columned structure outside the temple, huddled against its eastern wall. In Gus van Beek's measured words it was

a mausoleum constructed of well-cut limestone on an almost square building plan . . . Around the walls are tiers of ten burial compartments for a total of sixty bodies, and at least two chambers below the floor . . . Whether these compartments were used for inhumations or served as ossuaries is not known; the fact is that few bones have been found in any South Arabian tombs but this may be due to ancient plundering. Grave goods were put in the tombs, and offerings were placed outside the burial chambers, indicating a belief in an afterlife, and the continuing reverence for the dead by the community. We can reasonably assume that these burial customs and beliefs existed at the time of the Queen of Sheba, and perhaps one day archaeologists will be fortunate enough to find her own tomb.[3]

Before circumstances forced the team to flee across the desert, they found—and left behind in the mausoleum—two fragments of what was possibly a single stone slab. Only later did anyone realize their importance. They were inscribed ". . . *Yata' ['a]mar Bayyin, son of Yakrubmalik Watar*" and ". . .]*Sumhu'alay Ya[nuf. . .*"⁴ These were names traditionally reserved for Sabean royalty. Was the mausoleum, then, a royal tomb? Regrettably (the team being literally under the gun at the time), no one had a clear recollection of the circumstances of this discovery. What appeared to be two pieces of a broken grave marker might instead be fragments of a nonfunerary inscription that happened to mention royalty.

From the 1950s on, archaeologists visited the Mahram Bilqis, though only to look. No permits to dig were granted. Wistfully, they wondered what lay buried within and without the temple's ellipse. Though the surrounding terrain was to the eye even and unbroken, it had a curious dark gray stain. This could be evidence of disturbed earth, where a deeper stratum had long ago been brought to the surface by human activity. Or the stain could be meaningless.

In the early 1990s, Yemen's level of chaos eased, and a proposal was made to the government jointly by the Deutsches Archäologisches Institut and the American Foundation for the Study of Man (established by Wendell Phillips and after his untimely death kept alive by his dedicated sister Merilyn). An American team would excavate within the ellipse; the Germans would dig the stained area beyond the walls. The proposal was accepted, and, under the direction of Burkhard Vogt, the Germans arrived first on the scene—and were stunned and elated to find, just inches below the gray-stained surface, roof slabs of the first of an untold number of multiple-story, labyrinthine mausoleums. Here was a sunken city of the dead, crisscrossed by lanes, with staircases leading to entrances at different levels. Though looters had long ago left the interior of the tombs a jumble, they were filled—packed by the thousands—with shrouded Sabeans. Many were dust and bones, others well preserved.

Vogt's associates, Holgar Hitkin and Iris Gerlach, recovered and catalogued a host of grave goods: miniature animals, sacrificial plates, Egyptian-style figurines and scarabs, and beauty aids. Wherever death might take them, Sabean women would have their cosmetic bowls, eyeshadow, and lipstick. There were inscriptions, none royal, though one identified a servant of two mukarribs. Haunting alabaster faces gazed from niches in limestone stelae.

Vogt's team is uncovering what by any measure is an enormous cemetery. Twenty thousand or more interments may lie in an ellipse embracing the temple of the Mahram Bilqis, itself an ellipse.

Where, then, might the Sabeans' royal tombs be? Logic would suggest that they are close to—or even within—the temple's walls. At an archaeology conference, I queried the leader of the American team, Bill Glanzman.

"Logic?" he repeated and laughed. "Logic? From the Sabeans? You anticipate anything they've done—*anything*—and you can be

Mahram Bilqis funerary stelae

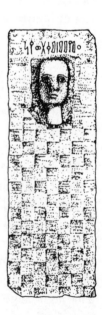

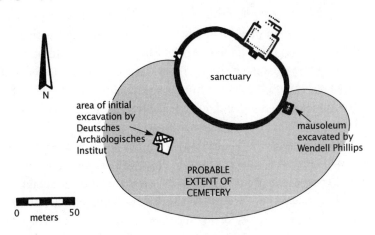

Mahram Bilqis necropolis

certain it'll be different. They'll fool you every time. You have an expectation? They'll defy it."

"But there appears to be quite a cemetery . . ."

"Oh, yes, but I doubt if there were any burials within the temple
walls. There is an old Semitic proscription against that. At Jerusalem, for instance, you find no biblical-era burials within the Old
City walls."

"No exceptions?"

"Logically, no."

"But about logic, you said . . ."

"Yes, I did. So I suppose there *could* be tombs. I hope not," he said
with a furrow of his brow. "They're a nightmare. To dig them properly slows you down, way down. Takes forever. We'll have problems
enough without tombs."

"But if it was the tomb of a certain queen?"

"That," he said with a grin, "would be different. Oh, my, would
that be different!"

He filled me in on his preliminary survey of the Mahram Bilqis and the many challenges his team would face in clearing its vast oval. We discussed what I had long heard from other archaeologists: that to focus on finding the queen of Sheba's tomb would be to almost certainly guarantee failure. It's an archaeological axiom that if you set out to find a specific something, you almost never do, but if you keep an open mind and don't get agitated, you are very likely to come upon something equally important.

We agreed that this was the way it should be, or at least we pretended that it was. The queen of Sheba's tomb could be within or near the Mahram Bilqis, or it could be up in the mountains at Sirwah, possibly beneath that site's Temple of 'Ilumqah. Or her final resting place may be lost for all time. Even if the royal tombs of Saba are found, it might be impossible to sort out which was hers among the resting places of a hundred and fifteen mukarribs and kings, their queens, children, and retainers.

We don't even know her name . . .

And yet . . .

An inscription discovered either by accident or by design could give a name to a queen watched over by the god 'Ilumqah as she journeyed to a faraway land. There could be a low relief of a woman on a camel. And what a find it would be if it mentioned ᙢ◉ᙢ𝌑ᖾ∏ᖾ𐊌1ᖾ —"Solomon son of David."

The American and German teams closing in on the mysteries of Ma'rib cannot help but ask, as the Yemeni poet Naswan al-Himyari asked eight hundred years ago,

> Where are the kings? A thousand kings have sunk into the dust and now rest under the ground in vaults and in tombs.
> Their monuments all through the land still tell of their deeds, and their fame is spread like the wafting fragrance of amber.
> Or where indeed is Bilqis, ruler of a renowned throne, whose palace once surpassed all others?[5]

APPENDIXES

NOTES

BIBLIOGRAPHY

ACKNOWLEDGMENTS

INDEX

APPENDIX 1

The Names of Sheba

"Sheba" is a land, a tribe, and a state—but *not* a queen's proper name. The queen of Sheba is like the queen of England. As for her actual personal name, different accounts offer:

Aurora Consurgens "The Rising Dawn," the queen of Sheba's designation in alchemical lore, which also invokes her as "the South Wind."

Bal'amah or Bashama A less commonly used Arabic alternative to Bilqis. This is probably a female version of the biblical "Balaam who journeyed to the tents of Israel and was overwhelmed by them and their God." Like Sheba, Balaam was left breathless. Both "Balaam" and "Bal'amah" may spring from the three-letter root *blm*, which has been taken to signify "incense" ("balsam" is derived from this root).

Biliqisu Sungbo A west African folk figure identified with the queen of Sheba. Pilgrims still venerate her grave in a Nigerian jungle clearing.

Bilqis (or Balkis) The Arabic—and most common—name for our queen. A little derisively, it has been suggested that Bilqis derives from the Greek word for "concubine"—*pallakis*—which was Hebraicized as *pilgesh*, then translated into Arabic as "Bilqis." In an alternative interpretation, the name is derived from a variant of the root *blm* (as with Bal'amah, above).

Eteye Azreb This is "Queen of the South," as rendered in Ge'ez, Ethiopia's ritual language.

Habashia A mysterious east African figure whose name may be a variant of "Abyssinia" (an ancient name for Ethiopia).

Makeda Our queen in Ethiopia's national saga, the *Kebra Nagast*. The name is derived from the shared Arabic and Ge'ez *malkat*, "queen."

Malkath Her name in Jewish folklore, derived from the Hebrew *malkah*, "queen."

Nikaule (or Nikaulis) Her name in Josephus's *Antiquities of the Jews*. This may be a corruption of Nitocris, a name shared by Babylonian and Egyptian queens in the *Histories* of Herodotus. Or Nikaule could be an elaboration of Nike, the classical world's Winged Victory.

Queen of the South The appellation for the queen of Sheba in Matthew 12:42 and Luke 11:31.

Sybilla A name inspired by the notion that she was a sybil, one of a class of pagan oracles who advised the Babylonians, Egyptians, Greeks, and Romans.

Beyond this, the queen of Sheba has been confused with the New Testament's Candace (derived from *kandake*, a Nubian term for queen mother); Zenobia, queen of Palmyra; and Lilith, in Judaism a witch of witches (as recounted in Appendix 3).

Chronology of the Sabean (Sheban) State

c. 6000 B.C.	Arabian peninsula repopulated following 12,000 years of extreme aridity.
c. 5000–3000 B.C.	Burials in the Stone Age necropolis of al-Alam, where rock lines may have guided early caravans as they traded in salt, obsidian, and possibly incense.
c. 2500–1700 B.C.	Egyptian expeditions to the land of Punt, recently identified as the coastal plains of southern Arabia.
c. 2400 B.C.	Artificial irrigation under way at Ma'rib.
c. 1500 B.C.	Just west of Ma'rib, dam built to completely block the Wadi Adana.
c. 1400–1200 B.C.	Development of Epigraphic South Arabic alphabet and script.
c. 1300–1100 B.C.	Domestication of the camel in southern Arabia.
c. 1200 B.C.	Earliest known formal rulers of Saba; beginnings of mercantile state.
c. 1100 B.C.	Invention of the camel saddle.
c. 1000 B.C.	Sabean caravans initiate long-range incense trade.
c. 980–950 B.C.	Earliest and latest possible dates for reign of King Solomon of Israel.

c. 970–940 B.C. Earliest and latest possible dates for queen of Sheba's reign, which may be linked to rule of one of the following Sabean mukarribs (dates estimated by Kenneth Kitchen):
Yada'il Yanuf, son of Karibil, c. 990–970 B.C.
Dhamar'alay, c. 970–955 B.C.
Yakrubmalik, son of Dhamar'alay, c. 955–940 B.C.
Yada'il Bayyin I, son of Dhamar'alay, c. 940–925 B.C.

c. 955–945 B.C. The queen of Sheba journeys north to Jerusalem.

c. 715 B.C. Construction of the final Great Dam of Ma'rib.

c. 690 B.C. Enlargement of Ma'rib's city wall to its maximum perimeter.

650–350 B.C. Construction of temple of Mahram Bilqis (overbuilding earlier structures).

c. 500 B.C. Temple of 'Ilumqah at Sirwah under construction (probably on site of earlier structures).

300–200 B.C. Decline of Sabean state; rise of rival state of Ma'in to the north.

A.D. 50–500 Rise of Christianity; decline of southern Arabian incense trade.

A.D. 340 Breach and repair of Ma'rib's Great Dam.

c. A.D. 615 Irreparable collapse of Great Dam.

1843 Joseph-Thomas Arnaud is first Westerner to visit Ma'rib.

1869 Joseph Halevy is first Westerner to visit Sirwah.

1882–94 Epigrapher Eduard Glaser makes four trips to Ma'rib to copy and translate numerous Sabean inscriptions.

1947   Ahmed Fakhry is first modern archaeologist to investigate Ma'rib and Sirwah.

1951–52   American Foundation for the Study of Man, led by Wendell Phillips, undertakes excavation of Mahram Bilqis but is forced to flee Yemen.

1997   Deutsches Archäologisches Institut team, led by Burkhard Vogt, begins excavation in and around Ma'rib, focusing on necropolis outside walls of Mahram Bilqis.

1998   American Foundation team, led by William Glanzman, surveys interior of Mahram Bilqis, with long-term excavation planned for the next decade.

APPENDIX 3

Demon Sheba

In pursuing the queen of Sheba, my hope had been to research her legend and then put it behind me so that I might focus on a flesh-and-blood historical queen. I thought I had achieved this—only to be increasingly troubled by portrayals of her as a creature of darkness, a vamp, a demon queen. A touchstone of this image is Karl Goldmark's opera *Die Königin von Saba,* in which she drives her hapless lover to his death and threatens Solomon with a "dread hour of vengeance." And in Gustave Flaubert's *The Temptation of St. Antony* she mercilessly torments the poor monk, then skips away along the shore of the Red Sea.

Our queen is creepily grotesque in *The Labyrinth of the World and the Paradise of the Heart,* a 1623 allegorical novel by the Prague writer Comenius (Jan Amos Komensky). When Solomon, accompanied by his sages, approaches Sheba's throne, he discovers her veil to be a spider web. She is Wisdom become Vanity. Her cheeks are painted with cracked red rouge; her hands are scabby and her body bloated; she reeks of asafetida.

From the 1600s to the present, in literature and lyrics, the flames of hell often lick at Sheba's soul.

What was the source of this portrayal? At first I had no idea, but I began to suspect that a malign Sheba might derive from some lesser-known folklore of Judaism, Christianity, or Islam. Christianity, I thought, would not be the most likely source, given her pious role in medieval legend and Renaissance art—but what about that goose foot? It was uncomfortably close to the devil's cloven hoof, and in England of olde, Sheba appears as a hobgoblin "Devil's Dame." As far as Islam and its storytellers were concerned, Sheba was one of their own, and the Koran quotes her acceptance of a single God: "Now I submit with Solomon to Allah, Lord of the Creation." Still, she was the daughter of a djinn.

As for Jewish folklore, the few relevant texts available in English were difficult to comprehend, if not impenetrably opaque. They contained allusions to Kabbalist texts written in Aramaic, centuries after that language ceased to be spoken, apparently to preserve secret knowledge. I'm by nature suspicious of secretive activities and lore. And I learned that a Kabbalist connection lurked behind Flaubert's bizarre queen of Sheba. The author was acquainted with one Eliphas Levi, a Kabbalist devotee in the occult revival that infatuated France in the nineteenth century.

Needing guidance, I spoke with several Reformed and Orthodox rabbis in Los Angeles and found that they regarded the story of Sheba's visit to Solomon as a straightforward encounter, a court affair of an emerging Israelite monarchy. Beyond that they were surprised that anyone would think to demonize the queen of Sheba.

I sought rabbis dwelling on the further mystical shores of Judaism, and in the United States and then Israel, I found several who allowed that they could answer my questions—but wouldn't. I traveled to the Israeli mountain town of Safed, a center since the sixteenth century of the swirling and flashing mysticism of the Kabbalah, which speaks of angels wrestling with demons to wring order from chaos. Did Sheba figure in this struggle? When I phoned ahead from Jerusalem, a Safed sage promised me insights, but when I tracked him down he said simply and firmly, "I cannot light a lamp for you."

I realized that to learn anything of the demonization of the queen of Sheba, I would have to do it on my own. Finding a piece of the puzzle here, another there, I came to accept that my picture would never be complete; I sensed a body of lore transmitted orally, never committed to paper.

I ultimately understood that the rabbis I had badgered had reason to be evasive. My apologies if I have misinterpreted their closely held beliefs.

Scholars who have touched at all on the dark side of Sheba cite the *Targum Sheni,* of the late fifth century A.D. This curious and rambling commentary on the book of Esther unexpectedly veers from the character of Esther to that of Sheba, who is depicted as a woman assuming a role that is rightfully a man's. Sheba is bold, she is manipulative, she is hardly the Jewish ideal of a dutiful wife or nurturing mother. She is the woman men have in mind when they mutter, "Who does she think she is, the queen of Sheba?" Yet in the *Targum Sheni* she is hardly demonic. That was yet to come. Researching ever more obscure texts, I found, was like groping my way through an old-time carnival's House of Fright. At first, as with the *Targum Sheni,* what I found would scare only the terribly timid or little children.

But wait.

"My mother!" shrieks the turbaned man, the object of his cry the queen of Sheba. But who is he? In the early medieval manuscript *Pseudo ben Sira* (*pseudo* because the document is attributed to a fictitious Babylonian courtier), the turbaned man is the wicked king Nebuchadnezzar. Such a mother-son relationship is historically impossible, of course, for Nebuchadnezzar reigned in the fifth century B.C., long after Sheba. Even so, in the text's margin a notation by one "Rashi" confirms that Solomon disastrously erred when "he had intercourse with her [Sheba] and she gave birth to Nebuchadnezzar who destroyed the temple." Were it not for this villainous offspring of the queen of Sheba, Solomon's temple might yet stand, and there would have been no heart-wrenching exile to Babylon, Nebuchadnezzar's land!

And so Sheba is cast . . . as the cause of unending sorrow to the people of Israel.

And Sheba is a sorceress or, less charitably, a witch. In the words of one of the few scholars who have plumbed her dark side, "a witch of the filthiest sort."[1]

This is revealed in the *Zohar* ("Book of Splendor"), the core text of Kabbalah. Allegedly compiled to preserve privileged knowledge after the final destruction of Solomon's temple, the *Zohar* was in reality composed in a stylized form of Aramaic by the Spanish Kabbalist Moses de Leon around A.D. 1280. In a passage in Book III, Sheba plies Solomon not only with riddles, but with a pointed query as to the ways of witchcraft. She is obsessed by the magical serpents said to have sprung from the bones of the heathen seer Balaam. The passage reads:

> We [the Kabbalists] have found in the Book of Ashmodai [a sorcerer at Solomon's elbow] which he gave to King Solomon that anyone who desires to make powerful enchantments, if he knows where the rock where Balaam fell, will find there snakes formed from the bones of that wicked one, and if he kills one he can make certain enchantments with its head and others with its body, and others again with its tail, there being three kinds in each one. One of the questions the Queen of Sheba asked Solomon was how to take hold of the bones of the serpent of three enchantments.[2]

The text that follows promises that whoever possesses these serpents will be rendered impervious to all weapons, for they cast a spell on all who might wield them. In recounting this, the *Zohar* states, "There are secret mysteries which should not be revealed," but then capitulates with ". . . only in order that the Companions [fellow Kabbalists of Moses de Leon] here should know the hidden ways of the world I have revealed them." That Sheba was a witch or worse is implied in a subsequent book of the *Zohar*, in a dense and convoluted passage determining that she must surely be a שָׂעִיר (se'ir), a category of demon that rises from the desert and works mischief in towns and cities.

First witch . . . now demon.

The ill a demon Sheba is capable of is revealed in *Sefer Pardes Rimmonim*, an elaboration of the *Zohar* by the Spanish rabbi Moses Cordovero. He portrays her as spreading diphtheria; he asserts that she *is* diphtheria. Her great and evil moment will come when she stalks the streets of Rome at the End of Days.

As if this weren't enough, there is a final fright in the mystical darkness of the Kabbalah. Cordovero goes on to equate Sheba with Lilith, Adam's legendary wife before Eve, who left her husband, refused the order of God's angels to return, and became a witch of witches—a demon queen, a harlot, vampire, the devil's grandmother . . . and his wife.

Did the rabbi Cordovero dream up this identity? It's doubtful. There is evidence that a Sheba-Lilith amalgam had long been brewing as a tenet of the Kabbalah and Jewish mysticism. The notion hovers between the lines of the *Zohar*. And there is a *targum* (commentary) whose lost original could date to Old Testament times. It facilely translates Job 1:15 as: "Suddenly, Lilith queen of Smaragd ["emerald" in Greek] fell upon them [Job's oxen and donkeys] and carried them off." In truth, the line reads: "Sabeans swept down on them and carried them off." There is no mention *at all* of Lilith.

The Sheba-Lilith equation would explain, at least in part, why I had knocked for naught on the doors of synagogues in Los Angeles, Jerusalem, and Safed. Lilith is as frightening as a woman can be, seething with vengeance and unbridled promiscuity. Entering the bedrooms and dreams of men who sleep alone, she couples with them; she stalks mothers at the hour of childbirth; she strangles infants in their cradles. She is a monster and she is beautiful, with beautiful hair. By day Lilith's refuge is a cave on the shore of the Red Sea, set in a wasteland of thorns and nettles, drenched in blood.[3] As Isaiah 34:14 describes:

Wild cats will meet hyenas there,
the hairy demons will call to each other,
there too will Lilith take cover
seeking rest.

But she doesn't rest. She consorts with lascivious demons and gives birth to endless *lilim*, demon children, even though God punishes her with the loss of a hundred a day. And every night she rages forth to seduce mortals and kill their children.

Tangled in Lilith's thicket, the queen of Sheba was reviled by Kabbalists near and far. A Polish manuscript begins, "As is well known, the queen of Sheba is a demon" and blames her for blocking the light of the moon as she wings on evil errands. She is a "mother of demons" in an Italian text, and in Germany she is featured in "Namen der Schadenstifter und Draussenbefindlichen"— lists of "troublemakers and outsiders"—which were compiled from the fourteenth century well into the nineteenth.

In the Rhineland city of Worms, a Kabbalist by night in his attic is reputed to have called forth a riotously dressed Sheba, along with her clanging and clanking army. "They danced and they jumped and they went away," the account relates, specifying that this feat must be done alone, in a clean and tidy room, either after Shabbat or on a Wednesday night, by reciting a precisely worded incantation that has since been misplaced. Just as well.

The spiral of superstition that demonized the queen of Sheba and Lilith was just that, superstition, and was apart from mainstream Jewish belief. But what a pervasive superstition! Throughout Europe, protection against Lilith was sought in the magic of amulets bearing the likeness of the three angels dispatched by God to wrest the demon queen from her Red Sea lair. The angels failed in that mission; the amulets apparently gave them a second chance to still her power.

*Amulet to ward
off Lilith*

Another bit of magic was the belief that tying a red ribbon to a crib or baby carriage would keep Lilith, merged with Sheba, at bay. A few days after I learned of this superstition, I happened to be returning to my Los Angeles office after lunch with an old friend, Gary Moscowitz. Services were letting out in the neighborhood's several synagogues, including one given to Kabbalah. The sidewalks were teeming with men in prayer shawls, modestly dressed wives, and children, many in baby carriages. No ribbons on the first few, but then I spied one across the street and another coming our way. I hesitated, but Gary did not. "Excuse me, ma'am," he forthrightly began, asking if Sheba or Lilith meant anything to the parents.

Guardedly the mother and father exchanged glances and, after some hesitation, replied that they were aware of both women—and the protection offered by a red bow. But their child's bow, they assured us, was decorative, nothing more.

I hoped so. I'd come to admire Sheba as the very antithesis of a Lilith. A woman with eyes shining, not as coals but as stars.

Alchemical Sheba

In the sixteenth and the seventeenth century in Europe, there were not one but two fantastical queens of Sheba. Along with a Kabbalistic queen of darkness there was a transcendent, alchemical queen of the dawn. Demon and angel, she was both. And nowhere is this duality clearer than in the brooding, magical city of Prague.

A white mist rose from the river Vltava and swirled about skeletal trees as I wandered the City of the Dead, the cemetery of old Prague's Jewish Josefov Quarter. Weatherworn headstones canting upward through a blanket of fallen leaves recorded the births and deaths of Kabbalists whose arcane writings had significantly contributed to the demonization of the queen of Sheba.

From the Josefov Quarter I walked west. As I neared the river, mist became fog and muffled whatever now haunts the city ("Sex, drogy a rokenrol," a splash of graffiti suggested), freeing me to imagine the nexus of sixteenth-century Prague: the mad and melancholy King Rudolf II. A gloomy soul, Rudolf dressed only in black, never laughed or even smiled, and was obsessed by the occult. He sought the counsel of Kabbalists—and alchemists. Some two hundred alchemists, it was reported, were at one time or another in his employ.

Wiping my glasses to read the blue enamel street signs, I found my way to the steps to Rudolf's Hradcany Castle, curving upward into foggy white nothingness. The stairs led to a plaza and a gate, then another gate, where two workmen were resetting paving stones. One stamped his feet and the other repeatedly sneezed as they directed me down an unsigned alley to a small door at the base of a stout, round tower with a conical cap. This was the Mihulka, the castle's Powder Tower. It was unlocked, and a spiral of stone stairs led up to where in recent centuries gunpowder was stored and cannon-balls cast. Prior to that, the tower housed the laboratories of mad Rudolf's court alchemists. Their rusted iron furnaces, their Latin-labeled crocks, their long-nosed glass flasks, had been saved and were on display.

Studying this arcane paraphernalia, I thought of how desperate the craft of a practicing alchemist must have been. Rudolf II's court drew them from all Europe. They were of two persuasions: the de-luded and those who would delude. The latter—mountebanks and rogues—cleverly and not so cleverly falsified the transformation of base metals into precious substances. They would, for example, the-atrically stir a liquid in a hot crucible with a hollow wand sealed by a wax plug; when the plug melted, it released hidden ounces of gold. Scrutinized by King Rudolf and his court physician, quite a number of alchemists were unmasked as charlatans and either dropped into "the Jug," as the castle's oubliette was known, or thrown to the bears in the dry moat below the Powder Tower.

On the other hand, earnest alchemists—true believers—struggled for days and months and years to bring about their sublimations, cal-cinations, cerations, lixiviations, and transmutations. It was rumored that in the Powder Tower they were on the verge of producing riches beyond imagining. Their elixirs could bend moonbeams; they lit fires in the firmament; they possessed toads that could make emer-alds explode. In reality, fumes and heat yellowed the alchemists' bloodshot eyes, which "dripped red as mulberry juice." Their lungs were clogged and their minds and bodies poisoned. Yet in their delir-ium and sweat, they believed success was within their reach. Their books, in Arabic, Hebrew, or, most commonly, Latin, told them so: *De Alum et Salubus; Ars Arcani; Rosariius Minor de Alchemia; Tractus Aureus de Lapide; Artis Auriferae.*

In the worn and stained parchment pages of these books, a woman both beautiful and wise beckoned them on: the queen of Sheba.

An Arab alchemical sage, Abufalah of Syracuse, who was consulted and trusted by all who followed him, related that the queen of Sheba had inherited the philosophers' stone—the talisman that can transform anything into anything—from a mysterious first husband. He had apparently rattled around their palace, gathering up everything "made of copper, tin, iron and lead, and all kinds of metals that were in the house, and he cast them into a fire, and then he scraped off a little from that Stone over the metals, and out came pure gold from the fire, purified seven fold.[1]

This may have been the world's first alchemical act, which the queen of Sheba duly appreciated. "She took the Stone and put it in her treasury to be her greatest treasure and the most precious thing." Later she gave the stone to her second husband, King Solomon, who was said to have confirmed the gift in his book *Sefer haMaspun* ("The Compass").

Solomon was celebrated as the king of alchemy and Sheba the queen, whereupon she became identified with several key elements and forces. Illustrating this, *De Alum et Salubus* ("The Book of Alum and Salts") offers the formula:

$$X\ \dagger\ \delta\ \Upsilon\ \frown\ D$$

That is, copper + salt + quicksilver + urine ⇒ sublimated ⇒ purified silver.

Of these substances, salt, quicksilver, and silver were *all* believed to be blessed and symbolized by Sheba. Further, it was she who mystically assured the critical act of sublimation; in *De Alum et Salubus* she is quoted, "I am the mediatrix of the elements, making one to agree with another." In this role she was known, from the earliest days of alchemy, as "the South Wind," the wind that stirs and transforms elements, the wind of alchemical and spiritual wisdom.

And she was also *Aurora consurgens,* "the dawn rising." Alchemists and their apprentices labored through the night so that a critical step in their conjurings would occur at dawn, a moment of gladness when "all evil odors and vapors that infect the mind fade away and weaken." That magical moment was symbolized by Sheba: "I am the most prudent virgin coming forth as the Dawn, shining exceedingly elect as the sun, fair as the moon, beside what is hid within."[2]

In this dizzying alchemical syzygy, the queen of Sheba is held to be ever pure and glorious, virtuous and innocent. She is "the whole magistery of the work." No one in Rudolf II's tower—or wherever alchemical furnaces glowed or retorts bubbled—would remotely

Solomon and Sheba as the King and Queen of Alchemy. She stands upon the moon, symbol of silver. (from Rosariius Minor de Alchemia, Berne, 1545)

think of darkening her reputation. That would be an act as witless as transmuting silver back to salt or gold to lead.

I descended from the Powder Tower thinking of King Rudolf's two hundred alchemists—as odd a legion as would ever be beholden to Sheba—and how they ultimately and inevitably failed their deranged king. But they never forsook their mystical queen.

Off to the west, a scythe of silver light burned through the day's mist, and the faint strains of a ragtag street band drifted up to Hradcany Castle from somewhere in the city below, oompah with hints of rokenrol.

Had I exhausted Sheba's lore and legend?

By no means, for myth is ever-inventive and clever in its conceits, even though its elements may have little to do with any conceivable reality—as in Kabbalah, as in alchemy.

I felt the way the late-sixteenth-century alchemist Johannes Grasseus must have, when he concluded a paean to the queen of Sheba: "This is the chaste, wise and rich Queen of Sheba, veiled in white. No human heart can sufficiently investigate all this."[3]

Notes

1. In the Monasteries of the East

1. The name Saba—or Sheba in English—appears in various contexts in the Middle East. In this case, it is the proper name of the monastery's sainted first abbot and has no connection with the biblical queen of Sheba.
2. Jerome Murphy-O'Connor, *The Holy Land: An Archaeological Guide from Earliest Times to 1700*, p. 43.
3. There is a history of unruly or naughty monks being exiled to St. Katherine's. A pilgrim in the 1800s described the monastery as "a kind of asylum for the rascally priests of the Greek Church." In the early 1920s, intrepid traveler Augusta Dobson saw the monastery as "a sort of penal settlement, where monks guilty of criminal offences, those troublesome to the Church by reason of unorthodox opinions, or lunatics were sent, to keep them safely out of the way."
4. Lesley Hazleton, *Where Mountains Roar*, p. 76. For a wry discussion of the personalities of the monks of St. Katherine's, see John Lloyd Stephens, *Incidents of Travels in Egypt, Arabia, Petraea, and the Holy Land*. Originally published in 1837, this stands as just about the best-ever journal of travels in the Middle East. Stephens sums up, "So far as I could judge, they [the monks] seemed perfectly contented; but they were, for the most part, mere drones and sluggards, doing little good for themselves

or others, and living idly upon the misapplied bounty of Christian pilgrims. I do not mean to say that they were bad men. Most of them were too simple to be bad; and, if there was evil in their nature, there was no temptation to do evil; and after all, the mere negative goodness which does no harm is not to be lightly spoken of, in a world so full of restlessness and mischief as this of ours" (p. 198).

2. I Kings 10

1. In our filmmaking, the Jerusalem Bible was a prime resource. Newly translated in Israel under the direction of Père Roland de Vaux, it is notable for its accuracy and its sense of the language and poetry of the original Hebrew and Greek.

3. Songs of Sheba

1. Although a number of scholars doubt the presence of scribes and the keeping of administrative records in Solomon's era, a convincing case for this is made by David W. Jamieson-Drake in his *Scribes and Schools in Monarchic Judah*.
2. Flavius Josephus, *Josephus: The Antiquities of the Jews*, p. 180.
3. Scholars have scoured the Song of Songs for topical allusions that would allow them to date the poems. Most of what they've found points to a period immediately after the Exile (the Jews' captivity in Babylon beginning in 587 B.C.). Some allusions appear older, as in the line "Lovely as Tirzah are you, my darling" (6:4). Tirzah was a short-lived capital of the house of Israel that rose and fell close to the time of Solomon. The upshot is that *fragments* of the work might have been composed in Solomon's time—and extensively reworked centuries later.
4. This and the following quotes are from Marie-Louise von Franz, ed., *Aurora Consurgens*, pp. 33, 53–55, and 145–47. The manu-

script of the *Aurora* was discovered in the Bibliothèque Nationale in Paris by psychoanalyst Carl Jung. Textual allusions date it to about A.D. 1240–1280.

5. The other queens who appear in the Bible—Esther, Vashti, sixty or more in Solomon's harem, and the Candace in the New Testament—are all wives of kings with no apparent temporal power.

6. Sixtus of Sienna, *Bibliotheca Sancta* (Frankfurt, 1575), p. 331.

4. The Desert Queen

1. The word "Semitic" was originally a benign academic term, coined in 1781 to describe the descendants of Noah's son Shem, that is, those who live in the Middle East, Arabs and Jews alike.

2. George Sale, ed., *The Koran*, p. 322.

3. This is the explanation by medieval commentator Ahmed ibn Mohammed al-Tha'labi of a difficult line in the Koran (quoted in Jacob Lassner, *Demonizing the Queen of Sheba*, p. 193).

4. Abu Mohammed ibn 'Abd Allah Kisa'i, *Tales of the Prophets*, p. 308. There is wonderful lore describing Solomon's journeys by carpet and the virtues and follies he observed. At one point he descends to dine with the King of the Ants (thus giving the Koran's chapter on Sheba its name) and learns "that the King of the most numerous army on earth is content to dine on the leg of a locust." Another time he prowls a city destroyed because its people thought themselves the equal of God. (This city was almost certainly inspired by legends of the lost city of Ubar— which a team that included Kay and me discovered in the Sultanate of Oman in 1990–1991.) Solomon beholds an inscription that bears the name of Ubar's most notorious king, Shaddad ibn 'Ad (see Louis Ginzberg, *The Legends of the Jews*, p. 571).

5. The "Garden of the Two Paradises" harks back to the Koran, which relates: "For the natives of Sheba there was . . . a garden

on their left and a garden on their right. We [God and the Prophet Muhammad] said to them: 'Eat of what your Lord has given you and render thanks to Him' . . . But they gave no heed. So we unloosed upon them the waters of the dam and replaced their gardens by two others bearing bitter fruit, tamarisks, and a few nettle shrubs. Thus we punish them for ingratitude: for we punish the ungrateful" (Sura of Sheba, 34:15–16). As elsewhere in the Koran and the Bible, scores with the wicked are settled— be they the inhabitants of Sodom and Gomorrah, Ubarites, or the entire world before the Flood.

6. Al-Kisa'i writes of Solomon's ring set with a seal carved at the beginning of time: "This seal was Adam's while he was in Paradise; but, when he was expelled, the ring flew from his finger and returned to Paradise, where it remained until Jibril brought it down to Solomon" (*Tales of the Prophets*, p. 301). Later the ring was snatched by the djinn Sakhr the Rebellious, a forerunner of Mephistopheles. Sakhr thereupon transformed himself into Solomon and wreaked havoc upon his harem and treasury. The real Solomon—now changed into Sakhr's form—wandered through his kingdom. When he told people he was the king, they called him a liar and threw dung at him. Reaching a riverbank, he begged a fish from a fisherman, only to be rebuffed. But then God cast compassion into the fisherman's heart, and he grudgingly offered Solomon one of his catch. Lo and behold—Solomon's stolen ring glittered in the guts of the fish! (How it got there is another story.)

7. The insertion of direct quotes from the Koran (here Sura 27: 30) in these tales is customarily shown by the Arabic equivalent of italics. That such quotes are few and far between in the legend of Solomon and Sheba indicates how much the tale evolved in the centuries after its revelation in the Koran in the late 600s A.D.

8. Flax is bent by the wind. It is woven into clothing for the poor

and shrouds for the dead. Birds feed on its seeds, and the plant's fiber is plaited to make fish traps.

9. To puzzle out the Lot family tree, see Genesis 11–19.
10. Angelo S. Rappoport, *Ancient Israel: Myths & Legends*, p. 124.
11. Abu Mohammed ibn Jabir Tabari, *The History of al-Tabari*, vol. 3, p. 152.
12. In al-Tha'labi's genealogy, the king Sharahil—who is unrelated and evil in most accounts—is her father. In that case she might have acceded to the throne by heredity rather than by assassination (not as good a story but perhaps closer to the truth).

5. With Eyes Shining As Stars

1. Paul F. Watson, "The Queen of Sheba in Christian Tradition," p. 138.
2. In this sculpture Moses has horns, a result of the Vulgate Bible's mistranslation of "the face of Moses radiant" as "the face of Moses with horns." And why, one might ask, is the queen of Sheba in the company of Moses? The answer lies in a tangent of her legend in which she is mistaken for Moses' second wife, Miriam.
3. A shift of foot from that of a beast to that of a bird may have been abetted by a German monk's scribal error in which *pes asinus* (ass-footed) was rendered as *pes anserinus* (goose-footed).
4. Honorius Augustodunensis, "De Imagine Mundi," p. 110.
5. An excerpt from a devotional poem cited in James B. Pritchard, ed., *Solomon and Sheba*, pp. 136–37.
6. Jacobus's tale was told and retold and inventively embroidered. An Ethiopian account entitled *The Thirteen Pains of the Cross* relates that before coming to Jerusalem, the queen of Sheba killed an evil serpent, and its splattered blood raised an ugly, hornlike growth on her leg. But when her leg bumped the tree spanning the pond, the horn fell off. Astounded by this miracle,

Solomon carried the wood to his temple, where he and the queen each placed a coin on it and called down a curse on anyone who might steal the money. Following their lead, Solomon's twenty-eight royal successors also placed coins on the wood, so that ultimately there were thirty coins—which were stolen to pay Judas for his treachery!

7. True Cross cycles were promoted by the Franciscans, then powerful in northern Italy. After the Crusades, the order had been given custody of a number of holy sites in Jerusalem, to the chagrin of dispossessed Muslim landowners. Anxious to promote the legitimacy of their claims, the fathers seized upon the *Legenda Aurea*. The legend of the True Cross, they found, could be divided into fifteen scenes, and to their delight thirteen of them took place in contested Jerusalem.

8. Jacobus de Voragine, *The Golden Legend*, vol. 4, translated by William Caxton, p. 170. In a variant of the *Legenda Aurea*, the queen tells Solomon the same thing, but later, "upon her return to her own country she [Sheba] wrote to Solomon that upon this tree [bridging the pond] would one day be hanged the man whose death would put an end to the kingdom of the Jews" (*The Golden Legend of Jacobus de Voragine*, translated by Granger Ryan and Helmut Ripperger, p. 270).

Knowledge of a text that inspired a painter can considerably enhance our understanding of Christian art. Leonardo's *Last Supper*, for instance, takes on new meaning if one knows that the painting depicts the moment when Christ tells his Disciples that one of their number will betray him before dawn.

9. The appellation "queen of the South" is confusing in that Sheba's city is frequently given as "Kitor, to the East." An explanation for this is that the Bible's "east" often means far away—as far as the beholder stands from the rising sun. A familiar instance of this is the allusion in Genesis to "the land of Nod to the east of Eden" (4:16).

10. The role of the queen of the South in the Last Judgment, as one might expect, is soft-pedaled in contemporary Christian thought. It's not a favorite of Bible study groups. In churches that calendrically recite the Gospels, the passage is read only once a year, to the few who might gather for Evensong on the third Wednesday in Lent.

11. Throughout Europe, a number of black Virgins have *Nigra sum sed formosa* inscribed beneath their feet—"I am black but beautiful," the queen of Sheba's entrance line (in medieval perception) in the Song of Songs. Such are the black Virgins enshrined in Rome's oldest church, Santa Maria in Trastevere, and in Sicily's sanctuary of the Madonna Nera of Tindari, the island's most popular place of pilgrimage. I visited the Madonna Nera and learned that she had arrived in a raging storm, when a ship from the East went aground on a nearby shore. Only by offloading her crate could the vessel be refloated. Today in her opulent church, the blind remove their smoked glasses; crutches are laid aside. A *Registry of Miracles* lies open. Floating high above the main altar, the Madonna Nera wears not a crown but a cylindrical cap typical of the East; her rose cape is covered with flowerlike stars. Depending on the light and angle of view, her dark almond eyes are stern, alarmed, or haughty— but hardly compassionate. They gaze across time, their intensity defying their imprisonment in wood, plaster, and paint. She is more a queen of the East—and South—than of the West. *Nigra sum sed formosa.*

12. The dynamic of a strong Sheba and a weak Solomon is repeated in the glass and statuary of a number of European cathedrals. At Chartres it is reflected in the symbolic figures crouching beneath their feet. Sheba's is a muscular, pugnacious fellow; Solomon's is a simpering little gnome, so weak that a pedestal, not the gnome, bears the corpulent king. Solomon gazes off into space, studiously avoiding Sheba's sidelong glance.

6. Touched by the Queen

1. Prior to Handel, several settings for the biblical Song of Songs, notably by Palestrina and Boyce, may have portrayed an unnamed queen of Sheba. Bach's Cantata no. 65 is titled "From Sheba Many Men Be Coming," but what he had in mind was "Three kings with incense, gold and myrrh, from afar. Allelulia!"

2. This and the following quotes are from Karl Goldmark, *Notes from the Life of a Viennese Composer*, pp. 83–240.

3. In a review as excessive as the ballet, a correspondent for the *New York Times* wrote, "The final orgy of the thousand-odd people on the stage at La Scala works up into a deafening tumult of sound and paroxysm of rhythm that finds a par only in the Dionysian climaxes of the *Sacre du Printemps*. Respighi has pounded out this uproar with an insistence little short of sardonic fury . . . At the Scala premiere it brought the audience to its feet in a frenzy of excitement that burst into an interminable ovation."

4. Barnum and Bailey's *Tribute of Balkis* featured Sheba's name in Jewish and Arab folklore, evidence that someone had done a modicum of research. The title may also have been chosen to distance the offering from the previous (and tattered) John Robinson production.

5. Handwritten recollections of Chester Pray's campfire talk and testimony regarding subsequent events are filed under case no. 484 in the Inyo County Courthouse, Independence, California.

6. Though it was believed lost, I discovered a sketchy report written by Goldfield embalmer Frank T. Dunn, which I reviewed with pathologist Richard Horowitz of Cedars-Sinai Hospital in Los Angeles. There appear to have been two discrete wounds. Horowitz suspected murder.

7. Concern for Chester Pray's demise faded as, in July of 1913, a

relentless heat wave consumed the region. In Death Valley the mercury topped 129 degrees for five consecutive days, then edged up to 135 (in the shade!), the hottest sustained temperature ever recorded anywhere on earth.

8. *Inyo Register*, Feb. 26, 1914. The conclusion of this article indicates that Jack Salsberry may have consorted with Diamondfield Jack Davis, a "walking arsenal" known to carry a brace of revolvers, a Bowie knife, and a sawed-off shotgun under his signature long black coat. If Salsberry had any reservations about dry-gulching Chester Pray, Diamondfield Jack would be the man to help him out—and cut himself in on the Queen of Sheba mine.

9. Betty Blythe did not lightly assume Sheba's crown. "Such a woman," she felt, "was Joan of Arc, Madame de Maintenon, Schumann-Heink in our time. Women of Sheba's type formed stepping stones in woman's progress. She was the first suffragist. Put on a desert isle, Sheba would build a hut—not of reeds—but of flowers, preferring to die rather than not to express herself in those things that make for color, the bloom and the music of life" (*Movie Weekly*, Nov. 19, 1921, p. 11).

10. Film historian Kevin Brownlow has searched without success for a print of Edwards's *The Queen of Sheba*, as has the director Blake Edwards, J. Gordon's talented grandson. All that survive are posters and a tantalizing sheaf of production stills.

11. A 1959 movie, *Solomon and Sheba*, had its own share of tragedy. Rehearsing a sword fight, Tyrone Power, playing Solomon, was felled by a heart attack at the age of forty-four. Much of the film was reshot starring a bewigged Yul Brynner, which allowed director King Vidor to use Power's wide shots. Like J. Gordon Edwards, Vidor never made another film.

12. Gustave Flaubert, *The Temptation of St. Antony*, pp. 84–89, abridged.

13. This and the following quotes are from Thomas B. Aldrich, *The Queen of Sheba*, pp. 57–58 and 72.

7. O Jerusalem!

1. Melville, *Journal of a Visit to Europe and the Levant*, p. 154.
2. Murphy-O'Connor, *The Holy Land: An Archaeological Guide*, p. 36.
3. The Roman-Jewish historian Flavius Josephus described Sheba as "a woman, queen of Egypt and Ethiopia; she was inquisitive into philosophy, and one that on other accounts also was to be admired" (*Antiquities of the Jews*, p. 180).

8. Looking for Solomon

1. Julius Wellhausen, *Prolegomen zür geschichte Israels*, p. 322.
2. A fine example of concocted history is the *Legenda Aurea* of Jacobus de Voragine, discussed in Chapter 5. The book's preposterous tales, sanctified by the medieval Church, were ridiculed by the Renaissance.
3. Two years later, in 1911, Temple Mount archaeology hit a low ebb—and came to a sudden and lasting halt—when, acting on the "telepathic guidance" of a clairvoyant, Captain Montague Brownslow Parker stole by night into the Dome of the Rock and battered away with a sledgehammer at the marble cover of its "Well of the Souls," attracting the attention of an Arab watchman and, within hours, all Jerusalem.
4. Scholars generally agree that in the form we know it, the book of Kings was compiled no earlier than 583 B.C., the year the Jews exiled to Babylon returned to Jerusalem—and needed to codify their beliefs and understand their past.
5. Other examples of biblical quirkiness that could have been—

but weren't—edited out: the reference to gods, not God, in Genesis 6:2–4; God called "Satan" in I Chronicles 21:1; the weird "blood bridegroom" story in Exodus 4:24–26; and in Judges the wretched story of an innocent woman cast to a lusting and murderous mob (20:4–6).

6. Yigal Yadin, *Hazor: the Rediscovery of a Great Citadel of the Bible*, p. 202.

7. Israel Finkelstein, "The Archaeology of the United Monarchy: An Alternate View," p. 185.

8. Finkelstein holds that "a full-blown state is characterized by a well-stratified society, one directed by a specialized public administration led by a ruling stratum which extends beyond the immediate kinship circles of the ruler. Writing systems are characteristic of full-blown states as are organized industrial production and the erection of monumental structures that serve both propaganda and legitimization goals as well as practical functions" ("State Formation in Israel and Judah," p. 39). In Finkelstein's view, Jerusalem met these criteria a century or even two *after* Solomon's reign.

9. Zabibi and Samsi

1. In both Hebrew and Arabic *Bir-Sheba* can be taken as "the well of Sheba." Prior to my journey, I had asked a couple of scholars about this. "Interesting, you may be onto something," said one. The other suggested I look at Genesis 21:25–33, in which it is evident that Beersheba was actually *Bir-sheeva*, which meant either "the well of the seven" or "the well of the oath"—referring to the oath confirming a treaty between Abraham and Abimelek the Philistine.

2. Arabist Nigel Groom suggests another possibility: "Perhaps he [King Solomon] was just bewitched by the daughter of a north

Arabian group of Sabeans who were passing through with a trad-ing caravan" (letter to the *London Times*, May 17, 1997).

3. Our investigations were focused only in part on the queen of Sheba. Our broader scope was the sweep of civilization in northern Arabia from earliest times on. Martha Joukowsky was particularly intent on learning more about the empire of the Nabateans—stretching from north of Medina to Damascus—that from the second century B.C. to the second century A.D. dominated the incense trade.

10. Further Suspects

1. As Joe Zias had pointed out in Israel, the Bible "has its feet very much on the ground." Once an event was set down, later scribes and redactors made few changes in its essential content. There was embroidery, to be sure, but it stopped well short of fabrica-tion.

2. Harry St. John Philby, *The Queen of Sheba* (published posthu-mously), p. 35.

3. Hinting of a southern Arabian queen of Sheba, the Bible offers a clue that at first passed me by. It was not a "Eureka, this is it!" clue, but one worth considering. Both Matthew and Luke al-lude to the queen of Sheba as "the queen of the South." It hap-pens that a common Hebrew word for "south" is יָמִין , *ymyn*. That is, Yemen. Could "the queen of the South" have been a queen of Yemen?

11. The Caliph's Command

1. The tour was organized by Pierre and Patricia Bikai, director and associate director of the American Center of Oriental Re-search in Amman, Jordan.

2. Lest anyone doubt that an Arab queen could be formidable, consider (with a grain of salt) what Boccaccio tells us of Zenobia. Born in A.D. 240, she was a child of the wilderness, a huntress who, "girding on a quiver, pursued and slew goats and stags with her arrows. Then, when she had become stronger, she dared come to grips with bears and pursued or lay in wait for leopards and lions, killing or capturing them." She took a keen interest in the Arab queens who had preceded her and who had held their own in a Semitic male-oriented world. Along with strength, "Zenobia had a beautiful body . . . She also had beautiful dark eyes and white teeth." Enemies feared the glint of those eyes, as she and her army brought to heel neighboring Persians, Saracens, and Armenians. "She never spoke to her soldiers without wearing her helmet, and she very seldom used a chariot while on expeditions. She more often rode on horseback and sometimes would walk for three or four miles with the soldiers ahead of the flags. Nor did she scorn drinking with her captains." With an audacity that stunned the world, Zenobia invaded and conquered all Egypt, then looked to Rome, only to meet her match in the Emperor Aurelian, a hardened ex-soldier. Apprehending her, Aurelian had her bound in golden chains and carried off to Rome, yet out of admiration he spared her life, exiling her to a villa in Tivoli.

3. This and the following quote are from Richard Burton, trans., *The Book of a Thousand Nights and a Night*, vol. 6, pp. 114–15.

4. The notion of veiling goes as far back as an Assyrian law code enacted under Tiglath-pileser I in the 1100s B.C. It reads in part: "The daughter of a lord whether it is with a shawl or a robe or a mantle must veil themselves . . . A harlot must not veil herself; her head must be uncovered; he who has seen a harlot veiled must arrest her, produce witnesses and bring her to the palace tribunal . . . they shall flog her fifty times with staves and pour

pitch on her head" (James B. Pritchard, ed., *Ancient Near Eastern Texts*, p. 163).

5. Astarte's key role in the pantheon of Palmyra is not immediately apparent, for she is a subversive goddess given to many guises, attributes, and epithets. In inscriptions and iconography, she is identified by her own name *('strt)*, but she also masquerades as Allat, *blty*, *b'ltk*, *gd* of Yedi'ebel, and *gd* of Tadmor. In his *Pantheon of Palmyra*, Javier Teixidor concludes that all are variations of Astarte, queen of heaven.

12. To Far Arabia

1. In a study comparing costs of living in the 1990s and two thousand years ago, archaeologist Gus Van Beek calculated that frankincense sold for the equivalent of $1,200 a pound.

2. The archaeologists' name for the hegemony of Hadramaut, Qataban, Saba, and a fourth state—Ma'in—is the *Sayhad*. We had hoped to visit Ma'in, but it was in a region closed to outsiders.

3. Albert Jamme, *The Al-'Uqlah Texts*, p. 49.

4. As the bedouin knew of Sheik Zabayr, Shakespeare and his contemporaries knew of their ancient and virtuous queen. In *Henry VIII*, John Cranmer praised the infant Princess Elizabeth as . . .

"A pattern to all princes living with her,
And all that shall succeed. Saba [Sheba's queen] was never
More covetous of wisdom and fair virtue
Than this pure soul shall be" (Act V, scene 5).

Elizabethan George Wither offered the love sonnet

I loved a lass, a fair one
As fair as e'er was seen;

> She was indeed a rare one,
> Another Sheba queen.

13. A Trail of Ruins

1. *Pliny: Natural History,* vol. 12: xxxii; vol. 6: xxxii.
2. Noted, with unaccustomed admiration, by Harry St. John Philby in "The Land of Sheba" (Part 1), p. 127.
3. *Pliny: Natural History,* vol. 12: xxxii.
4. For a discussion of betyls, see *The Road to Ubar,* chapter 13. Ubar, incidentally, would be a good example of a hajar, with its sha'b encompassing its tenting grounds, oasis, and croplands.
5. L. S. Vasilyev, quoted in Andrey Korotayev, *Ancient Yemen,* p. 3.
6. Hajar bin Humeid was discovered in the course of a 1949 ramble by Aden's political agent, Nigel Groom. (Groom later wrote *Frankincense and Myrrh,* a classic—and still the best—account of Arabia's incense trade.) Van Beek and Dragoo's work was under the auspices of adventurer-scholar Wendell Phillips and the American Foundation for the Study of Man. Though Phillips's prime objective was the Moon Temple of the Queen of Sheba, farther west at Ma'rib, his pioneering team dug as well at Timna' and, this one season, at Hajar bin Humeid.
7. A worst-case scenario for the origin of the southern Arabian alphabet would be a 692 B.C. date for Hajar bin Humeid's stratum Q, an 850 B.C. date for Stratum S and its monogram, and a 1050 B.C. date for the origin of writing and civilization in southern Arabia.
8. Gus Van Beek, "The Land of Sheba," p. 60.
9. Luqman is the name of a mythical Arabian personality, variously a vagabond, slave, shepherd, carpenter, tailor, Aesoplike writer of fables, and vizier. He was said to have been the treasurer of Ubar and the builder of the great dam that watered the queen of Sheba's charmed city of Kitor.

10. It is possible that the site of "Luqman" was ancient Harib, mentioned in a badly damaged inscription discovered at Hajar bin Humeid, nine miles east as the crow flies. The text recounts that a king of Qataban and his son had "roofed the road [built a staircase?] between the house of them both, [called] Harib, and its well Bahrun [the oval lake below?]."

11. The Pliny citation is in Andrew Crichton, *History of Arabia*, vol. 1, p. 115. Agatharchides is quoted in Christian J. Robin, "The Rise and Fall of Ancient Kingdoms," p. 22.

14. City of Divine and Mysterious Pleasure

1. Abu Mohammed al-Hamdani, quoted in "Marib," by W. W. Muller, in *Encyclopedia of Islam*, vol. 6: 565–66.

2. Jurgen Schmidt, "The Sabaean Irrigation Economy of Marib" in *Yemen: 3000 Years of Art and Civilization in Arabia Felix*, ed. Werner Daum, p. 55.

3. Phrase from an inscription translated by Albert Jamme in his *Sabean Inscriptions from Mahram Bilqis*, p. 36.

4. A Sabean tablet matter-of-factly records the construction of a house "up to a level of six ceilings with six storeys, and they have added two [further] storeys and all the store rooms and its terrace." This inscription, in the Sana'a National Museum, describes a widespread high-rise architecture still surviving in the villages and cities of today's Yemen.

5. According to the storyteller al-Sha'bi, the queen of Sheba's Salhan palace had seven doors, five hundred columns, and "a ceiling of marble slabs arranged in order and joined together with lead so that the entire ceiling looked as if it were a single slab . . . At each corner of the palace was a gold cupola that extended towards the sky . . . She had something of everything bestowed upon her."

6. The likelihood that there actually was a monumental Sabean

throne is enhanced by the fact that there was less than a one-hundred-year gap between the reign of M'a'adikarib III—the last king to sit on Saba's throne—and the account of Sheba's throne in the Koran.

7. This and the following quotes are from Strabo, *The Geography of Strabo*, vol. 16: iv.

8. For a discussion of "Taboos on Quitting a House," see James G. Frazer, *The Golden Bough*, p. 200.

9. Eduard Glaser quoted in Brian Doe, *Southern Arabia*, p. 61.

10. These and the following quotes are from articles in the *New York Times* and *Los Angeles Times* in the mid-1950s and from Wendell Phillips, *Qataban and Sheba*, pp. 210–320. In early 1975, on behalf of the National Geographic Society, I had several conversations with Phillips, having no idea he was in ill health. He died later that year, at the age of forty-four, a loss to adventure and archaeology.

15. Chiseled in Stone

1. A Karibil-Karibilu synchronism is backed up by an additional Sabean-Assyrian connection that gives a date of 715 B.C. to the reign of the mukarrib Yatamar Bayyin I.

2. Albert Jamme, *Sabean Inscriptions from Mahram Bilqis*, p. 269.

3. That Sirwah was a first capital of the Sabeans has been suggested by the southern Arabian scholars Ahmed Fakhry, Brian Doe, and Nigel Groom. As evidence of this, epigrapher Jacques Ryckmans cites an edict "sent to the tribe of Sirwah, that *possessed* the territory of the city of Ma'rib" (*L'Institution Monarchique en Arabie Méridionale avant l'Islam*, p. 177).

4. Our space images had given us an advance look at Sirwah. We saw that Incense Road routes could have gone north via *either* Ma'rib or Sirwah, with the Sirwah route passing through the re-

ported but unexcavated sites of Yala and Khirbat Jid'an. Also, the possible shift of the Sabean throne from Sirwah to Ma'rib made sense according to our space images, which revealed Sirwah to be in a protected mountain valley with limited water resources. The surrounding drainage was a modest 120 square miles (300 square kilometers). No matter how clever and efficient its water-works, Sirwah could not support a population of more than a few thousand. As the Sabeans prospered and multiplied, their capital almost inevitably would have had to move to Ma'rib, where a drainage of nearly 4,000 square miles (10,000 square kilometers) could be funneled to water crops for a city of 30,000 or more.

16. A Secret of the Sands

1. Similar burials across Arabia, from the Sinai Peninsula to eastern Oman, have been dated to 3400–4200 B.C. (middle to late Bronze Age).
2. In 1936, on a clandestine trip across the Saudi Arabian border into the Ramlat Sabateyn, Harry Philby passed al-Alam but was unaware of its landmark stone lines. He mentioned the site's tombs but didn't think that they were Neolithic. He had the romantic notion that here were the graves of the last of the Sabeans, who, after the collapse of their great dam and their civilization, fled to the desert.

17. The Glory of Kings

1. Miguel F. Brooks, trans., Kebra Nagast, pp. 31–32.
2. In subsequent pages of the Kebra Nagast, Ethiopia embraced Judaism. This did happen historically, though not necessarily in the era of Solomon and Sheba. Ethiopian Judaism certainly dates to the diaspora after the fall of Jerusalem to the Romans in

A.D. 70 and may extend well back into Old Testament times, judging from the practices and rituals of the Beta Israel (Ethiopia's "House of Israel"), some of which antedate Josiah's reforms of the mid-600s B.C.

18. The Holy City of Aksum

1. E. Littmann, trans., *The Legend of the Queen of Sheba in the Tradition of Axum*, p. 28. This quote is from a manuscript that may contain older material than the better-known *Kebra Nagast*.
2. Since "the queen of Sheba" is a title referring to a people and a land rather than a personal name, one would expect that if she came from Ethiopia, historically there would have been an Ethiopian region called Saba—but there wasn't. Here is an indication that, though she was adopted by the Ethiopians, her homeland was the Arabian state of Saba.
3. Miguel F. Brooks, trans., *Kebra Nagast*, pp. 62–63.
4. There is some indication in the Bible that *something* happened to the Ark in Solomon's reign. Prior to his death it is cited more than two hundred times; following his death it is rarely mentioned.
5. If future archaeology rules out an Arabian colonization of Ethiopia in the tenth century B.C., it is still possible that the queen of Sheba was a Sabean figure—who was popularized in Ethiopia a few centuries later.

20. The Road to Sirwah

1. As it happened, I first heard of Sirwah as a fourteen-year-old growing up in Providence, Rhode Island. In town to deliver a lecture at Brown University, Ahmed Fakhry had come to our house for dinner. At once intense and full of good humor, he

was busy at the time translating a number of inscriptions he had
recorded at Sirwah.

21. *In the House of the South Wind*

1. Sheik Ahmed's kidnapping–public works synergy is quite distinct from kidnapping and bombing in the name of fundamen-
   talism and the jihad, or holy war, that, beginning with the 1998
   murder of four tourists near Aden, has racked Yemen.
2. The summer–winter palace theory of Sirwah and Ma'rib is hazily suggested in several inscriptions and in the lament of the pre-
   Islamic poet Alkama': "Gone are the kings of Sirwah and
   Ma'rib/Who could ever in this world feel secure?"
3. The identity of the biblical "he" who named Solomon's pillars is
   unclear; in I Kings it appears to be Hiram, a bronze worker; in II
   Chronicles it is Solomon. The names Jacin and Boaz are obscure; they possibly mean "it is firm" and "it is strong." Coinci-
   dentally, the name of the Sabean moon god—'Ilumqah—may
   mean "he is strong." A promising avenue of research would be a
   comparison of the religious architecture and paraphernalia of
   ancient Israel and Yemen. A Sabean temple at al-Masagid, for
   example, appears to replicate the floor plan of Solomon's temple, as described in the Bible. And his temple's cauldron of the
   "Great Sea" has a parallel in an enormous cauldron—the largest
   known to have been cast in antiquity—unearthed at the Qatabanian capital of Timna'.
4. This and the following quotes (including those by al-Hamdani
   and al-Khaisey) are from Ahmed Fakhry, *An Archaeological
   Journey to Yemen*, pp. 30–32.
5. The sketch in the text is based on stone fragments in the Aden
   Museum, as well as a Sabean altar drawn by scholar-explorer
   Eduard Glaser—there being an ancient similarity between altars and thrones as godly dwelling places. Aksumite thrones sur-

viving in Ethiopia—which may well be derivative of Sabean models—reinforce this interpretation.

22. Sheba and Solomon

1. For a portrait of Neolithic settlements in southern Arabia, see Alessandro de Maigret, *The Bronze Age Culture of Hawlan at-Tiyal and al-Hada*.
2. Punt, the source of Egyptian Queen Hatshepsut's incense and spices, is the subject of a bas relief in her mortuary temple in Luxor's Valley of the Queens. In recent years the Deutsches Archäologisches Institut, under the direction of Burkhard Vogt, has unearthed evidence that Punt was a crescent of southern Arabian coastal plain stretching from today's As-Sabya on the Red Sea to Aden on the Indian Ocean.
3. Menwai is named and portrayed on a canopic jar in the Egyptian collection of New York's Metropolitan Museum of Art. Interestingly, a Sabean alabaster face in the museum's Near Eastern collection has near-identical features.
4. Proto-Sinaitic appears as graffiti scratched in the desert varnish of boulders and rock faces of the Sinai peninsula. Here is a sampling of letters.

Letter	Egyptian	Proto-Sinaitic	Epigraphic South Arabic	Represents
a				bull's head
b				house
h				prayer
m				water
n				serpent

Though southern Arabia's script harks back to Egyptian hieroglyphics, its language is closer to the Semitic tongues of the Fertile Crescent.

5. As an intermediate step in long-range trade, it is probable that
   Sabean goods changed hands a number of times along what
   would become the Incense Road. From tribe to tribe, cargoes
   would have been sold and resold and transferred from one caravan to the next.

6. It is possible that the "gold" of "gold, frankincense and myrrh"
   was not gold at all but a grade of frankincense. Jacques Ryckmans makes a case for this in his article "De l'or, de l'encens et
   de la myrrhe."

7. James B. Pritchard, *Solomon and Sheba*, p. 9. As an example of
   this usage, Pritchard cites the unambiguous case of Lot's eldest
   daughter (in Genesis 19:31–32) telling her sister, "There is not a
   man in the land to come to [*bw'*] us in the way they do the world
   over. Come [*bw'*], let us ply our father with wine and sleep with
   him." Further examples are in Genesis 16:2, 30:3, and 38:8; Deuteronomy 22:3; and II Samuel 16:21.

8. The Sabeans later bamboozled the Romans into believing
   that their land was the source of peppercorns (actually from
   India), fine silks (from China), and cinnamon (from Indo-
   nesia).

Epilogue. Sheba's Tomb

1. *Pliny: Natural History*, vol. 12: xxx.

2. Abu Mohammed al-Hamdani, *The Antiquities of South Arabia*,
   pp. 90–92.

3. Van Beek, "The Land of Sheba," pp. 62–63.

4. Recorded as inscriptions Ja 824 and 825 in Jamme, *Sabean Inscriptions from Mahram Bilqis*, p. 244. Brackets in such inscriptions traditionally signify broken-off sections that can sometimes

be inferred. In this case, it is a safe guess that "Ya" is the beginning of "Yanuf."

5. Quoted in *Yemen: 3000 Years of Art and Civilization in Arabia Felix*, ed. Werner Daum, p. 212.

Appendix 3. Demon Sheba

1. Lou H. Silberman, "The Queen of Sheba in Judaic Tradition," in *Solomon and Sheba*, ed. Pritchard, p. 80.
2. This and the following quote are from *The Zohar*, trans. Harry Sperling and Maurice Simon, vol. 5:276–77.
3. Flaubert's *The Temptation of St. Antony* cannily captures the Sheba-Lilith amalgam: the character is Sheba, but the locale is Lilith's haunt on the desert shore of the Red Sea.

Appendix 4. Alchemical Sheba

1. This and the following quote are from Raphael Patai, *The Jewish Alchemists*, p. 102.
2. Marie-Louise von Franz, *Aurora Consurgens*, pp. 138–39.
3. Johannes Grasseus, "Arca Arcani" in *Theatrum Chemicum* (Strasbourg, 1616), vol. 6: 314.

Bibliography

Abbot, Nabia. "Pre-Islamic Queens." *American Journal of Semitic Languages and Literature* 58, no. 1 (Jan. 1941).

———. "Women and the State on the Eve of Islam." *American Journal of Semitic Languages and Literature* 58, no. 3 (July 1941).

Abdallah, Yusuf. "Der Sonnengesang von Saba: Ein Stück religioser Literatur aus dem antiken Jemen." In *Die Königin von Saba*, ed. Werner Daum. Stuttgart: Belser Verlag, 1988.

Ackerman, James S. "Knowing Good and Evil: A Literary Analysis of the Court History in 2 Samuel 9–20 and 1 Kings 1–2." *Journal of Biblical Literature* 109, no. 1 (Spring 1990).

Ahlstrom, Gosta W. *The History of Ancient Palestine from the Palaeolithic Period to Alexander's Conquest.* Sheffield, Eng.: Sheffield Academic Press, 1992.

Ahroni, Y., M. Evenari, L. Sanan, and N. H. Tadmor. "The Ancient Desert Agriculture of the Negev." *Israel Exploration Journal* 10 (1960).

Albright, William F. "The Excavation of the Temple of the Moon at Marib (Yemen)." *Bulletin of the American Schools of Oriental Research* 128 (Dec. 1952).

Aldrich, Thomas B. *The Queen of Sheba.* Boston: Houghton Mifflin, 1877.

Angelini, Alessandro. *Piero della Francesca.* Milan: Scala/Riverside, 1995.

Augustodunesis, Honorius. "De Imagine Mundi." In *Abhandlungen* der philosophisch-philologischen Classe der königlich. Munich: Bayrischen Akademie der Wissenschaften, 1835.

Barker, Barbara M. *Bolossy Kiralfy, Creator of Great Musical Spectacles: An Autobiography.* Ann Arbor, Mich.: UMI Research Press, 1988.

Beebe, H. Keith. "The Dromedary Revolution." *Occasional Papers of the Institute for Antiquity and Christianity* 18 (May 1990).

Beeston, A. F. L. "Some Features of Social Structure in Saba." In *Studies in the History of Arabia*, ed. Abd al-Rahman T. al-Ansary. Riyadh, Saudi Arabia: University of Riyadh Press, 1979.

————. "Women in Saba." In *Arabian and Islamic Studies: Festschrift R. B. Serjeant*, ed. Robin L. Bidwell and G. Rex Smith. New York: Longmans, 1983.

————. "The Religions of Pre-Islamic Yemen." In *L'Arabie du Sud, Histoire et Civilization*, vol. 1: *Le Peuple Yemenite et Ses Racines*, ed. Joseph Chelhod. Paris: G.-P. Maisonneuve et Larose, 1984.

————. "Pre-Islamic Yemeni Inscriptions." In *Yemen: 3000 Years of Art and Civilization in Arabia Felix*, ed. Werner Daum. Innsbruck: Pinguin-Verlag, 1988.

Bent, Theodore. *The Sacred City of the Ethiopians.* London: Longmans, Green, 1893.

Bernstein, Burton. *Sinai: The Great and Terrible Wilderness.* New York: Viking Press, 1979.

Biella, Joan C. *Dictionary of Old South Arabic: Sabaean Dialect.* Cambridge, Mass.: Scholars Press, 1982.

Birnbaum, Chiarola. *Black Madonnas: Feminism, Religion and Politics in Italy.* Boston: Northeastern University Press, 1993.

Boardman, John, et al., eds. *The Cambridge Ancient History.* New York: Cambridge University Press, 1984.

Boccaccio, Giovanni. *Concerning Famous Women.* Translated by Guido A. Guarino. London: George Allen & Unwin, 1963.

Bowen, Richard L., Jr., and Frank P. Albright, eds. *Archaeological Discoveries in South Arabia*. Baltimore: Johns Hopkins University Press, 1958.

Breton, Jean François. "Le Site et la Ville de Sabwa." *Syria* 68 (1991).

———. *Arabia Felix: From the Time of the Queen of Sheba*. Notre Dame, Ind.: University of Notre Dame Press, 2000.

Brooks, Miguel F., ed. and trans. *Kebra Nagast*. Lawrenceville, N.J.: Red Sea Press, 1996.

Brown, Sarah. *Stained Glass in Canterbury Cathedral*. Canterbury, Eng.: Cathedral Gifts, 1995.

Brownlow, Kevin. *The Parade's Gone By*. New York: Alfred A. Knopf, 1968.

———. *Hollywood: The Pioneers*. New York: Alfred A. Knopf, 1968.

Brunner, Ueli. "Die Erforschung der antiken Oase von Marib mit Hilfe geomorphologischer Untersuchungsmethoden." *Archäologische Berichte aus dem Yemen* 2 (1982).

Budge, E. A. Wallis. *A History of Ethiopia*. London: Methuen, 1928.

———. *The Queen of Sheba and Her Only Son Menyelek*. London: Oxford University Press, 1932.

Bulgarelli, Grazia M. "Evidence of Paleolithic Industries in Northern Yemen." In *Die Königin von Saba*, ed. Werner Daum. Stuttgart: Belser Verlag, 1988.

Bulliet, Richard W. *The Camel and the Wheel*. Cambridge, Mass.: Harvard University Press, 1975.

Burton, Richard F., trans. *The Book of a Thousand Nights and a Night*. London: Printed by the Burton Club for Private Subscribers Only, 1885.

Calderon de la Barca, Pedro. *El Arbol del Mejor Fruto*. In *Obras Completas*, ed. Angel Valbuena Prat. Madrid: Aquila, 1952.

———. *La Sibylla del Oriente y Gran Reina de Saba*. In *Las Comedias*, ed. J. J. Keil. Leipzig: Ernest Fischer, 1829.

Caton-Thompson, Gertrude, and E. W. Gardner. "Climate, Irrigation, and Early Man in the Hadramaut." *Geographical Journal* 93, no. 1 (Jan. 1939).

Chelhod, Joseph, ed. *L'Arabie du Sud, Histoire et Civilization.* Paris: G.-P. Maisonneuve et Larose, 1984.

Clapp, Nicholas. *The Road to Ubar.* Boston: Houghton Mifflin, 1998.

Cleuziou, Sergei, et al. "De Peuplement Pre- et Protohistorique du Système Fluviantile Fossile du Jawf-Hadramawt au Yemen." *Paleorient* 18, no. 2 (1992).

Cleveland, Ray L. *An Ancient South Arabian Necropolis: Objects from the Second Campaign in the Timna' Cemetery.* Baltimore: Johns Hopkins University Press, 1965.

Cohen, Rudolph. "The Fortresses King Solomon Built to Protect His Southern Border." *Biblical Archaeological Review* 11, no. 3 (May–June 1985).

Conover, Richard E. *Give 'Em a John Robinson.* Xenia, Ohio: Richard E. Conover, 1965.

Crichton, Andrew. *History of Arabia, Ancient and Modern.* 2 vols. Edinburgh: Oliver & Boyd, 1834.

Cross, Frank Moore. *Canaanite Myth and Hebrew Epic.* Cambridge, Mass.: Harvard University Press, 1973.

Dan, Joseph, ed. *The Christian Kaballah.* Cambridge, Mass.: Harvard University Press, 1977.

Daum, Werner, ed. *Die Königin von Saba.* Stuttgart: Belser Verlag, 1988.

———. *Yemen: 3000 Years of Art and Civilization in Arabia Felix.* Innsbruck: Pinguin-Verlag, 1988.

Davies, Philip. *In Search of Ancient Israel.* Sheffield, Eng.: Academic Press, 1992.

———. "'House of David' Built on Sand." *Biblical Archaeology Review* 20, no. 4 (July–Aug. 1994).

———. "What Separates a Minimalist from a Maximalist? Not Much." *Biblical Archaeology Review* 26, no. 2 (Mar.–Apr. 2000).

Dawood, N. J., trans. *The Koran*. Hammondsmith, Eng.: Penguin Books, 1974.

De Leon, Moses. *The Zohar*. Translated by Harry Sperling and Maurice Simon. London: Soncino Press, 1931–1934.

de Maigret, Alessandro. "The Yemeni Bronze Age." In *Yemen: 3000 Years of Art and Civilization in Arabia Felix*, ed. Werner Daum. Innsbruck: Pinguin-Verlag, 1988.

———. *The Bronze Age Culture of Hawlan at-Tiyal and al-Hada*. Rome: Ismeo, 1990.

———. *The Sabaean Archaeological Complex in the Wadi Yala*. Rome: Ismeo, 1988.

De Nerval, Gerard. "Histoire de la Reine du Matin et de Salomon Prince des Genies." In *Oeuvres*, ed. Henri Lemâitre. Paris: Garner Frères, 1958.

Department of Antiquities and Museums, Kingdom of Saudi Arabia. *An Introduction to Saudi Arabian Antiquities*. Riyadh: Ministry of Education, 1975.

Deribere, Maurice. *Au Pays de la Reine de Saba*. Paris: France-Empire, 1977.

Dever, William G. "Archaeology and the 'Age of Solomon': A Case Study in Archaeology and Historiography." In *The Age of Solomon: Scholarship at the Turn of the Millennium*, ed. Lowell K. Handy. Leiden: E. J. Brill, 1997.

———. "Save Us from Postmodern Malarkey." *Biblical Archaeology Review* 26, no. 2 (Mar.–Apr. 2000).

Dickson, H. R. P. *The Arab of the Desert*. London: George Allen and Unwin, 1959.

Doe, Brian. *Monuments of South Arabia*. London: Falcon-Oleander, 1983.

———. *Southern Arabia*. London: Thames & Hudson, 1971.

Donovan, Claire. *The Winchester Bible*. Toronto: University of Toronto Press, 1993.

Drewes, A. J. "The Lexicon of Ethiopian Sabaean." *Raydan* 3 (1980).

Duda, Dorothea. "Die Königin von Saba in der islamischen Miniaturmalerei." In *Die Königin von Saba,* ed. Werner Daum. Stuttgart: Belser Verlag, 1988.

Eph'al, Israel. *The Ancient Arabs.* Leiden: E. J. Brill, 1982.

Fakhry, Ahmed. *An Archaeological Journey to Yemen (March–May, 1947).* Cairo: Government Press, 1951.

Fatovitch, Rodolfo. "Remarks on the Pre-Aksumite Period in Northern Ethiopia." *Journal of Ethiopian Studies* 23 (Nov. 1990).

Fedele, Francesco G. "North Yemen: The Neolithic." In *Yemen: 3000 Years of Art and Civilization in Arabia Felix,* ed. Werner Daum. Innsbruck: Pinguin-Verlag, 1988.

Finkelstein, Israel. "Back to Megiddo." *Biblical Archaeological Review* 20, no. 1 (Jan.–Feb., 1994).

———. "The Archaeology of the United Monarchy: An Alternate View." *Levant* 28 (1996).

———. "Ethnicity and the Origin of the Iron I Settlers in the Highlands of Canaan: Can the Real Israelites Stand Up?" *Biblical Archaeology Review* 59, no. 4 (Dec. 1996).

———. "State Formation in Israel and Judah: A Contrast in Context, a Contrast in Trajectory." *Near Eastern Archaeology* 62, no. 1 (Mar. 1999).

Finster, Barbara. "Die Stadtmauer von Marib." *Archäologische Berichte aus dem Yemen* 3 (1982).

Flaubert, Gustave. *The Temptation of Saint Antony.* Trans. Kitty Mrosovsky. Ithaca, N.Y.: Cornell University Press, 1981.

Forster, Charles. *The Historical Geography of Arabia.* London: Duncan and Malcolm, 1844.

Fraser, Antonia. *Boadicea's Chariot: The Warrior Queens.* London: Weidenfeld and Nelson, 1968.

Frazer, James G. *The Golden Bough.* New York: Macmillan, 1923.

Freedman, David Noel, ed. *The Anchor Bible Dictionary.* Entries on Deuteronomistic History, Incense, Frankincense, Prehistory of

Arabia, and Religion of South Arabia. New York: Doubleday, 1992.

Gibb, H. A. R., et al., ed. *The Encyclopaedia of Islam.* Entries on Bilqis, Djinn, al-Hamdani, Ma'rib, Saba. Leiden: E. J. Brill, 1979.

Gibson, Shimon, and David M. Jacobson. "The Oldest Datable Chambers on the Temple Mount in Jerusalem." *Biblical Archaeologist* 53, no. 3 (1994).

———. *Below the Temple Mount in Jerusalem.* Oxford: Tempus Reparatum, 1996.

Giday, Belai. *Ethiopian Civilization.* Addis Ababa: Belai Giday, 1991.

Ginzberg, Louis. *The Legends of the Jews.* Philadelphia: Jewish Publication Society of America, 1987.

Glanzman, William. "Arabia and the Persian/Arabian Gulf." In Brian M. Fagan, ed., *Oxford Companion to Archaeology.* New York: Oxford University Press, 1996.

Goldmark, Karl. *Notes from the Life of a Viennese Composer.* New York: Albert and Charles Boni, 1927.

Gray, John. *I & II Kings: A Commentary.* London: SCM Press, 1970.

———. *Near Eastern Mythology.* New York: Peter Bedrick Books, 1982.

Green, William. "Strippers and Coochers—the Quintessence of American Burlesque." In *Western Popular Theater,* ed. David Mayer and Kenneth Richards. London: Methuen, 1977.

Greenslet, Ferris. *The Life of Thomas Bailey Aldrich.* Boston: Houghton Mifflin, 1908.

Grierson, Roderick, ed. *African Zion: The Sacred Art of Ethiopia.* New Haven: Yale University Press, 1993.

Grohmann, Adolf. *Göttersymbole und Symboltiere auf Südarabischen Denkmälern.* Vienna: Alfred Holder, 1914.

———. *Arabien.* Munich: C. H. Beck'schen Verlagsbuchhandlung, 1963.

Groom, Nigel. *Frankincense and Myrrh*. London: Longman, 1981.

Hadrani, Bilqis Ibrahim. "Die Königin Bilqis in der zeitgenössischen jemenitischen Dichtung." In *Die Königin von Saba*, ed. Werner Daum. Stuttgart: Belser Verlag, 1988.

Halpern, Baruch. *The First Historians*. University Park, Pa.: Pennsylvania State University Press, 1996.

Hamblin, Dora J. "Saudi Arabia Uncovers Its Past." *Smithsonian* 14, no. 6 (Sept. 1983).

al-Hamdani, Abu Mohammed. *The Antiquities of South Arabia*. Translated by Nabih Amin Faris. Princeton: Princeton University Press, 1936.

Hancock, Graham. *The Sign and the Seal*. New York: Simon & Schuster, 1992.

Handy, Lowell K., ed. *The Age of Solomon: Scholarship at the Turn of the Millennium*. Leiden: E. J. Brill, 1997.

Harding, G. Lankester. *Archaeology in the Aden Protectorates*. London: Her Majesty's Stationery Office, 1964.

Hazleton, Lesley. *Where Mountains Roar*. New York: Holt, Rinehart, and Winston, 1980.

Herberg, Werner. "Baukomplex B im Wadi Dana." *Archäologische Berichte aud dem Yemen* 3 (1982).

Herodotus. *Herodotus: The Histories*. Translated by Aubrey de Selincourt. New York: Penguin Books, 1985.

Hobbs, Joseph J. *Mount Sinai*. Austin: University of Texas Press, 1995.

Holladay, John S. "Kingdoms of Israel and Judah: Political and Economic Centralization in the Iron IIA-B (ca. 1,000–750 BCE)." In *The Archaeology of Society in the Holy Land*, ed. T. E. Levy. Leicester, Eng.: Leicester University, 1995.

Isaac, Ephraim, and Cain Felder. "Reflections on the Origins of the Ethiopian Civilization." In *Proceedings of the Eighth Interna-*

tional Conference of Ethiopian Studies. Addis Ababa: Institute of Ethiopian Studies, 1988.

Jacobus de Voragine. *The Golden Legend.* Translated by William Caxton. Hammersmith, Eng.: Kelmscott Press, 1892.

———. *The Golden Legend.* Translated by Granger Ryan and Helmut Ripperger. New York: Longmans, Green, 1941.

Jager, Otto A. *Antiquities of North Ethiopia.* Stuttgart: F. A. Brockhaus, 1985.

Jamieson-Drake, David W. *Scribes and Schools in Monarchic Judah.* Sheffield, Eng.: Almond Press, 1991.

Jamme, Albert. "An Archaic South-Arabian Inscription in Vertical Columns." *Bulletin of the American Schools of Oriental Research* 137 (1955).

———. *Sabean Inscriptions from Mahram Bilqis.* Baltimore: Johns Hopkins University Press, 1962.

———. *The Al-'Uqlah Texts.* Washington, D.C.: Catholic University of America Press, 1963.

Jankowski, A. *Die Königin von Saba und Salomo: Die anharische Version der Handschrift Berlin.* Hamburg: Buske, 1987.

Jaussen, J., and R. Savignac. *Mission Archaeologique en Arabia.* Paris: Ernest Leroux, 1909 and 1914.

Jerrers, Ann. *Magic and Divination in Ancient Palestine and Syria.* Leiden: E. J. Brill, 1996.

Jones, Alexander, ed. *The Jerusalem Bible.* Garden City, N.Y.: Doubleday, 1966.

Josephus, Flavius. *Josephus: The Antiquities of the Jews.* Translated by H. St. J. Thackeray and Ralph Marcus. Cambridge, Mass.: Harvard University Press, 1934.

Joukowsky, Martha. *A Complete Field Manual of Archaeology.* Englewood Cliffs, N.J.: Prentice-Hall, 1980.

Jung, Carl G. *Mysterium Coniunctionis.* Princeton: Princeton University Press, 1963.

Jung, Michael. *Religious Monuments of Ancient Southern Arabia*. Naples: Instituto Universitario Orientale, 1967–1982.

——. *Research on Rock Art in North Yemen*. Naples: Instituto Universitario Orientale, 1991.

al-Kalbi, Hisham. *The Book of Idols*. Translated by Nabih Amin Faris. Princeton: Princeton University Press, 1936.

Kenny, Vincent. *Herman Melville's Clarel: A Spiritual Autobiography*. Hamden, Conn.: Archon Books, 1973.

Kinglake, Alexander. *Eothen: Or Traces of Travel Brought Home from the East*. London: J. Ollivier, 1844.

al-Kisa'i, Mohammed ibn 'Abd Allah. *Tales of the Prophets*. Translated by W. M. Thackston, Jr. Boston: Twayne, 1978.

Kitchen, Kenneth A. *Documentation for Ancient Arabia*. Liverpool, Eng.: University of Liverpool, 1994.

——. "Sheba and Arabia." In *The Age of Solomon: Scholarship at the Turn of the Millennium*, ed. Lowell K. Handy. Leiden: E. J. Brill, 1997.

——. "The Patriarchal Age: Myth or History?" *Biblical Archaeology Review* 21, no. 2 (Mar.–Apr. 1995).

Klein-Franke, Aviva. "Die Königin von Saba in der judischen Überlieferung." In *Die Königin von Saba*, ed. Werner Daum. Stuttgart: Belser Verlag, 1988.

Kluger, Rivkah S. *Psyche and the Bible*. Zurich: Spring Publications, 1974.

Knappert, Jan. *Islamic Legends*. Leiden: E. J. Brill, 1985.

Knoppers, Gary. *Two Nations Under God: The Deuteronomistic History of Solomon and the Dual Monarchies*. Atlanta: Scholars Press, 1993.

Kobishchanov, Yuri M. *Axum*. University Park, Pa.: Pennsylvania State University Press, 1979.

Koehler, Ludwig, and Walter Baumgartner. *The Hebrew and Aramaic Lexicon of the Old Testament*. Leiden: E. J. Brill, 1994.

Koltuv, Barbara B. *The Book of Lilith*. York Beach, Me.: Nicolas-Hays, 1986.

———. *Solomon and Sheba: Inner Marriage and Individualism*. York Beach, Me.: Nicolas-Hays, 1993.

Korotayev, Andrey. *Ancient Yemen*. Oxford: Oxford University Press, 1995.

Lasine, Stuart. "Solomon and the Wizard of Oz: Power and Invincibility in a Verbal Palace." In *The Age of Solomon: Scholarship at the Turn of the Millennium*, ed. Lowell K. Handy. Leiden: E. J. Brill, 1997.

Lassner, Jacob. *Demonizing the Queen of Sheba*. Chicago: University of Chicago Press, 1993.

Lavin, Marilyn A. *Piero della Francesca*. New York: Harry N. Abrams, 1992.

———. *Piero della Francesca: San Francesco, Arezzo*. New York: George Braziller, 1994.

Lemche, Niels P. "On Doing Sociology with Solomon." In *The Age of Solomon: Scholarship at the Turn of the Millennium*, ed. Lowell K. Handy. Leiden: E. J. Brill, 1997.

Lemche, Niels P., and Thomas L. Thompson. "Did Biran Kill David? The Bible in the Light of Archaeology." *Journal for the Study of the Old Testament* 64 (1994).

Levi, Eliphas. *The Book of Splendours*. York Beach, Me.: Samuel Weiser, 1984.

Lingenfelter, Richard E. *Death Valley and the Amargosa: A Land of Illusion*. Berkeley: University of California Press, 1986.

Littmann, E. *The Legend of the Queen of Sheba in the Tradition of Axum*. Leiden: E. J. Brill, 1904.

Macdonald, Michael C. A. "North Arabia in the First Millennium B. C. E." In *Civilizations of the Ancient Near East*, ed. J. Sasson. New York: Scribner, 1995.

———. "Trade Routes and Trade Gods at the Northern End of

the 'Incense Road' in the First Millennium B.C." In *Profumi d'Arabia: Atti del Convegno*. Rome: "L'erma" di Bretschneider, 1997.

Mardrus, J. C. *The Queen of Sheba*. New York: Bernard G. Richards, 1925.

Malraux, André. *La Reine de Saba: une "Aventure Géographique."* Paris: Gallimard, 1993.

Maududi, S. Abula'la. *The Meaning of the Koran*, vol. 9: *Surah An-Naml—Surah Ar-Rum*. Lahore, Pakistan: Islamic Publications, 1993.

McKenzie, S. L. *The Trouble with Kings*. In *Vetus Testamentum*, Supplements 42. Leiden: E. J. Brill, 1991.

Melville, Herman. *Journal of a Visit to Europe and the Levant*. Edited by Howard C. Horsford. Princeton: Princeton University Press, 1955.

———. *Clarel: A Poem and Pilgrimage in the Holy Land*. London: Constable, 1924.

Millard, Alan. "King Solomon in His Ancient Context." In *The Age of Solomon: Scholarship at the Turn of the Millennium*, ed. Lowell K. Handy. Leiden: E. J. Brill, 1997.

Monroe, Elizabeth. "Arabia: St. John Philby's Contribution to Pre-Islamic Studies." In *Proceedings of the Seminar for Arabian Studies*. London: Seminar for Arabian Studies, 1973.

Morton, Paul K. *Geology of the Queen of Sheba Lead Mine, Death Valley, California*. San Francisco: California Division of Mines and Geology, 1965.

Moscati, Sabatino. *Ancient Semitic Civilization*. New York: G. P. Putnam's Sons, 1960.

Muller, Walter W. "Notes on the Use of Frankincense in South Arabia," in *Proceedings of the Ninth Seminar for Arabian Studies*. London: Seminar for Arabian Studies, 1976.

———. "Arabian Frankincense in Antiquity According to Classical

Sources." In *Studies in the History of Arabia*, vol. 1. Riyadh, Saudi Arabia: University of Riyadh, 1977.

———. "Outline of History of Ancient Southern Arabia." In *Die Königin von Saba*, ed. Werner Daum. Stuttgart: Belser Verlag, 1988.

Munro-Hay, Stuart C. *Excavations at Aksum*. London: British Institute of Eastern Africa, 1989.

Murphy-O'Connor, Jerome. *The Holy Land: An Archaeological Guide from Earliest Times to 1700*. Oxford, Eng.: Oxford University Press, 1980.

Na'aman, Nadav. "Cow Town or Royal Capital? Evidence for Iron Age Jerusalem." *Biblical Archaeology Review* 23, no. 4 (July–Aug. 1997).

Noya, Sergio, ed. *L'Arabie Avant L'Islam*. Aix-en-Provence, France: Edisud, 1994.

O'Leary, De Lacy. *Arabia Before Muhammad*. London: Kegan Paul, Trench, Trubner, 1927.

Ostoia, Vera K. "Two Riddles of the Queen of Sheba." *Metropolitan Museum Journal* 6 (1972).

Overstreet, William C., Maurice Grolier, and M. Toplyn, eds. *The Wadi Al-Jubah Project: Geological and Archaeological Reconnaissance in the Yemen Arab Republic*. Washington, D.C.: American Foundation for the Study of Man, 1988.

Pankhurst, Richard. "Die Königin von Saba in der äthiopischen Tradition." In *Die Königin von Saba*, ed. Werner Daum. Stuttgart: Belser Verlag, 1988.

Parker, Kim I. *Wisdom and Law in the Reign of Solomon*. Lampeter, Wales: Mellen Biblical Press, 1992.

Parr, Peter J., G. Lankaster, and J. E. Dayton. "Preliminary Survey in N.W. Arabia, 1968." *Bulletin of the Institute of Archaeology* (University of London) 8–10 (1970–71).

Patai, Raphael. *The Hebrew Goddess*. New York: Avon Books, 1978.

———. *The Jewish Alchemists*. Princeton: Princeton University Press, 1994.

Philby, Harry St. John. "The Land of Sheba." *Geographical Journal* 92 (1938).

———. *Sheba's Daughters*. London: Methuen, 1939.

———. *The Land of Midian*. London: Ernest Benn, 1957.

———. *The Queen of Sheba*. London: Quartet Books, 1981.

Phillips, Wendell. *Qataban and Sheba*. New York: Harcourt, Brace, 1955.

Pirenne, Jacqueline. *La Grèce et Saba*. Paris: Imprimerie Nationale, 1955.

———. Review of Gus Van Beek's Hajar Bin Humeid report. *Syria* 51 (1974).

———. "The Chronology of Ancient South Arabia—Diversity of Opinion." In *Yemen: 3000 Years of Art and Civilization in Arabia Felix*, ed. Werner Daum. Innsbruck: Pinguin-Verlag, 1988.

Pliny the Elder. *Pliny: Natural History*. Translated by H. Rackham. Cambridge, Mass.: Harvard University Press, 1986.

Pope, Marvin. *The Song of Songs*. New York: Doubleday, 1977.

Price, David. *Essay toward the History of Arabia*. "Arranged from the Tarikh Tebry and other authentic sources." London: printed by the author, 1824.

Pritchard, James B., ed. *Ancient Near Eastern Texts*. Princeton: Princeton University Press, 1955.

———. *Solomon and Sheba*. London: Phaidon Press, 1974.

Ptolemy, Claudius. *Claudius Ptolemy: The Geography*. Translated by Edward L. Stevenson. New York: Dover, 1991.

Rappoport, Angelo S. *Ancient Israel: Myths and Legends*. New York: Bonanza, 1987.

Raswan, Carl R. *Black Tents of Arabia*. Boston: Little, Brown, 1935.

Retso, Jan. "The Domestication of the Camel and the Establishment of the Frankincense Road from South Arabia." *Orientalia Suecana* 60, no. 198 (1991).

Ripellino, Angelo M. *Magic Prague*. London: Picador, 1995.

Ripinsky, Michael M. "The Camel in Ancient Arabia." *Antiquity* 49, no. 196 (Dec. 1975).

Ritmeyer, Leen, and Kathleen Ritmeyer. *Secrets of Jerusalem's Temple Mount*. Washington, D.C.: Biblical Archaeology Society, 1998.

Robin, Christian. "Religion of South Arabia." In *The Anchor Bible Dictionary*, ed. David N. Freedman. Vol. 6. New York: Doubleday, 1992.

———. "The Rise and Fall of Ancient Kingdoms." In *Version Originale. Le Trimestriel de Réflexion. The Arabian Peninsula*, no. 3, ed. C. Desjeunes. Paris: Version Originale, 1993.

Robin, Christian, and I. Gajda, eds. *Arabia Antiqua: Early Origins of South Arabian States*. Rome: Instituto Italiano per il Medio et Estremo Oriente, 1966.

Ryckmans, Jacques. *L'Institution Monarchique en Arabie Méridionale avant l'Islam*. Louvain, France: Publications Universitaires, 1951.

———. "De l'or, de l'encens et de la myrrhe." *Révue biblique* 52 (1951).

———. "Biblical and Old South Arabian Institutions: Some Parallels." In *Arabian and Islamic Studies: Festschrift R. B. Serjeant*, ed. Robin L. Bidwell and G. Rex Smith. New York: Longmans, 1983.

———. "The Old South Arabian Religion." In *Yemen: 3000 Years of Art and Civilization in Arabia Felix*, ed. Werner Daum. Innsbruck: Pinguin-Verlag, 1988.

Sale, George, ed. *The Koran*. London: Thomas Tegg and Son, 1838.

al-Saleh, Khairat. *Fabled Cities, Princes and Jinns*. London: Peter Stone, 1985.

Sass, Benjamin. *Studia Alphabetica: On the Origin and Early His-

tory of the Northwest Semitic, South Semitic and Greek Alphabets. Göttingen: Vanderhoeck und Ruprecht, 1991.

Saud, Abdullah Saud. "The Domestication of Camels and Inland Trading Routes in Arabia." *ATLAL* 14 (1996).

Schmidt, Jürgen. "Ancient South Arabian Sacred Buildings." In *Yemen: 3000 Years of Art and Civilization in Arabia Felix,* ed. Werner Daum. Innsbruck: Pinguin-Verlag, 1988.

Schmidt, Jürgen, Ulrich Brunner, and Mathias Gerig. "Marib." *Archäologische Berichte aus dem Yemen* 1 (1982).

Schneider, Laurie. "The Iconography of Piero della Francesca's Frescoes Illustrating the Legend of the True Cross in the Church of San Francesco in Arezzo." *Art Quarterly* 32, no. 1 (Spring 1969).

Scholem, Gershom. "Peraqim adashim me'inyane Ashmodai v-Lilit." *Tarbiz* 19 (1948).

———. *Kabbalah.* New York: Meridian, 1978.

———. "Lilith und die Königin von Saba." In *Die Königin von Saba,* ed. Werner Daum. Stuttgart: Belser Verlag, 1988.

Scott, R. B. Y. "Solomon and the Beginnings of Wisdom in Israel." In *Wisdom in Israel and in the Ancient near East,* ed. M. Noth and D. Winton Thomas. Leiden: E. J. Brill, 1955.

Sedov, Alexander V. "On the Origin of the Agricultural Settlements in Hadramawt." In *Arabia Antiqua: Early Origins of South Arabian States,* ed. Christian J. Robin. Rome: Ismeo, 1996.

Seigne, Jacques. "Le Château Royal de Shabwa: Architecture, Techniques de Construction et Restitutions." *Syria* 68 (1991).

Seipel, Wilfried, ed. *Jemen: Kunst und Archäologie im Land der Königin von Saba.* Vienna: Kunstlerhaus, 1998.

Seller, Abednego. *The Antiquities of Palmyra Built by King Solomon.* London: S. Mith & B. Walford, 1705.

Serjeant, Robert B. *South Arabian Hunt.* London: Luzac, 1983.

Serjeant, Robert B., and Ronald Lewcock. *San'a: An Arabian Islamic City.* London: World of Islam Festival Trust, 1983.

Seters, John Van. *Abraham in History and Tradition*. New Haven: Yale University Press, 1975.

Shahid, I. "The *Kebra Nagast* in the Light of Recent Research." *Le Museon* 89 (1976).

Shanks, Hershel. "Face to Face: Biblical Minimalists Meet Their Challengers." *Biblical Archaeology Review* 23, no. 4 (July–Aug. 1997).

———. "Where Is the Tenth Century?" *Biblical Archaeology Review* 24, no. 2 (Mar.–Apr. 1998).

al-Sheik, Khalil. "Das Bilqis-Motiv in der modernen arabischen Literatur." In *Die Königin von Saba*, ed. Werner Daum. Stuttgart: Belser Verlag, 1988.

Silberman, Lou H. "The Queen of Sheba in Judaic Tradition." In *Solomon and Sheba*, ed. James B. Pritchard. London: Phaidon Press, 1974.

Silberman, Neil Asher, Israel Finkelstein, David Ussishkin, and Baruch Halpern. "Digging at Armageddon." *Archaeology* 52, no. 6 (Nov.–Dec. 1999).

Smith, W. Robertson. *Kinship and Marriage in Early Arabia*. London: Adam and Charles Black, 1903.

Snowden, Frank M., Jr. *Blacks in Antiquity*. Cambridge, Mass.: Harvard University Press, 1970.

Solle, Dorothee, Joe H. Kirchberger, and Herbert Haag. *Great Women of the Bible*. Grand Rapids, Mich.: William B. Eerdmans, 1994.

Sprenger, Alois. *Die Alte Geographie Arabiens*. Amsterdam: Meridian, 1966.

Stiegner, Roswitha G. "Die Königin von Saba in der jemenitschen Legende." In *Die Königin von Saba*, ed. Werner Daum. Stuttgart: Belser Verlag, 1988.

Strabo. *The Geography of Strabo*. Translated by Harold L. Jones. Cambridge, Mass.: Harvard University Press, 1983.

al-Tabari, Abu Mohammed ibn Jabir. "The Children of Israel."

Translated by William M. Brinner. In *The History of al-Tabari,* vol. 3, ed. Edshan Yar-Shater. Albany: State University of New York Press, 1989.

Teixidor, Javier. *The Pantheon of Palmyra.* Leiden: E. J. Brill, 1979.

Thompson, Thomas L. *The Historicity of the Patriarchal Narratives.* Berlin: Walter de Gruyter, 1975.

———. *Early History of the Israelite People.* Leiden: E. J. Brill, 1992.

———. *The Mythic Past.* New York: Basic Books, 1999.

Tibbetts, G. R. *Arabia in Early Maps.* Cambridge, Eng.: Falcon-Oleander, 1978.

Ullendorff, Edward. "The Queen of Sheba." *Bulletin of John Rylands Library* 45, no. 1 (Sept. 1962).

———. *Ethiopia and the Bible.* London: British Academy by Oxford University Press, 1968.

———. *The Ethiopians: An Introduction to a Country and People.* Oxford: Oxford University Press, 1973.

———. "The Queen of Sheba in Ethiopian Tradition." In *Solomon and Sheba,* ed. James B. Pritchard. London: Phaidon Press, 1974.

Van Beek, Gus W. "A Radiocarbon Date for Early South Arabia." *Bulletin of the American Schools of Oriental Research* 143 (Oct. 1956).

———. "Frankincense and Myrrh." *Biblical Archaeologist* 23, no. 3 (Sept. 1960).

———. *Hajar bin Humeid.* Baltimore: Johns Hopkins University Press, 1969.

———. "The Rise and Fall of Arabia Felix." *Scientific American* 221, no. 6 (Dec. 1969).

———. "The Land of Sheba." In *Solomon and Sheba,* ed. James B. Pritchard. London: Phaidon Press, 1974.

———. "South Arabian History and Archaeology." In *The Bible and* the Ancient Near East: Essays in Honor of William Foxwell Albright. Winona Lake, Ind.: Eisenbrauns, 1979.

Volkoff, Oleg V. D'ou Vint la Reine de Saba? Cairo: l'Institut Français d'Archéologie Orientale, 1971.

Von Franz, Marie-Louise. Aurora Consurgens: A Document Attributed to Thomas Aquinas on the Problems of Opposites in Alchemy. New York: Pantheon, 1966.

Von Uthmann, Jorg. "Salomo und die Königin von Saba: Ein Gipfeltreffen mit Folgen." In Die Königin von Saba, ed. Werner Daum. Stuttgart: Belser Verlag, 1988.

Von Wissmann, Hermann. Über die Frühe Geschichte Arabiens und das Entstehen des Sabaerreiches. Vienna: Osterreichischen Akademie der Wissenschaften, 1975.

———. Das Grossreich der Sabaer bis zu Seinem Ende im Pruhen 4. Jh. v. Chr. Vienna: Osterreichischen Akademie der Wissenschaften, 1982.

Warner, Marina. "In and Out of the Fold: Wisdom, Danger, and Glamour in the Tale of the Queen of Sheba." In Out of the Garden: Women Writers on the Bible, ed. C. Buchmann and C. Spiegel. New York: Fawcett Columbine, 1994.

———. From the Beast to the Blonde. New York: Farrar, Straus, and Giroux, 1994.

Watson, Paul F. "The Queen of Sheba in Christian Tradition." In Solomon and Sheba, ed. James B. Pritchard. London: Phaidon Press, 1974.

Watt, W. Montgomery. "The Queen of Sheba in Islamic Tradition." In Solomon and Sheba, ed. James B. Pritchard. London: Phaidon Press, 1974.

Wellhausen, Julius. Prolegomen zür geschichte Israels. Berlin: Druck und Verlag von Georg Reimer, 1895.

Whalen, Norman M., and David W. Pease. "Early Mankind in Arabia." Aramco World 43, no. 4 (July–Aug. 1992).

Wightman, G. J. "The Myth of Solomon." *Bulletin of the American Schools of Oriental Research* 277/278 (Feb.–May 1990).

Yadin, Yigal. *Hazor: the Rediscovery of a Great Citadel of the Bible.* New York: Random House, 1975.

Yeats, William Butler. *The Collected Poems.* London: Macmillan, 1963.

Zarins, Juris. "The Camel in Ancient Arabia: A Further Note." *Antiquity* 52 (1978).

———. "Pastoral Nomadism in Arabia: Ethnoarchaeology and the Archaeological Record—a Case Study." In *Pastoralism in the Levant*, ed. O. Bar-Yosef and A. Kahznov. Madison, Wis.: Prehistory Press, 1992.

———. "Prehistory of Arabia." In *The Anchor Bible Dictionary*, vol. 1, ed. David N. Freedman. New York: Doubleday, 1992.

Zehren, Erich. *The Crescent and the Bull.* New York: Hawthorne Books, 1962.

Zohar, M. "Pastoralism and the Spread of the Semitic Languages." In *Pastoralism in the Levant*, ed. O. Bar-Yosef and A. Kahznov. Madison, Wis.: Prehistory Press, 1992.

Acknowledgments

Looking for Sheba, I was and am thankful that the world we live in has mysteries and conundrums for all who are curious. Years from now I'll be learning more of her biblical, Koranic, goose-footed, painted-by-the-masters, alchemical, Kabbalistic, Last Judgmental, operatic, star-of-the-circus, archaeological self. It was harrowing and sublime to follow her trail to distant sands.

I had the good fortune to make the acquaintance of two icons of southern Arabian archaeology, the late Ahmed Fakhry and the late Wendell Phillips. Through the perseverance of Wendell's sister Merilyn and her husband, Gordon Hodgson, his American Foundation for the Study of Man is again active in Yemen. For their time and advice, I thank AFSM stalwarts Gus Van Beek, Father Albert Jamme, Bill Overstreet and, especially, Bill Glanzman.

Sifting through the many accounts touching on the queen meant spending time in a host of libraries, including the UCLA Research Library in Los Angeles and the Huntington Library in San Marino, California; the Wisconsin Historical Society Circus World Archives in Baraboo, Wisconsin; the Oriental Collection of the New York Public Library; the Rockefeller and John Hay libraries at Brown University; the Library of the School of African and Oriental Studies in London; the Rockefeller Library in Jerusalem; and the collection of the American Institute of Yemeni Studies in Sana'a, Yemen.

My gratitude to Peter Parr and Nanina Shaw Reade for organizing the annual Seminar for Arabian Studies at the University of London, where Jan Retso, Kenneth Kitchen, Michael Macdonald, and Holgar Hitken offered advance looks at their research.

Back in the United States, Klaus and Gabrielle Brill translated dense German treatises, Paul Boorstin lent a hand with French texts, Bonnie Stalls clarified arcane Arabic phrases, and Brown University's Bill Wyatt set my hopeless high school Latin straight.

As the legend of the queen of Sheba spun into uncharted terrain, the following were most helpful: the late H. Keith Beebe of Occidental College; Marvin Sweeney of Claremont Theological Seminary; Death Valley rangers Kari Coughlin and Linda Green; Beverly Harry, clerk of the Inyo County Court House; Bill Meracher, curator of the Central Nevada Museum; Daniel Kasser, Shenandoah Valley vintner of Makeda Ethiopian honey wine; and Jay Soloff of Columbia Wine and Spirits, now importing La Reine Pédauque vintages to America. I thank two cousins: Lucy Buckley, who with her mom, Alfreda Parisi, filled me in on the Black Virgin of Tindari, and Pardon Tillinghast of Middlebury College, one of the world's few practicing hagiographers. Fred Dahlinger, Jr., was an encyclopedia of the American circus, and long-time carnival operator Al Stencil was versed in hootchy-cootch. Veering back to the realm of the sacred, Cherry Johnstone of Canterbury Cathedral shared insights into the medieval mind and recalled that as a child she had been at the side of Emperor Haile Selassie of Ethiopia when he visited the cathedral and longingly gazed at its stained rondel of Sheba and Solomon, murmuring, "It's true, you know . . . It's true . . ."

My gratitude to Jesuit Father Bill Fulco, for permission to use his new and spirited translation of the Song of Songs.

And it was a pleasure to work with the Jet Propulsion Laboratory's Ron Blom and Bob Crippen as they processed and analyzed space images of the Ramlat Sabateyn region of southern Arabia.

For aid, advice, and inspiration as I roamed the Middle East, I am indebted to Herb Krosney, Joe Zias, and Israel Eph'al in Israel, and to Pierre and Patricia Bikai, M. Ali Bouri, and the Baron brothers in

Syria. As deputy minister of education, Dr. Sa'ad A. al-Rashid welcomed us to Saudi Arabia and put us in the capable hands of Dr. Abdullah Saud al-Saud, director general of the kingdom's research center and museums, and Dr. Hussein Ali Abul al-Hasan, senior archaeologist. Elizabeth Thornhill and Ambassador Wyche Fowler of the U.S. Embassy in Riyadh were most helpful. And a very special thanks to scholar of Islam Michael Wolfe.

I received good advice from Kathryn Bard and Rudolfo Fatovitch, archaeologists working in Ethiopia, and for help in Yemen I am indebted to Noha Sadek of the American Institute of Yemeni Studies and Mohammad Osman of al-Mamoon International Tours. For getting myself and my traveling companions to the Middle East and back, I thank Melanie Mueller and Lori Giovenco of Space Age Travel of Los Angeles, and Irma Turtle and Jan Misseri of Turtle Tours in Carefree, Arizona.

My wife, Kay, and daughters Cristina and Jennifer were ever accepting of my faraway rambles, and joined me when they could. Additional moral support and insights were offered by Werner Daum, Nigel Groom, Alan Jutzi, Myles Hymes, Harrison Engle, Ben Bennett, Steven Lopuck, John, Louise, and Christopher Brinsley, Ron and Merle Mardigian, Artemis and Martha Joukowsky, and a writer beyond compare, Qoholeth.

Twenty years ago, Kay and I were descending a mountain trail west of Petra in Jordan when a lone figure approached from the other direction. He introduced himself as Bob Ivey from Los Angeles, and ever since that time he and his wife, Jill Bowman, have shared our interest in the Middle East. As attorney and agent, Bob has represented both *The Road to Ubar* and *Sheba: Through the Desert in Search of the Legendary Queen*. He introduced me to Harry Foster of Houghton Mifflin, who on both books was a pleasure to work with, as was Peg Anderson. For their consummate editing, the text is far the better. And I thank Kristen Mellon and Anne Chalmers for their realization of the book's line drawings and graphic design.

Illustration Credits

Index